Jejueo

Jejueo

The Language of Korea's Jeju Island

Changyong Yang, Sejung Yang, and William O'Grady

 University of Hawai'i Press
Honolulu

Printed in the United States of America

26 25 24 23 22 21   6 5 4 3 2 1

Library of Congress Cataloging-in-Publication Data

Names: Yang, Changyong, author. | Yang, Sejung, author. | O'Grady, William, author.
Title: Jejueo : the language of Korea's Jeju Island / Changyong Yang, Sejung Yang, and William O'Grady.
Description: Honolulu : University of Hawai'i Press, [2020] | Includes bibliographical references and index.
Identifiers: LCCN 2019010536 | ISBN 9780824874438 (cloth ; alk. paper)
Subjects: LCSH: Jejueo language.
Classification: LCC PL945.C4 Y36 2020 | DDC 495.7/7—dc23
LC record available at https://lccn.loc.gov/2019010536

ISBN 978-0-8248-8988-3 (pbk.)

Cover photo by Sein Yang, a resident of Jeju Island.

Contents

Figures and Tables

Figures

Tables

Acknowledgments

In the course of our work on this book, we received help, advice, and support from many quarters.

The University of Hawai'i Press was supportive from the earliest days of this project, and we wish especially to acknowledge the work of Stephanie Chun, Cheryl Loe, our copyeditor Michael Sola, our compositor and kindred spirit Wanda China, and two anonymous referees whose comments and observations allowed us to make many improvements to our book. We are also grateful to Hye-yoon Choi for her help converting our manuscript to MS Word and to Joel Bradshaw, Cheri Ebisu, Maho Takahashi, Jennifer Kanda, Justin Kanda, and Hae-Sung Park for their technical assistance.

We owe a tremendous debt of gratitude to various speakers of Jejueo who helped us understand their language: Mi-Soon Byeon, Seongsu Huh, Jaehyu Yang, Seongpyo Yang, and residents of the Uigwili Noinhoegwan senior citizen's home. We also benefited from valuable comments and advice from Dong-Jae Lee, Ho-min Sohn, Brendan O'Grady and, especially, Miho Choo, whose insights helped shape this book.

The Center for Korean Studies at the University of Hawai'i at Mānoa has been generous in its support of this project, beginning with a Min Kwan-Shik Faculty Enhancement Award to subsidize the cost of publication. We particularly appreciate the efforts of Sang-Hyop Lee (center director), Sang-Yee Cheon, and Tae-Ung Baek, who offered encouragement and advice at every stage of the project's development. We are also grateful for logistical support from James Randall and Laurie Brinklow in the Island Studies Program and Pauline MacPherson in Robertson Library at the University of Prince Edward Island, where parts of this book were written.

This work was supported by the Core University Program for Korean Studies through the Ministry of Education of the Republic of Korea and the Korean Studies Promotion Service of the Academy of Korean Studies (AKS-2015-OLU-2250005).

Abbreviations and Translation Convention

Abbreviations

1	first person
2	second person
3	third person
ABIL	abilitive
ACC	accusative
ADV	adverb marker
AH	addressee honorific
AUX	auxiliary verb
CAUS	causative
CLAS	classifier
COMPL	completive
CON	connective
CONT	continuative
DAT	dative
DIR	directional
DST	distal deictic
EMPH	emphatic
EVI	evidential
EXC	excrescent
EXCL	exclamatory
GEN	genitive
HAB	habitual
INCH	inchoative
INSTR	instrumental
LOC	locative
LV	linking vowel
MEAS	measurement
NEG	negative

NMLZ   nominalizer
NOM   nominative
NPST   non-past
OBLG   obligative
ORD   ordinal
PASS   passive
PERS   person
PFV   perfective
PGEN   pseudo-genitive
PL   plural
PROSP   prospective
PRX   proximate deictic
SE   sentence ender
TOP   topic
x   represents an unexpressed subject, without regard for
          person or number
!   "!" is often used at the end of a sentence to mark an im-
          perative or propositive in informal speech.

Translation Convention

In translating Jejueo sentences that contain an unexpressed subject we will often use *s/he* ("she or he"), with the understanding that, depending on the context, other interpretations may also be possible, including first- and second-person pronouns as well as plurals. In cases where a first or second person pronoun is preferred (or even required), this is reflected in the choice of subject in the translation, even if it is not overtly expressed in the Jejueo sentence.

1

Jeju Island and Its Language

1. The Beginning

A very long time ago, three demigods emerged from the earth at a place on Jeju Island now known as Samseonghyeol, where three holes in the volcanic ground are still visible. Go, Yang, and Bu were eventually joined by three princesses, who arrived by sea along with horses, cows, and the seeds of several grains. The demigods each married a princess, creating three clans who went about the work of planting crops and raising animals. So begins the traditional story of the Jeju people.

Modern Jeju Island is rich in history and culture, all the more so because it is home to a unique language, about which little is known even within Korea, where its very existence is officially denied. A major goal of this book is to introduce readers to that language, so that it can assume its rightful place in the cultural and linguistic fabric of Korea.

We will concentrate in this first chapter on some general background issues, starting with the history of Jeju Island and some features of its culture. We then turn to an overview of its language, including the confusion and controversy that has surrounded its status. The remainder of the book is devoted to a close examination of the inner workings of the language, with a focus on its phonology and morphosyntax.

2. History and Culture

Jeju Island was created from volcanic eruptions some two million years ago, but did not become an island until much later—perhaps around twenty thousand years ago, when melting glaciers caused a precipitous rise in sea levels. Contemporary Jeju Island has an area of 1,847 square kilometers (714 square miles) and lies about sixty kilometers southwest of the Korean mainland. It is dominated by Mount Halla, an extinct volcanic crater whose height of almost two thousand meters makes it the highest mountain in South Korea. The climate is subtropical, with four distinct seasons, including a mild, dry winter and a warm, humid summer.

Early signs of human settlement on Jeju Island date to about ten thousand years ago. As the island's population grew, a small community evolved into a distinct civilization that came to be known as the Tamna Kingdom (탐라). Other early names for the island include Tangna (탁라), Seomna (섬나), and Tammola (탐모라).

It is not known precisely when the Tamna Kingdom was founded, but it was clearly well established by the early centuries of the first millennium AD. Historical records indicate extensive maritime trade with surrounding areas, as well as a precarious relationship with powers on the Korean mainland. In 476, Tamna entered into a tributary arrangement with the Baekje Kingdom, which controlled the southwestern part of the Korean peninsula. Later, in the seventh century, Tamna switched its allegiance to the newly ascendant Silla Kingdom, whose capital Gyeongju is located in the southeast of the Korean mainland.

Tamna briefly reclaimed its independence after the collapse of Silla in 935. However, just three years later, it fell under the control of King Taejong, founder of the Goryeo dynasty, which was to rule the Korean peninsula for the next four and a half centuries. The island was officially annexed in 1105, and was renamed Jeju 'province across the sea' in 1295.

In 1270, a battered army of rebels landed on Jeju Island—the survivors of a failed uprising against the Goryeo Kingdom, which had surrendered much of its authority to Mongolian invaders. The rebels were eventually pursued by a force of ten thousand Goryeo and Mongol troops, who annihilated them three years later. For the next one hundred years, the Mongols held sway over Jeju Island, intermarrying with the inhabitants, using the land to raise horses and livestock, launching raids against Japan, and finally turning on Goryeo itself. It was at this point, in 1374, that the Goryeo king Gongmin dispatched a large naval force to Jeju Island, successfully wresting it from Mongol control after a bloody battle.

A few years later, the Goryeo Kingdom gave way to the Joseon dynasty (1392–1897), which drew Jeju Island into its highly centralized administrative network in 1404. Under Joseon, Jeju Island lost what little remained of its autonomy, and its residents were subjected to many indignities and restrictions, including a prohibition against leaving the island, which was in effect from 1629 to 1825. Various uprisings, including one in 1862, another in 1898, and still another in 1901, were brutally suppressed.

The Japanese occupation of Korea (1910–1945) brought still more hardship to Jeju Island, but the worst was yet to come. In the spring of 1948, Jeju Island was in a state of turmoil. Amid deep resentment stemming from a wide range of grievances, rebels attacked several police stations and polling places on April 3—Sasam, or 4-3, as it came to be known. In the weeks and months that followed, soldiers and right-wing vigilantes dispatched by the national government inflicted terrible vengeance on the population of Jeju Island. Between fifteen thousand and thirty thousand people were killed (perhaps 10 percent of the population), and thousands of others fled into exile in Japan. Until the early 1990s, even the mention of the Jeju massacre was considered by the national government to be a treasonous act, subject to severe punishment, and the full facts did not come to light until a special truth commission issued its report in 2003.[1]

Modern Jeju Island is an autonomous self-governing province of a now democratic Republic of Korea. No longer a "land of rocks and wind," as it was once known, its fields of volcanic ash soil, bounded by stone fences, produce tangerines, grains, and vegetables of various sorts. Its natural beauty and ocean setting have made it a mecca for tourists, contributing to a vibrant economy and growing prosperity.

Thanks to its unique history and relative isolation, Jeju Island has a culture that distinguishes it from the Korean mainland, as well as from other parts of Asia. Two aspects of Jeju culture are especially visible and well known.

---

1. The report was commissioned in 2000 by President Kim Dae-jung and chaired by Prime Minister Goh Keon; it was received and approved in 2003 by President Roh Moo-hyun, who issued an official apology. The Korean version of the report can be found at http://www.jeju43peace.or.kr/pages.php?p=4_2_1_1, and an English translation at http://jeju43peace.or.kr/report_eng.pdf.

Large statues, known as *dolhaleubang* (돌하르방 'stone grandfathers'), dot the island. Standing up to eight feet tall and carved from volcanic rock, these gods of protection and fertility were first produced in the mid-1700s. They have become powerful symbols of the mystique of Jeju Island.

Jeju Island is famous too for its *haenyeo* (해녀) 'sea women,' also known as *jawmnye* (좀네), who for centuries have braved the cold and treacherous waters of the Korean Strait to dive, without scuba gear, for abalone and other creatures of the sea. Working year round, they make up to a hundred dives a day, often holding their breath for more than a minute as they descend to depths that can exceed thirty feet. Relatively few *haenyeo* still ply their difficult trade; their numbers have fallen from more than twenty-five thousand in the 1960s to fewer than five thousand today, most of whom are in their sixties or older (see S.-H. Choe 2014).

Other aspects of Jeju culture are less visible to the casual observer—its folklore, its traditional matriarchal family structure, its wedding and funereal practices, and its shamanistic rituals, with their unique music and dance. Perhaps most important of all, however, is its language.

3. The Language

The speech of Jeju Island goes by many names—*Jejueo* 'Jeju language,' *Jejumal* 'Jeju speech,' *Jejudomal* 'Jeju Island speech,' *Jeju jiyeogeo* or *Jeju bangeon* 'Jeju regional language,' and *Jeju satuli* 'Jeju dialect.' In recent years, *Jejueo* (pronounced *jay-joo-uh*) has been gaining popularity. It is used in the provincial government's 2007 Language Act and in the name of the *Jejueo Bojeonhoe* ('The Jeju Language Preservation Society').

The name *Jejueo* was first used by Ju-Myeong Seok (1947), and has since appeared in a number of important pieces of scholarship, including the dictionary prepared by Hyun et al. (1995, 2009), and grammars by Y.-b. Kang (2007) and J.-W. Ko (2011a,b). Somewhat ironically, however, *Jejueo* is actually the Korean name for the language of Jeju Island; it is not the name most commonly used by speakers of the language, who prefer *Jejumal* or *Jejudomal*. Nonetheless, *Jejueo* appears likely to be the name by which the language will be known in the future. For that reason, we will use it here.

Jejueo has two major varieties, one spoken in the northern half of the island (and perhaps more influenced by Korean) and the other spoken in the southern half. There is no "standard" variety, however, and we will for the most part ignore differences among individuals and speech communities. The more important issue for now relates to whether Jejueo deserves to be called a language.

For much of modern history, the distinction between language and dialect has been a matter of politics in much of the world. The speech of a bigger or more powerful community is called a language, whereas the speech of a smaller or less influential group is labeled a dialect. Max Weinreich (1945) summed up this view with a famous aphorism: "A language is a dialect with an army and a navy."

Both Koreas have long maintained, independently of each other, that Korean national identity is embodied in a shared single indigenous language. "The ideology of one nation, one race and one language," writes S. Lee (2013, 233), "has gradually emerged over the course of Korean history." Indeed, as King (2007, 229) observes, it has now become "central to modern concepts of Korean national identity." A similar sentiment was expressed in 1984 by Kim Il-Sung, the founder of the North Korean state:

> Language is one of the most important common features defining a nation. No matter whether people have the same blood and live on the same territory, if their languages are different, they cannot be said to be one people. (cited by King 2007, 224)

Consistent with these views, the National Institute of the Korean Language and the Korean Ministry of Education have consistently classified Jejueo as a nonstandard dialect of Korean rather than a separate language—a practice that has been followed by many linguists as well (e.g., King 2006, 276ff.; Yeon 2012, 168–185; Sohn 1999, 74ff.; J.-h. Kim 2016, 110; among many others). But other considerations point in a very different direction.

For the most part, modern linguistics rejects politically motivated definitions of language-hood, grounding the distinction between dialect and language on linguistic considerations. The best-established criterion of this type is comprehensibility: if two varieties of speech are not mutually intelligible, they are classified as separate languages (Hockett 1958; Casad 1974; Gooskens 2013). Of course, the distinction is not always clear-cut, as Hockett and others have acknowledged, and it is widely recognized that mutual intelligibility is sometimes a matter of degree (see Okura 2015 for a review). However, this does not mean that no cases are sufficiently clear to invite a consensus. Many are, and the status of Jejueo and Korean appears to fall into that category.

Reports that monolingual Korean speakers have difficulty understanding Jejueo date back to at least the 1500s. Kim Jeong, the author of the *Topography of Jeju Island* (published in 1552) and a visitor to the island for fourteen months starting in the summer of 1520, made one of the earliest surviving comments on the island's speech. He noted that he had encountered many unfamiliar words and expressions but that, with time, he was able to learn the language "like a child learning the language of barbarians." Eighty years later, in 1601, Kim Sangheon spent six months on Jeju Island as a secret inspector for the national government. He too was struck by what he heard there, complaining in his travelogue *Namsalok* that he had trouble understanding the islanders' speech, which he compared to the "sound of a bird."

A two-hundred-year ban on travel to the mainland that began in 1629 increased the island's isolation, further deepening the linguistic divide between Jejueo and Korean. It is no surprise that today's visitors report that they cannot understand Jejueo at all—an observation that is occasionally seconded in the linguistic literature (e.g., Cho, Jung, & Ladefoged 2000, 110).

In order to investigate the comprehensibility of Jejueo more thoroughly, we conducted an experiment designed to assess the ability of different groups of monolingual Korean speakers to understand Jejueo. The findings have been reported in detail in earlier work (Yang et al. 2019); we offer a somewhat less detailed account here.

4. Classifying Jejueo

A total of fifty-six participants took part in the study: ten native speakers of Jejueo, whose results on the comprehension test serve as a baseline against which to measure the performance of other participants, and forty-six monolingual speakers of Korean who had no significant previous exposure to Jejueo—twenty-three from Seoul, eleven from the southern city of Yeosu in South Jeolla, and twelve from the southeastern city of Busan in South Gyeongsang province. (Both Yeosu and Busan have distinctive speech varieties of their own that depart from the Seoul standard.) Because most fluent speakers of Jejueo are middle-aged or older and because age is in general an important factor in psycholinguistic studies, all participants were between the ages of fifty-two and sixty-eight.

The centerpiece of the experiment was a silent video that depicted a series of events that began with a man on a ladder picking pears (the "pear story," created by Chafe 1980). Several fluent native speakers of Jejueo watched the video and described the events in Jejueo as they unfolded. The most fluent versions of the story were then merged into a single script that eliminated false starts, pauses, incomplete sentences, and the like. In a final step, the script was read aloud by a highly fluent female speaker, creating an auditory recording that was a minute and nine seconds in length.

Participants first listened to the narrative without interruption. The narrative was then replayed in five segments, varying in length from one to three sentences. After each segment, the participants were asked to respond in writing to one or more questions designed to test their understanding of what they had just heard. Both the questions (nine in all) and the responses were given in Korean.

Table 1.1 reports the mean percentage of correct responses by each participant group. As can be seen here, there is a large difference between the success rate of the native speakers of Jejueo (89.12 percent correct) and the performance of the other three groups, which ranged from a mere 6 to 9.92 percent.[2] Evidently, Jejueo was not intelligible to monolingual speakers of Korean, regardless of whether they speak Seoul Korean or one of the regional varieties found in the southern part of the Korean peninsula.

Table 1.1 **Percentage (%) of correct responses to the comprehension questions**

JEJUEO NATIVE SPEAKERS	SEOUL	YEOSU	BUSAN
89.21	9.92	6.00	6.14

This conclusion is further reinforced by the results of a self-assessment survey that we conducted in conjunction with our experiment. The survey asked the participants to rate their ability to understand Jejueo by circling the appropriate number on a scale that ranged from 0 ("not at all") to 5 ("quite a bit") to 10 ("everything"). (See figure 1.1.)

---

2. An analysis of variance showed that the effect of region on the test scores is significant, $F(2, 43) = 3.997$, $p = .03$. However, post hoc comparisons using the Bonferroni adjustment indicated that the mean percentage correct for Yeosu and Busan did not differ significantly from each other or from the score for Seoul [(Seoul and Yeosu ($p = .07$); Seoul and Busan ($p = .09$)].

0	1	2	3	4	5	6	7	8	9	10
not at all					quite a bit					everything

Figure 1.1   Self-assessment scale

The survey question was posed three times in the course of the comprehension experiment: once right before participants heard the narrative, a second time right afterward, and a final time after they had finished responding to the comprehension questions. Table 1.2 presents our findings.

Table 1.2   Self-assessment scores for comprehension (scale of 0 to 10)

SURVEY QUESTION	JEJU ISLAND	SEOUL	YEOSU	BUSAN
Before experiment	8.0	1.78	1.72	1.16
After narrative	8.1	0.65	0.27	1.08
After questions	8.3	0.41	0.30	0.75

Here again, we see a sharp contrast between the Jejueo speakers and the Korean monolinguals. The former group indicated a strong ability to understand Jejueo from the beginning (8 on our 0-to-10 scale) and slightly increased that assessment as they progressed through the experiment. In contrast, the three groups of monolingual Koreans acknowledged at the outset that they had a very limited ability to understand Jejueo (less than 2 out of 10), and ended up lowering their self-assessment in the course of the experiment to less than 1 on our scale—the equivalent of "almost nothing."

Still, more research is called for, and we continue to explore the issue of comprehensibility as a criterion for language-hood, both in a Korean setting and in an international context. A study of the latter type, reported by Yang, O'Grady, et al. (2019), is worth mentioning here. In order to establish a baseline against which to measure the performance of the participants in our Jejueo study, we investigated the extent to which Norwegian is comprehensible to speakers of Dutch. (Norwegian and Dutch are related but uncontroversially distinct Germanic languages.) Using a methodology and materials comparable to those for the Jejueo study, we tested the intelligibility of Norwegian to twenty-eight native speakers of Dutch, none of whom had significant previous exposure to the language.

The average success rate for the Dutch speakers on the comprehension questions for Norwegian was 9.89 percent, which falls into the same range as the success rate of the monolingual Korean speakers in our study of Jejueo.[3] Moreover, a self-assessment survey similar to the one used in the Jejueo study yielded comparable results. Before the study began, the Dutch speakers estimated their ability to comprehend Norwegian at 2.3 on average (on our 0-to-10 scale). They then lowered their mean self-assessment to 1.18 after hearing the narrative, and lowered it still further to 1.05 after trying to respond to the comprehension questions.

These findings leave little room for doubt: Jejueo and Korean are distinct languages, just as Norwegian and Dutch are.

5. The Koreanic Language Family

There is much still to learn about the origin of Jejueo, but it is clearly related to Korean. One sign of this is the existence of systematic phonetic correspondences in the lexical items of the two languages. The words in table 1.3 illustrate one such correspondence, involving Jejueo *j* (/tʃ/) and Korean *g* (/k/) in front of the vowel *i*. (The words from each language are written using the system of Romanization recommended by the National Institute of the Korean Language; see chapter 2 for details.)

Table 1.3   A phonetic correspondence between Jejueo and Korean

Jejueo	Korean	Meaning
jil (질)	*gil* (길)	'path, road'
jipeuda (지프다)	*gipda* (깊다)	'deep'
jimchi (짐치)	*gimchi* (김치)	'kim chee'

As illustrated in table 1.4, the lexicon of Jejueo and Korean reveals a mixture of similarities and differences, as one would expect from related languages—including French and Spanish, German and Dutch, or Mandarin and Cantonese. (A short bidirectional diction-

---

3.   By way of further comparison, Jensen's (1989) study of the mutual intelligibility of Spanish and Portuguese as they are spoken in South America, which used a methodology similar to ours (comprehension questions about orally presented passages), yielded a success rate in the 50–60 percent range.

ary [Jejueo–English and English–Jejueo], prepared as a companion to this volume, is available at https://sites.google.com/a/hawaii.edu /jejueo/dictionary.)

Table 1.4   Jejueo and Korean vocabulary

JEJUEO	KOREAN	MEANING
bam (밤)	*bam* (밤)	'night'
bi (비)	*bi* (비)	'rain'
swe (쉐)	*so* (소)	'cow'
abang (아방)	*abeoji* (아버지)	'father'
badang (바당)	*bada* (바다)	'sea'
nang (낭)	*namu* (나무)	'tree'
gojang (고장)	*kkoch* (꽃)	'flower'
sanggoji (상고지)	*mujigae* (무지개)	'rainbow'
jiseul (지슬)	*gamja* (감자)	'potato'

A sizeable number of morphemes and words in the two languages are identical: *bam* (밤) 'night,' *bi* (비) 'rain,' *ga-da* (가다) 'go,' *o-da* (오다) 'come,' *bo-da* (보다) 'see,' *meog-da* (먹다) 'eat,' and so on. Korean has of course influenced Jejueo over the years, but many shared items, like the ones just mentioned, are the same in Middle Korean, from which both Jejueo and Korean descended. These items reflect common provenance; they do not show that Jejueo is a dialect of Korean. There are many identical or near-identical words in Spanish and Italian, too, yet neither is a dialect of the other. Mutual intelligibility, not the number of "similar" words, is the decisive factor.

It is also common to find words in Jejueo that have close cognates in Korean but a different use. For example, the Jejueo verb *gawm-da* (곱다) 'wash' looks almost identical to Korean *gam-da* (감다), but the two differ in their meaning: washing the body in Jejueo versus washing just hair in Korean. There are also words like *sichida* (시치다) 'clean, wash' that are now considered archaic in Korean, but are still in everyday use in Jejueo.[4] Phenomena of this sort are commonplace in language families around the world, from Germanic and Romance to Polynesian and Chinese. They do not, in and of themselves, establish that one language is a dialect of another.

Morphology, too, shows similarities and differences. Some suffixes are identical in the two languages, such as the case markers *-i*

---

4.   Interestingly, the word has apparently also been retained in the speech of Jeolla province.

and *-eul,* both from Middle Korean. But matters are very different when we consider the past progressive (past continuative). Whereas Korean makes use of the subordinating conjunction *-go* in combination with the existential verb *iss(-da)* and the perfective suffix *-eoss,* Jejueo employs the continuative suffix *-eoms* and the past-tense suffix *-eon,* neither of which has a direct counterpart in modern Korean. (A complete list of abbreviations can be found on pp. xi–xii.)

Korean:

*Nongbu namu sim-**go**   **iss-eoss**-eo.* (농부 나무 심고 있었어)
farmer   tree   plant-CON be-PFV-SE
'A farmer was planting a tree.'

Jejueo:

*Nongbani nang singg-**eoms-eon**.* (농바니 낭 싱겂언)
farmer   tree   plant-CONT-PST
'A farmer was planting a tree.'

Many more similarities and differences will unfold as a fuller picture of Jejueo emerges in the chapters that follow.

What is clear even now, though, is that Korea has two very different varieties of speech within its borders. The two are similar in ways that show that they descended from a common source and must therefore be related to each other. Yet, despite those similarities, they are not mutually intelligible and must therefore be considered separate languages. The only way to make sense of this situation is to acknowledge that Korea is home to a language family, which we can call "Koreanic," that consists of at least two members—Korean and Jejueo.[5]

6. Jejueo Today

It is not yet clear whether Jejueo and Korean diverged from each other to the point of mutual unintelligibility in the Old Korean period (prior to 1000 AD) or in the Middle Korean period (1000 to

---

5. This choice of family name does not imply that Jejueo is a variety of Korean any more than saying that English is a Germanic language implies that it is a variety of German. It is possible that the Koreanic family contains a third member: some linguists believe that the traditional variety of speech of North Korea's Hamgyeong province may not be mutually intelligible with Korean.

1600), as we assume. However, the more recent history of Jejueo is relatively easy to reconstruct.

After centuries as the primary language of Jeju Island, Jejueo began to lose ground following the Second World War. As C. Yang (2014) explains, there were a number of reasons for the decline. The aftermath of the 4-3 incident resulted in the death or exile of a very large proportion of the island's population, as well as the destruction of more than half of the island's four hundred traditional villages. In the years that followed, the status of Jejueo was further undermined by an influx of tens of thousands of people from the Korean mainland. A national curriculum was implemented in 1955, and Korean became the official language of education. In the following decades, the local and national governments strongly promoted Korean as the language of national unity, and it gradually became the language of work and education on Jeju Island, although Jejueo continued to be used in many homes. The development of the island as a premier tourist destination made Korean even more important as the language of commerce, contributing further to the decline of Jejueo.

In 2010, UNESCO (http://www.unesco.org/languages-atlas) classified Jejueo as critically endangered, a classification reserved for languages whose youngest fluent speakers are grandparents or great-grandparents. According to UNESCO estimates, Jejueo is spoken by five thousand to ten thousand Jeju Islanders, about 1 to 2 percent of the total population of six hundred thousand. However, these estimates may well be overly optimistic, as many elderly Jeju Islanders who were once speakers of Jejueo are no longer fluent in the language and cannot use it for extended conversations. Younger residents of Jeju Island are, of course, even less proficient in the language.

A 2014 survey of 502 native Jeju Islanders by C. Yang asked participants to estimate their ability to speak and comprehend Jejueo on a scale of 1 (low) to 5 (high). The results for the portion of the survey dealing with comprehension are summarized in figure 1.2, which shows a strong correlation between proficiency in the language and age of the speaker.

The true picture may in fact be even bleaker, as there is reason to think that the participants' self-assessments were inflated. Yang, O'Grady, and Yang (2017) conducted a study that measured the ability of sixty-five Jeju Islanders, aged twenty to thirty, to understand prerecorded Jejueo sentences constructed from basic vocabulary. Each sentence was pronounced twice, once by a male speaker and

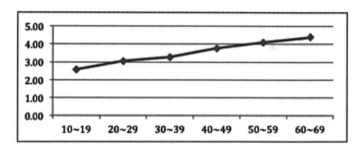

**Figure 1.2   Self-assessment of Jejueo comprehension
ability (502 participants)**

once by a female speaker, both of whom were in their seventies and
highly fluent. The job of the participants was to paraphrase each
sentence in written Korean right after hearing it—a task that drew
heavily on their comprehension skills.

Before listening to the test sentences, the participants were asked
to estimate their ability to comprehend Jejueo on a scale of 1 to 5. At
the conclusion of the task, they were asked to estimate their fluency
a second time on the same scale. The results suggest that participants
initially overestimated their ability to understand Jejueo: their mean
pretest self-assessment of 3.23 on the 5-point scale fell to 2.13 after
they heard actual Jejueo sentences—a statistically significant decrease
[t (126.46) = 5.47, $p < .0001$]. Moreover, this reassessment was for the
most part supported by relatively low scores on the translation task:
even young adults who grew up on Jeju Island had trouble understanding the language's distinctive vocabulary and suffixes.

By all estimates, then, Jejueo is in grave peril. Its fluent speakers
are elderly, and younger people either do not use it at all or speak a
heavily Koreanized version (Yang 2018). Sadly, the plight of Jejueo is
only worsened by confusion and misunderstanding about its nature
and status—matters that we hope to clarify in this book.

7. The Book

Jejueo is by no means an undocumented language. Quite to the contrary, in its guise as a "dialect" of Korean, it has been the object of
careful study by a number of distinguished linguists, who have produced helpful dictionaries and grammatical analyses, almost always in
Korean. A list of many of these contributions can be found at https://
sites.google.com/a/hawaii.edu/jejueo/more-about/bibliography.

In addition to drawing on data from published sources, we are fortunate to have been able to work with native speakers of Jejueo, from whom we have obtained valuable insights and judgments, on which we draw throughout the book. The description of the language that we offer is based largely on our own analysis of new and old information rather than a synthesis of previous scholarship. The end result is a picture of the language that resembles previous proposals in some respects and departs from them in others, most notably with respect to the system of verbal suffixes that express aspect, modality, tense, and sentence type.

This is the first comprehensive treatment of Jejueo in English and will therefore be one of the few sources of information about the language for readers not fluent in Korean. For that reason, it is tempting to cast our net as broadly as possible in terms of our coverage of the language. However, practical considerations have forced us to adopt a narrower focus, and we have deliberately chosen to forgo two lines of inquiry that might otherwise call for attention.

First, we have decided not to attempt a systematic treatment of matters relating to historical linguistics. It is well known that Jejueo has preserved certain phonological contrasts, vocabulary items, and grammatical morphology that reflect significantly earlier varieties of the language, some dating back to Middle Korean, if not farther. A proper compilation of these facts, and the commentary that they require, lies outside our areas of expertise, and we must leave this task to others. We look forward with interest and excitement to future developments in this area.

Second, we have decided not to undertake a point-by-point comparison of Jejueo and Korean. We are well aware of the value of comparative analysis, and we are all quite familiar with the phonology and morphosyntax of modern Korean. Yet, it is our feeling that Jejueo deserves its own treatment. Linguists think nothing of writing a book on Korean with no more than a passing mention of Jejueo; indeed, that is the standard practice. Yet, somehow, there is an unstated assumption that the less known Jejueo cannot be adequately studied if its features are not compared to those of Korean. We see the merits of using one language to understand another, and our understanding of Korean has no doubt informed our analysis of Jejueo, at least on occasion. However, we ask readers to allow us to give Jejueo its own book—a small gesture of respect to a language that has been so long in the shadows.

2

Phonology and Orthography

1. Introduction

This chapter focuses on the essentials of Jejueo phonology, orthography, and Romanization. We begin in section 2 by outlining the phonological inventory of Jejueo and some basic facts about its phonotactics. Section 3 describes the use of the Hangeul orthography to write Jejueo in a way that records key phonological and morphological information. We conclude with a survey of the language's most productive phonological processes.

In Romanizing Jejueo, we have followed the recommendations of the National Institute of the Korean Language (NIKL) for works of linguistic analysis. In adopting this practice, we set to the side the Yale system of Romanization that is favored by many linguists for writing in English about Korean. We do this with some reluctance and only because we anticipate a readership that will include non-linguists who are unfamiliar with the Yale system and will perhaps be more at ease with spellings such as *Jeju* than *Ceycwu*. Nonetheless, like the Yale system, the version of the NIKL system that we use posits a one-to-one correspondence between Roman letters and the symbols of Hangeul; it is therefore substantially different from the Romanization seen on street signs and place names, which puts more emphasis on pronunciation.

2. Phonemes

The phonology of Jejueo clearly reflects its membership in the Koreanic language family. This is especially evident in its inventory of
phonemic contrasts, illustrated here largely with the help of words
shared by Korean and Jejueo.

2.1 Consonants

A defining feature of the Koreanic consonant system is a series of
three-way contrasts involving plain, aspirated, and tense stops and
affricates. These contrasts are exemplified in table 2.1, starting with
the sound's symbol in the International Phonetic Alphabet (IPA), its
Romanization, the corresponding Hangeul symbol, and two examples in actual words. (Following Cho, Jun, & Ladefoged 2000, we use
the symbol * to indicate a tense consonant.)

Table 2.1   Jejueo stops and affricates

IPA Symbol	Roman-ization	Hangeul	Examples	
Labial stops:				
/pʰ/	p	ㅍ	*pe* (페) 'ticket'	*geonpung* (건풍) 'brag'
/p/	b	ㅂ	*be* (베) 'boat, belly'	*neobegi* (너베기) 'width'
/p*/	pp	ㅃ	*ppe* (뻬) 'bone'	*nawmppi* (놈삐) 'radish'
Dental stops:				
/tʰ/	t	ㅌ	*tawl* (틀) 'seaweed'	*gungtungi* (궁퉁이) 'idea'
/t/	d	ㄷ	*dawl* (돌) 'moon'	*gudeul* (구들) 'room'
/t*/	tt	ㄸ	*ttawl* (똘) 'daughter'	*butteo* (부떠) 'from'
Velar stops:				
/kʰ/	k	ㅋ	*kada* (카다) 'mix, burn'	*sawngki* (숭키) 'vegetable'
/k/	g	ㄱ	*gada* (가다) 'go'	*gagebi* (가게비) 'frog'
/k*/	kk	ㄲ	*kkada* (까다) 'peel'	*nikkeob* (니껍) 'bait'
Affricates:				
/tʃʰ/	ch	ㅊ	*chada* (차다) 'salty'	*guche* (구체) 'shame'
/tʃ/	j	ㅈ	*jada* (자다) 'sleep'	*imje* (임제) 'owner'
/tʃ*/	jj	ㅉ	*jjada* (짜다) 'weave'	*gujjag* (구짝) 'straight'

Jejueo also has a typologically unusual contrast between a lax,
lightly aspirated *s* and a tense counterpart, another signature feature
of Koreanic phonology (table 2.2).

Table 2.2   Dental fricatives

IPA Symbol	Roman-ization	Hangeul	Examples	
/s/	s	ㅅ	*sawl* (술) 'flesh'	*gawse* (ㄱ세) 'scissors'
/s*/	ss	ㅆ	*ssawl* (쑬) 'uncooked rice'	*seolsswe* (설쒜) 'gong'

There are three nasal consonants in Jejueo: labial *m*, dental *n*, and velar *ng* (table 2.3). (The velar nasal cannot occur syllable-initially.)

Table 2.3   Nasals

IPA Symbol	Roman-ization	Hangeul	Examples	
/m/	m	ㅁ	*ma* (마) 'fog'	*mawseum* (ㅁ슴) 'mind'
/n/	n	ㄴ	*neu* (느) 'you'	*musin* (무신) 'which'
/ŋ/	ng	ㅇ	*nang* (낭) 'tree'	

A palatal variant of *n* (IPA symbol: [ɲ]), occurs in front of *i* or *j*, as in *inyeog* (이녁) 'oneself' (P.-h. Hyun 1962).

The liquid *l* is pronounced as a flapped *r* between vowels, but as a clear-*l* sound elsewhere (table 2.4). (It does not occur word-initially in native words.)

Table 2.4   The liquid *l*

IPA Symbol	Roman-ization	Hangeul	Examples	
/l/	l	ㄹ	*jil* (질) 'road'	*saleum* (사름) 'person'

A voiceless glottal fricative /h/ rounds out the set of Jejueo consonants. It can occur word-initially and word-internally, but not at the ends of words (table 2.5). Some scholars report the presence of a voiced glottal fricative phoneme (IPA symbol: /ɦ/) (K.-W. Kim 2001; Y.-b. Kang 2007; P.-h. Hyun 1979, 1982, cited in Y.-b. Kang 1983, 30), an apparent reflex of a voiced velar fricative in Middle Korean (e.g., I. Lee & Ramsey 2000, 286; K.-M. Lee & Ramsey 2011, 143ff.). We know of no cases in contemporary Jejueo where this sound has a contrastive function; however, it can be heard as a variant of /h/

when it occurs between *l* and a vowel (Y.-b. Kang 2007; P.-h. Hyun et al. 2009).[1]

Table 2.5   The glottal fricative *h*

IPA SYMBOL	ROMAN- IZATION	HANGEUL	EXAMPLES
/h/	*h*	ㅎ	*haw-da* (ᄒᆞ다) 'do' *mohi-da* (모히다) 'nonglutinous'

    ilhe (일헤) 'seventh day' [ilɦe]   *meolhi* (멀히) 'wild grapes' [məlɦi]
    gawlhi (ᄀᆞᆯ히) 'chain'   [kɒlɦi] *mulhe* (물헤) 'paint'   [mulɦe]

For a different phonetic outcome in the patterns in table 2.5, see the discussion of sonorant doubling in section 4.2.2.

2.2 Vowels

The vowel phonemes of the variety of Jejueo used by older speakers can be represented as shown in table 2.6. (This is essentially the system posited by Cho, Jun, Jung, & Ladefoged 2001.)

Table 2.6   Jejueo vowels

	IPA SYMBOL	ROMAN- IZATION	HANGEUL	EXAMPLES
Front vowels:				
High:	/i/	*i*	ㅣ	*iluhuje* (이루후제) 'later'
Mid:	/e/	*e*	ㅔ	*eyeom* (에염) 'side, near'
Low:	/æ/	*ae*	ㅐ	*saengi* (생이) 'bird'
Central vowels:				
High:	/ɨ/	*eu*	ㅡ	*eus-da* (읏다) 'not have, not exist'
Mid:	/ə/	*eo*	ㅓ	*eomeong* (어멍) 'mother'
Low:	/a/	*a*	ㅏ	*abang* (아방) 'father'
Back vowels:				
High:	/u/	*u*	ㅜ	*uyeong* (우영) 'house garden'
Mid:	/o/	*o*	ㅗ	*olabang* (오라방) 'older brother'
Low:	/ɒ/	*aw*	ㆍ	*geuljaw* (글ᄌᆞ) 'letter'

---

1. Symbols written between slashes represent phonemes—contrastive sounds that can be used to distinguish between words: e.g., /pe/ 'boat' versus /pʰe/ 'ticket.' Throughout this book, symbols written between square brackets represent allophones, the various actual pronunciations of phonemes.

As table 2.6 indicates, at least some varieties of Jejueo have retained a vowel not found in contemporary Korean. *Alae a* (literally
'lower *a*') can be traced back to Middle Korean (K.-M. Lee 1993, 146;
Ogura 1944, 456–458). Its precise character today is a matter of controversy, and it is variously represented as mid back unrounded /ʌ/,
mid back rounded /ɔ/, low central /ɐ/, and low back rounded /ɒ/
(P.-h. Hyun 1962; W.-J. Hyun 1988; Y.-H. Park 1988; S.-c. Jung 2000;
Cho et al. 2001; K.-W. Kim 2001; W.-B. Kim 2006; D.-H. Ko 2008; S.-D.
Moon et al. 2015). For the sake of exposition, we will represent the
vowel as /ɒ/, without committing to the details of its phonetic real-
ization. In the absence of an official Romanization convention, we
use the digraph *aw* to represent this vowel. In many words, *alae a* alternates with *o*: *ttawsi* (뜨시) versus *ttosi* (또시) 'again,' *nawmppi* (놈삐)
versus *nomppi* (놈삐) 'radish,' and so on. This alternation is manifested in many of the examples used throughout this book.

Some older speakers of Jejueo maintain a contrast between *e*
(ㅔ) and *ae* (ㅐ) (W.-B. Kim 2005; D.-H. Ko 2008). Based on a study
of sixty native speakers born prior to 1950, S.-D. Moon et al. (2015)
conclude that the distinction has been maintained primarily in word-
initial syllables.

semi (세미) 'spring (water)' /semi/
sæmi (새미) 'a kind of rice cake' /sæmi/

However, there seems to be no clear contrast between the two vowels
in the speech of most younger speakers (Cho et al. 2001).

In sum, the vowel quadrangle for older fluent speakers of Jejueo
can be depicted as shown in figure 2.1, with nine separate vowels,
represented by their phonetic symbols.

/i/	/ɨ/	/u/
/e/	/ə/	/o/
/æ/	/a/	/ɒ/

**Figure 2.1 The "vowel quadrangle"
for Jejueo (older fluent speakers)**

For younger or less fluent speakers, there are just seven vowels, ar-
ranged as shown in figure 2.2.

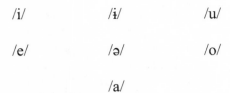

/i/   /ɨ/   /u/

/e/   /ə/   /o/

/a/

**Figure 2.2 The "vowel quadrangle"
for Jejueo (younger and less fluent
speakers)**

A word of caution is called for before proceeding. Because our system of Romanization for both vowels and consonants makes use of digraphs (*ng, eu, ae, aw*), there is some danger of ambiguity in certain cases. When this happens, we use a dot to indicate a syllable break.

Digraph (no dot):   Distinct letters (separated by a dot):
gonengi (고넹이) 'cat'   *en.gida* (엔기다) 'be hugged'
neu (느) 'you'   *me.uda* (메우다) 'fill'

2.3 Glides

Jejueo has two on-glides: *y* and *w*, each of which can combine with a following vowel to create a diphthong (table 2.7). The *y* can occur with all vowels except *i* and *eu*; *w* can appear with all vowels except *eu*, *u, o*, and *aw*. (The double *alae a* symbol indicates *alae ya*.)

Table 2.7   Jejueo glides

y	*w*
yesugjekkillag (예숙제낄락) 'quiz, riddle'	*walida* (와리다) 'be in a big hurry'
yagaegi (야개기) 'neck'	*wenchag* (웬착) 'left side'
yole (요레) 'here, this place'	*wiyeom* (위염) 'danger'
yawla (ᄋᆞ라) 'several'	*weollyeog* (월력) 'calendar'

Hangeul and the standard Romanization maintain the historical contrast between the diphthongs *yae* (얘) and *ye* (예), now both pronounced *ye*, as well as the distinction among *wae* (왜), *we* (웨), and *oe* (외), now all pronounced *we* (S.-D. Moon et al. 2015). This homophony has proven problematic, leading S.-D. Moon et al. (ibid. 90) to propose that the contrast no longer be made in writing. Nonetheless, we will opt in this book for the more conservative orthographic practice.

Both Hangeul and the standard Romanization include the digraph *ui* (ᅴ), corresponding to the Middle Korean diphthong /ɨj/. However, the diphthong itself has been all but lost. S.-D. Moon et al. (2015) report that *eu* is a possible reflex in word-initial position, with *i* heard elsewhere; *ui* was given a diphthongal pronunciation just 10 percent of the time by male speakers and not at all by females.

*ui*nam (의남) 'fog'	can be pronounced *eunam*
bas-dui (밧듸) 'in the field'	usually pronounced *batti*
moui-da (모의다) 'nonglutinous'	usually pronounced *moida*

2.4 Phonotactics

The maximally complex phonetic syllable in Jejueo consists of a single consonant in the onset position, a vowel or diphthong, and a single consonant in the coda position.

V only:	*aw* (ᄋ) 'yes'
CV:	*ma* (마) 'fog'
CVC:	*pen* (펜) 'side'

A medial consonant (other than *ng*) in a VCV pattern is pronounced at the onset of the second syllable even if that creates a mismatch between syllables and morphemes. (A hyphen represents a morpheme boundary; a dot represents a syllable boundary.)

gob-a (곱아) pronounced *go.ba*

hide-SE

'hide'

dawl-eumin (돌으민) pronounced *daw.leu.min*

run-if

'if (I) run'

We return to this issue in section 3.

2.5 Prosody

As observed by S.-C. Jung (1999, 545; 2000, 82) and K.-W. Kim (2001, 34), vowel length, stress, and tone are not used contrastively in Modern Jejueo. Moreover, Jejueo is prosodically somewhat similar to the Seoul variety of Korean, with accentual phrases whose basic tonal pattern is Low-High-Low-High (S.-H. Lee 2014). However, there are also substantial differences, which we will not attempt to describe here; for discussion see W.-b. Shin (2015) and Y.-l. Ko (2009).

3. Orthography

Jejueo does not have a literary tradition, and until recently was usually not written by its speakers. With efforts to preserve and revitalize the language now underway, considerable attention has been devoted to developing and refining an orthography. There is a consensus that Jejueo can and should be written using Hangeul, the uniquely Korean script developed in the fifteenth century by King Sejong the Great. Two special features define this orthography.

First, Hangeul is a deep (or morphophonemic) orthography: it favors morphological transparency over pronunciation by providing (where possible) a single spelling for each morpheme. Thus, the Jejueo word for 'chicken' has the spelling (둑 ~ *dawg*), even when it is pronounced 'dawng,' as in the second example below.

둑 (*dawg*) 'chicken'   [tɒk]
둑눈 (*dawg-nun*) 'chicken eye'   [tɒŋnun]

A second key feature of Hangeul orthography, whether it is used for Korean or for Jejueo, is that letters are organized into blocks.

Korean: Jejueo:
만 들 다   멩 글 다
man.deul.da   *meng.geul.da*
'make'   'make'

But there is an important proviso here, which was codified for Korean in 1933 and is central to the modern orthography. When there is a mismatch between syllable boundaries and morpheme boundaries, the latter typically win out. The perfective form of 'give' in Korean is a case in point, since the final consonant of the aspectual suffix *-eoss* (었) is pronounced at the beginning of the next syllable; see the discussion of phonotactics in section 2.4.

주었어   *ju-eoss-eo* pronounced *ju.eo.sseo*

    give-PFV-SE

    'gave'

Although pronounced *ju-eo-sseo* (주어써), the word is written *ju-eoss-eo* (주었어) in order to maintain the integrity of each of its component morphemes. Put simply, morphology takes precedence over phonology.

The situation in Jejueo is somewhat more complicated. Because the language is understudied, it is often unclear where the morpheme boundaries lie. As a result, a number of researchers adopt the de facto practice of grouping letters into phonetic syllables, especially in the case of verbal morphology. This has led to spellings such as the following, which obscure the presence of the continuative suffix *-ams* (앎).

> 터주암서 (*teoju-**am**-seo*) pronounced *teo.ju.am.seo*
> 'making a hole (in clothes/shoes)'

In contrast, we follow the practice of representing a word's composition in a more transparent manner, in accordance with the basic principles of modern Hangeul orthography.

> 터주앎어   *teoju-**ams**-eo*
>
> make.a.hole-CONT-SE
>
> 'making a hole (in clothes/shoes)'

As we will see in more detail in later chapters, adherence to the principle of morphological transparency reveals many facts about word structure that would otherwise be obscured, especially in the case of verbs. This in turn promises to simplify the teaching and learning of Jejueo—an important consideration for efforts to revitalize the language. For a detailed discussion of this matter, see Yang et al. (2019).

4. Phonological Processes

The phonological processes that modify pronunciation in Jejueo can be divided into two classes: those that are "Koreanic," in the sense of also being widely manifested in Korean, and those that occur primarily or exclusively in Jejueo. We will deal with each in turn. (In order to keep the chapter as accessible as possible, we will use phonetic transcription only when the effects of phonological processes are not evident in the Hangeul spelling and/or the Romanization.)

4.1 Phonological Processes Shared with Korean

4.1.1 Voicing

Plain stops and affricates (Romanized as *b*, *d*, *g*, and *j*) are at most partially voiced in initial position. However, they are fully voiced when they occur between two vowels, or between a sonorant and a vowel. (This subtlety is not captured by Hangeul or by our system of Romanization—hence the need for IPA notation.)

b (ㅂ):	*baleu* (바르) 'sea'	[parɨ]
	i baleu (이 바르) 'this sea'	[ibarɨ]
	jin baleu (진 바르) 'long sea'	[tʃinbarɨ]
d (ㄷ):	*donggos* (동곳) 'icicle'	[toŋgot]
	i donggos (이 동곳) 'this icicle'	[idoŋgot]
	jin donggos (진 동곳) 'long icicle'	[tʃindoŋgot]
g (ㄱ):	*gadal* (가달) 'leg'	[kadal]
	i gadal (이 가달) 'this leg'	[igadal]
	jin gadal (진 가달) 'long leg'	[tʃingadal]
j (ㅈ):	*jumenggi* (주멩기) 'pocket'	[tʃumeŋgi]
	i jumenggi (이 주멩기) 'this pocket'	[idʒumeŋgi]
	jin jumenggi (진 주멩기) 'long pocket'	[tʃindʒumeŋgi]

Aspirated consonants remain voiceless in all contexts; tense consonants appear to manifest modest voicing in intervocalic positions, but are otherwise voiceless.

4.1.2 Neutralization in final position

A signature feature of Koreanic languages is the neutralization of various consonant contrasts at the end of a syllable. The neutralization is manifested in two ways. First, because consonants are not released in syllable-final position, voicing, aspiration, and tensing are lost in Jejueo. Thus *p* (ㅍ) and *b* (ㅂ) are both pronounced as an unreleased *p*-like sound at the end of a syllable, *g* (ㄱ) and *kk* (ㄲ) are both pronounced as an unreleased *k*-like sound, and so on. (The diacritic symbol ˺ marks an unreleased consonant.)

b (ㅂ):	*kob* (콥) 'nail'	pronounced [kʰop̚]
p (ㅍ):	*sseop* (썹) 'leaf'	pronounced [s*əp̚]
g (ㄱ):	*beonjjig* (번찍) 'clear'	pronounced [bəndʒ*ik̚]
kk (ㄲ):	*bakk* (밖) 'outside'	pronounced [pak̚]

Second, affricates and fricatives end up being pronounced in syllable-final position as if they were *t*, the closest corresponding stop.

s (ㅅ):	*naws* (낯) 'face,'	pronounced [nɒt̚]
j (ㅈ):	*nawj-gog* (낯곡) 'low and'	pronounced [nɒt̚ k*ok]

4.1.3 Tensing

Lax consonants are predictably tensed when they occur right after an obstruent. This effect is not represented in either Hangeul or the standard Romanization. (A hyphen in the examples below marks a morpheme boundary.)

*yeog-**b**ul* (역불) 'on purpose'	bold-faced consonant is pronounced ***pp***
*nog-**d**i* (녹디) 'mung beans'	bold-faced consonant is pronounced ***tt***
*nob-**s**e* (놉세) 'wind from east or west'	bold-faced consonant is pronounced ***ss***
*gag-**j**i* (각지) 'bean pod'	bold-faced consonant is pronounced ***jj***
*dawd-**d**ang* (돋당) 'run + suffix'	bold-faced consonant is pronounced ***tt***
*jolab-**g**og* (조랍곡) 'sleepy + suffix'	bold-faced consonant is pronounced ***kk***
*gob-**j**u* (곱주) 'hide + suffix'	bold-faced consonant is pronounced ***jj***
*aj-**g**e* (앚게) 'sit + suffix'	bold-faced consonant is pronounced ***kk***
*daws-**s**u-da* (돗수다) 'warm + suffixes'	bold-faced consonant is pronounced ***ss***

Tensing may sometimes also occur when a lax consonant follows a nasal at a morpheme boundary within a compound.

    bam-jil (밤질) 'night road'   bold-faced consonant
                                                is pronounced *jj*
    nang-gaji (낭가지) 'tree branch'   bold-faced consonant
                                                is pronounced *kk*

Jejueo also commonly tenses the first consonant of a verbal suffix when the final consonant of the stem is a nasal (S. Oh et al. 2015, 30).

    gawm-ge (곰게) 'wash+ suffix'   pronounced *gawmkke*
    geun-dang (근당) 'rake + suffix'   pronounced *geunttang*
    geom-su-da (검수다) 'black + suffix'   pronounced *geomssuda*

There is no comparable tensing for nominal suffixes (S. Oh et al. 2015, 30).

    mawm-gwang (몸광) 'gulfweed + with'   pronounced *mawmgwang*
    sanggun-deole (상군더레)   pronounced *sanggundeole*
      'skilled woman-diver + to'

4.1.4 Aspiration

    A lax consonant can be aspirated under a variety of conditions. The most systematic and regular examples involve the merger of a lax consonant with a following /h/ to create a single aspirated consonant. In the first example below, for instance, the final consonant of *seodab* (서답) 'laundry' is converted into the corresponding aspirated stop when the word combines with *hawda* (ᄒ다) 'do.'

    seodab-haw-da (서답ᄒ다)   pronounced *seodapawda*
      'do the laundry'
    angjag-haw-da (앙작ᄒ다) 'cry a lot'   pronounced *angjakawda*
    menttag-haw-da (멘딱ᄒ다) 'smooth'   pronounced *menttakawda*

The effects of this process are not represented in either Hangeul or the standard Romanization, both of which use a two-consonant sequence, as in the examples above, rather than a single aspirated consonant.

    Merger and aspiration also take place when *h* precedes a lax consonant, a much less common pattern. This happens in a small number of words whose root ends in a "hidden" *h*, which is not directly pronounced but which merges with the lax consonant in the onset of the next syllable to yield an aspirated consonant.

joh-gog (좋곡) 'good + suffix'   pronounced *jo-kog*
noh-da (놓다) 'put + suffix'   pronounced *no-ta*

4.1.5 Nasalization

An obstruent that immediately precedes a nasal consonant undergoes nasalization.

dawg-nun (독눈) 'chicken's eye'   pronounced *dawngnun*
sawdab-makke (수답마께) 'laundry stick' pronounced
                                                          sawdammakke
yawp-mun (욥문) 'side door'   pronounced *yawmmun*
bas-nalog (밧나록) 'dry-field rice plant' pronounced *bannalok*

4.1.6 *n* insertion

An *n* is added to the beginning of the second component of
certain compounds if that item's initial sound is *i* or *y*. (The added
n is represented orthographically in only some of the compounds
that undergo this process.) In the final example below, *s* (a 'pseudo-
genitive' marker to be discussed in chapter 3) is nasalized to *n* under
the influence of the *n* that is inserted in front of *yagegi*, yielding two
n sounds where previously there had been none.

dam-il (담일) 'stone-fence work'   pronounced *damnil*
jawm-nyeo (줌녀) 'woman diver'   pronounced *jamnyeo*
  (*nyeo* < *yeo*)
ssog-ib (쏙입) 'inner leaf'   pronounced *ssongnib*
guj-in il (궂인 일)   pronounced *gujinnil*
  'unpleasant/hard work'
dwi-s-yagegi (뒷야게기) 'back of neck' pronounced *dwinnyagegi*

The phenomenon is not without exceptions, however; *n*-insertion
does not take place in the following examples.

dog-yag (독약) 'poisonous drug'   pronounced *dogyag* or
                                                          dokkyag
ses-imo (셋이모) 'second eldest aunt'   pronounced *settimo*

4.1.7 Palatalization

The dental fricatives /s/ and /s*/ are palatalized in front of /i/
or /j/.

sili (시리) 'rice cake steamer'   pronounced *shili* [ʃiri]
sim (심) 'power'   pronounced *shim* [ʃim]

A much less common form of palatalization affects *d*, but only when it occurs in front of an affixal *-i*.

mawd-i (묻이) 'eldest child'   pronounced *mawji*
gudum-bad-i (구둠받이) 'dustpan'   pronounced *gudumbaji*

4.1.8 Irregular verbs

There are various types of irregular verbs. One major class of this type is characterized by the conversion of a stem-final *d* (ㄷ) into *l* (ㄹ) in front of a vowel.

gawd-da (굳다) 'speak':
    gawd-gog (굳곡) 'speak and,' but *gawl-eumin* (굴으민) 'if (s/he) speaks' and *gawl-eunan* (굴으난) 'because (s/he) speaks'
dawd-da (돋다) 'run, go':
    dawd-gog (돋곡) 'run and,' but *dawl-eumin* (돌으민) 'if (s/he) runs,' *dawl-eunan* (돌으난) 'because (s/he) runs'

In another important class of irregular verbs, a stem-final *b* is deleted in front of a suffix that begins with *u* and undergoes lenition to *w* in front of any other vowel.

gob-da (곱다) 'pretty':
    gob-gog (곱곡) 'pretty and,' but *go-unan* (고우난) 'because (s/he) is pretty,' *go-umin* (고우민) 'if (s/he) is pretty,' and *gow-an* (고완) 'pretty'
jub-da (줍다) 'sew':
    jub-gog (줍곡) 'sew and,' but *ju-unan* (주우난) 'because (s/he) sewed,' *ju-umin* (주우민) 'if (s/he) sews,' and *juw-eon* (주원) 'sewed'

4.1.9 Reduction of *i* to *y*

A stem-final *i* can be reduced to *y* when followed by a suffix that begins with a vowel.

dawl-a-ji-eos-jeo (돌아지엇저) 'be hung'   or *dawlajyeosjeo* (돌아졋저)
chu-li-eos-jeo (추리엇저) 'pay'   or *chulyeosjeo* (추렷저)
jeb-hi-eos-jeo (젭히엇저) 'be caught'   or *jebhyeosjeo* (젭혓저)

A further type of contraction, at least for some speakers, involves the reduction of *yeos* to *is*.

> *dawl-a-jy-eos-jeo* (돌아졋저) 'be hung'   pronounced *dawlajisjeo*
> *jeb-hy-eos-jeo* (젭혓저) 'be caught'   pronounced *jebhisjeo*
> *chuly-eo-by-eos-jeo* (추려볏저)   pronounced *chulyeobisjeo*
>   'completely pay'

4.2 Phonological Processes Not Shared with Korean

4.2.1 Aspiration within compounds and phrases

In compounds and phrases where the first root ends in a sonorant and the second root begins with a lax consonant, the consonant can sometimes be aspirated (J.-h. Kim 2014b, 103–105; J.-W. Ko 2011a, 33). Kim reports that the aspiration strategy is more common among elderly people, and that younger and more educated speakers prefer tensing. Aspiration is reflected in the Hangeul spelling (and in our Romanization), but tensing is not.

> *gawseul* (ᄀᆞ슬) + *jangma* (장마)   pronounced *gawseul changma*
>   'fall rainy season'   (ᄀᆞ슬 창마)
> *halmang* (할망) + *jib* (집)   pronounced *halmang jjib* or
>   'grandmother's house'   *halmang chib* (할망칩)
> *gwendang* (궨당) + *jib* (집)   pronounced *gwendang jjib* or
>   'relative's house'   *gwendang chib* (궨당칩)
> *mawm* (ᄆᆞᆷ) + *gug* (국) 'gulfweed   pronounced *mawm kkug* or
>   soup'   *mawm kug* (ᄆᆞᆷ쿡)
> *sul* (술) + *beng* (벵)   pronounced *sul ppeng* or *sul*
>   'alcohol bottle'   *peng* (술펭)
> *gwe* (궤) + *bang* (방)   pronounced *gwe pang* (궤팡)
>   'store room'
> *mawmul* (ᄆᆞ물) + *gawleu* (ᄀᆞ르)   pronounced *mawmul kkawleu*
>   'buckwheat powder (flour)'   or *mawmul kawleu* (ᄆᆞ물ᄏᆞ르)
> *an* (안) + *deule* (드레)   pronounced *an-tteule* or
>   'to the front'   *an-teule* (안트레)

At least some instances of this type of aspiration reflect a phenomenon that dates back to Middle Korean (J.-r. Hong 1998; K.-M. Lee & Ramsey 2011, 172, 183–184), which had a "hidden" *h* at the end of various noun stems. Although unwritten and never pronounced directly, the *h* has the effect of triggering aspiration of a following consonant.[2] Hong lists twenty such nouns, some of which appear in the list below.

dolh + *jaengi* (돓 + 쟁이)   *dol-chaengi* (돌챙이)
stone maker   'wall maker'

baleuh + *gwegi* (바릏 + 궤기)   *baleu-kwegi* (바르퀘기)[3]
  sea   meat   'fish'

anh + *geoli* (않 + 거리)   *an-keoli* (안커리)
inside house   'inner house'

nah + *do* (낳 + 도)   *na-to* (나토)
age   even   'even (his/her) age'

amh + *dosegi* (않 + 도세기)   *am-tosegi* (암토세기)
female pig   'sow'

joh +   *bab* (좋+밥)   *jo-pab* (조팝)
millet rice   'millet rice'

mah +   *ji-da* (맣 + 지다)   *ma-chi-da* (마치다)
rainy.season become-SE   'become rainy season'

However, not all cases of aspiration within Jejueo compounds can be explained in this way. As Hong notes, there is no reason to believe that *ppang* (빵) 'bread' has a hidden *h*; yet aspiration occurs in *ppang-chib* (빵칩) 'bakery.'

4.2.2 Consonant doubling

Under a variety of circumstances, a word-final consonant can be doubled when followed by a vowel-initial word or morpheme. In the following examples, a stem-final *n* or *l* is doubled when a locative marker is attached to a noun (S.-C. Jung 1998, E. Kang 2004, J.-W. Ko et al. 2014, 17).

---

2. As K.-M. Lee and Ramsey (2011, 171) observe, remnants of this process can be discerned in Modern Korean words such as *am-talg* 'hen, female chicken,' in which the unexpected aspiration in the word for 'chicken' (normally *dalg*) is a reflex of a historical hidden *h* in *am* 'female,' formerly *amh*.

3. This compound has a second variant, *baleus-gwegi* (바룻궤기), with a final *s* on *baleu* (an apparent instance of *sai sios*, which causes tensing in the following consonant); see chapter 3, section 5.2.

an-e (안에) 'inside'   pronounced *anne*
jil-e (길에) 'at the street'   pronounced *jille*

A similar effect can be heard in the names for January, July, and August, although it is not reflected in the spelling.

il-*weol* (일월) 'January': from *il* 'one' and *weol* 'month,'
    pronounced *il-lweol*
chil-*weol* (칠월) 'July': from *chil* 'seven' and *weol* 'month,'
    pronounced *chil-lweol*
pal-*weol* (팔월) 'August': from *pal* 'eight' and *weol* 'month,'
    pronounced *pal-lweol*

Sonorant doubling (accompanied by *h*-deletion) also occurs within compounds such as the following (K.-W. Kim 2001, 115–116; S. Oh et al. 2015, 35).

jeon**h**wa (전화) 'telephone'   pronounced *jeon.nwa*
man**h**wa (만화) 'comic book'   pronounced *man.nwa*
il-**h**awg-nyeon (일흑년) 'first grade'   pronounced *il.lawng.nyeon*
il**h**eum (일흠) 'name'   pronounced *il.leum*
il**h**eun (일흔) 'seventy'   pronounced *il.leun*

Doubling of an obstruent, which has the effect of tensing, can be observed at the boundaries within compounds and phrases. As illustrated in the following examples from S.- C. Jung (2001, 307), this process affects the final consonant of the first part of the compound when the second part begins with a vowel.

hangu**g**-*eumsig* (한국음식)   pronounced *hangukkeumsig*
  'Korean food'
ma**d**-adeul (맏아들) 'first son'   pronounced *mattadeul*
jiji**b**-ai (지집아이) 'girl'   pronounced *jijippai*
gaju**g** os (가죽옷) 'leather clothes'   pronounced *gajukkos*
da**b** alan (답 알안) 'knowing the   pronounced *dappalan*
  answer'

4.2.3 *l*-deletion

The phoneme /l/ is deleted from root-final position in verbs when it is followed by a suffix that begins with *u* or (as also happens in Korean) *n* (J.-W. Ko 2011a, 175). (The suffix -*u* in the following examples is an addressee honorific; see chapter 7, section 5.)

dawl-da (돌다) ·	*daw-u-da* (드우다) '(It is) sweet.'
eojil-da (어질다)	*eoji-u-da* (어지우다) '(She) is gentle.'
eol-da (얼다)	*eo-u-da* (어우다) '(It) is cold.'
jil-da (질다)	*ji-u-da* (지우다) '(It) is long.'
meol-da (멀다)	*meo-u-da* (머우다) '(It) is far.'
kkawneul-da (꼬늘다)	*kkawneu-u-da* (꼬느우다) '(It) is thin.'
bul-da (불다)	*bu-nan* (부난) 'because (it is) windy'
dawl-da (돌다)	*daw-nan* (드난) 'because (it is) sweet'
gal-da (갈다)	*ga-nan* (가난) 'because (you) ground it'
al-da (알다)	*a-nan* (아난) 'because (you) know'

4.2.4 Vowel harmony

As in Korean, certain verbal suffixes in Jejueo show an alternation between *eo* and *a* that is sensitive to the (final) vowel of the stem to which they attach. The examples in table 2.8 involve the past-tense suffix *-as/eos* (앗/엇), which is accompanied here by the sentence ender *-eo* (어).

Table 2.8   Vowel harmony in Jejueo

eo	*a*
meog-eos-eo (먹엇어) 'ate'	*gal-as-eo* (갈앗어) 'plowed'
sis-eos-eo (싯엇어) 'washed'	*gob-as-eo* (곱앗어) 'hid'
guj-eos-eo (궂엇어) 'was/is bad'	
geus-eos-eo (긋엇어) 'drew (a line)'	

The two languages differ in an interesting way: whereas in Korean, *a* is used only if the vowel in the preceding syllable is *a* or *o*, in Jejueo *a* is also found under various other conditions, which may reflect vowel harmony patterns in Middle Korean, as John Whitman notes:[4]

• (In the case of many verbs), if the stem ends with the vowel *aw* followed by a consonant.

yawg-as-eo (욱앗어)	*dawl-as-eo* (돌앗어)
mature-PFV-SE	run-PFV-SE
'S/he is mature.'	'S/he ran.'

---

4. We have observed considerable variation among speakers in how they implement vowel harmony. Further research is clearly called for.

*chawj-**as**-eo* (훛앗어)   but not: *gawj-**eos**-eo* (긎엇어)

look.for-PFV-SE   take-PFV-SE

'S/he looked for it.'   'S/he took it.'

- (In the case of certain verbs), if the stem ends with the vowel *eu* or *u* followed by the consonant *l*.

*menggeul-**as**-eo* (멩글앗어)   *beoseul-**as**-eo* (버슬앗어)

make-PFV-SE   earn-PFV-SE

'S/he made it.'   'S/he earned it.'

*jawdeul-**as**-eo* (즈들앗어)   *jawmul-**as**-eo* (즈물앗어)

worry-PFV-SE   get.dark-PFV-SE

'S/he worried.'   'It got dark.'

But not:

*deul-**eos**-eo* (들엇어)   *beomul-**eos**-eo* (버물엇어)

ask-PFV-SE   get.dirty-PFV-SE

'S/he asked.'   'It got dirty.'

- (In some cases and for some people) if the (final) vowel of the stem is *i* or *y*.[5]

*Ij-**a**-bul-eos-jeo.* (잊아불엇저)

forget-LV-COMPL-PFV-SE

'I completely forgot.'

*Mawl-**li**-ams-jeo* (몰리앖저), contractible to *mawl-ly-**a**ms-jeo* (몰럈저)

dry-CAUS-CONT-SE

'I am making (it) dry.' (J.-W. Ko 2011a, 97)

*Nawl-**li**-ams-jeo* (놀리앖저), contractible to *nawl-ly-**a**ms-jeo* (놀럈저)

fly-CAUS-CONT-SE

'I am making (it) fly.' (ibid.)

---

5. Use of *a* in this context was also an option in Middle Korean (K. Lee & Ramsey 2011, 162).

But not:

Jil-eos-eo (질엇어)   *Gow-a-jy-eos-eo.* (고와젓어)

watery-PFV-SE   pretty-LV-become-PFV-SE

'It is watery.'   'She became pretty.'

It is even possible to find *a* after a stem that ends in *u*, as in the case of the dysyllabic root in the verbs *eonju-da* 'gather' and *teoju-da* 'to make a hole in clothes/shoes.' In contrast, *ju-da* 'give' calls for *eo* for many speakers, although at least one of our consultants allows *a* here as well.

teoju-as-eo (터주앗어)   *ju-eos-eo* (주엇어)

make.hole-PFV-SE   give-PFV-SE

'made a hole (in clothes/shoes)' 'gave'

4.2.5 *y* insertion

An initial *y* is added to a verbal suffix that begins with the vowel *eo* when the stem ends in *e, ae,* or *aw.*[6]

Je-yeos-eo. (제엿어)   *Gae-yeos-eo?* (개엿어?)

fast-PFV-SE   mix.with.water-PFV-SE

'(It) was fast.'   'Did (you) mix (it) with water?'

Je-yeoms-eo (제엾어)   *Gwe-yeoms-eo.* (궤엾어)

be.fast-CONT-SE   boil-CONT-SE

'(It) is becoming fast.'   '(It) is boiling.'

Haw-yeoms-u-gang? (ᄒ엾우강?)   *Haw-yeos-eo.* (ᄒ엿어)

do-CONT-AH-SE   do-PFV-SE

'Are (you) doing (it)?'   '(S/he) did (it).'

One qualification is called for: there seems to be only one verb in contemporary Jejueo whose root actually ends in the phoneme *aw,* namely, *haw-da* (ᄒ다) 'do.' Other verbs that are spelled with *aw,* such as *saw-da* (ᄉ다) 'stand' and *chaw-da* (ᄎ다) 'wear a sword,' are pronounced as if the vowel were *a* and therefore do not manifest *y* insertion.

---

6. Contracted forms are also possible here: *je-s-eo* (젓어), *be-s-eo* (벗어), *he-ms-u-gang* (헶우강), and *he-s-eo* (헷어).

4.2.6 Umlaut triggered by a grammatical marker

The vowels *a*, *eo* and *o* typically undergo umlaut in (C)VC roots when a following derivational suffix contains *i* (table 2.9; K.-W. Kim 2001, 187). (Because the passive and causative suffixes used in most of these patterns are nonproductive, it is perhaps best to consider the umlaut found here to be diachronic rather than synchronic.[7])

Table 2.9   Umlaut in Jejueo

CHANGE	EXAMPLE	AFTER UMLAUT
a ⟶ e	*an-da*	*en-gi-da* (엔기다) 'be held'
eo ⟶ e	*meog-da*	*meg-hi-da* (멕히다) 'be eaten'
eo ⟶ e	*meog-da*	*meg-i-da* (멕이다) 'feed/make eat'
a ⟶ e	*kkakk-da*	*kkekk-i-da* (껨이다) 'be sharpened'
a ⟶ e	*jab-da*	*son-jeb-i* (손젭이) 'handle, door knob'
o ⟶ we	*nog-da*	*nweg-i-da* (눼이다) 'make melt'
o ⟶ we	*jjoch-da*	*jjwech-gi-da* (쮈기다) 'be followed'

Umlaut does not occur when the root ends in *l*, as in *sal-li-(u)-da* (살리(우)다) 'revive' (lit. 'make live') or *al-li-(u)-da* (알리(우)다) 'inform.'

4.2.7 Alternations involving initial vowels in suffixes

Like Korean, Jejueo has a variety of verbal suffixes that require an initial vowel when their stem ends in a consonant. The examples in table 2.10 illustrate an alternation of this type for *-min* (민) 'if' and *-meong* (멍) 'while.' Although *eu* is the default epenthetic vowel in these patterns, there are two additional options (S. Oh et al. 2015, 31): *i* when the stem-final consonant is *s*, *j*, or *ch*, and *u* after a stem-final labial consonant (table 2.11). The variant with *-u* is retained even when the stem-final *b* is dropped, as happens in irregular verbs like *dab-da* (답다) 'build,' where we find *da-umin* (다우민) and *da-umeong* (다우멍).

---

7. Moreover, umlaut sometimes fails to apply when the conditions for it appear to be met: the passive form of *ppob-da* (뽑다) 'pluck, pick' is *ppob-hi-da* (뽑히다), without umlaut.

Table 2.10   Epenthesis in Jejueo suffixes

STEM ENDING IN A VOWEL	STEM ENDING IN A CONSONANT
ka-min (카민) 'burn + if'	*an-eumeong* (안으멍) 'hug + while'
beolleu-meong (벌르멍) 'break +while'	*mid-eumin* (믿으민) 'believe + if'
o-meong (오멍) 'come + while'	*yawg-eumin* (욕으민) 'mature + if'
nawli-min (누리민) 'get out [of a vehicle] + if'	

Table 2.11   Additional options for epenthesis

STEM ENDING IN *s*, *j*, OR *ch*	STEM ENDING IN A LABIAL CONSONANT
nawj-imin (높이민) 'low + if'	*jawm-umin* (줌우민) 'put [into soup] + if'
guj-imin (궂이민) 'bad + if'	*sim-umeng* (심우멍) 'grab + while'
daws-imeong (돗이멍) 'hot + while'	*gob-umeng* (곱우멍) 'hide + while'
jus-imeong (줏이멍) 'pick + while.'	*deop-umeong* (덮우멍) 'cover + while'
joch-imeong (좇이멍) 'follow + while'	

4.2.8 Lenition of *b* to *w*

In Jejueo, as in Korean, a stem-final *b* in certain verbs undergoes lenition to *w*, as noted in section 4.1.8.

elub-da (에룹다) 'be difficult'   *eluw-a* (에루와) 'It is difficult.'
bib-da (빕다) 'pour'   *biw-a* (비와) 'Pour (it)!'

However, unlike Korean, Jejueo also allows lenition at word boundaries within noun compounds, as illustrated in the following two examples (S. Oh et al. 2015, 66).

dae   +   *bas* (대 + 밧) > *daewas* (대왓)
bamboo field   bamboo field

swe + *bang* (쉐 + 방) > *swewang* (쉐왕)
cow   room   barn

3

Nouns

1. Introduction

This chapter is devoted to a survey of nouns and their morphology. The first two sections examine the various types of nouns found in Jejueo; remaining sections focus on the form and function of nominal morphology.

2. Basic Nouns

Basic nouns refer to persons, objects, and substances. For the sake of convenience, we divide words of this type into two major subclasses—common nouns and proper nouns.

2.1 Common Nouns

Common nouns may have either countable or noncountable referents. Count nouns typically denote individuals and objects; they may occur with a determiner as well as with a plural marker (see section 3).

> *i   halmang-deol* (이 할망덜)
>
> this grandmother-PL
>
> 'these grandmothers'

Noncount nouns typically denote substances. They can occur with a determiner, but not with a plural marker.

geu gawlu (그 ᄀᆞ루)	*mosal* (모살)	*ssawl* (ᄊᆞᆯ)
'that powder'	'sand'	'rice'

2.2 Proper Nouns

Proper nouns are used to name individuals and places. (The first three names below are apparently Koreanic in origin, while the last three are Sino-Korean.)

San-gumbuli (산굼부리)	a crater located on the southeast side of Jeju Island
Dakkeune (다꼬네)	a village located on the north side of Jeju Island
Soesokkag (쇠소깍)	an estuary in Hyodon village (south side of Jeju Island)
Jejudo (제주도)	Jeju Province/Jeju Island
Hallagsan (할락산)	Mount Halla
Samseonghyeol (삼성혈)	the holes in the earth from which the three mythical founders of the Tamna Kingdom emerged

Proper nouns with a human referent can be accompanied by the vocative marker *a* (아) when used to call out to the person in question.

-*a* (아)

ALLOMORPHY: -*ya* (야) after a stem that ends in a vowel.
USAGE: Vocative marker.

*Gildong-**a*** (길동아)	*Jim-gae-**ya*** (짐개야)
Gildong-VOC	Kim-family-VOC
'Hey, Gildong'	'Hey, member of the Kim family'

3. Kinship terms

Kinship terms are often used instead of proper nouns as a matter of politeness, both to call people and to refer to them. The following list was compiled based on studies by J.-W. Ko (2011a), S.-J. Song (2007), and P.-h. Hyun et al. (2009).

3.1 Basic Kinship Terms

haleubang (하르방), *haleubaji* (하르바지), *haleubanim* (하르바님)
  'grandfather'

halmang (할망), *halmani* (할마니), *halmanim* (할마님)
  'grandmother'
abang (아방), *abaji* (아바지), *abanim* (아바님) 'father'
eomeong (어멍), *emi* (에미), *eomeoni* (어머니), *eomeonim* (어머님)
  'mother'
nampen (남펜), *seobang* (서방) 'husband'
gagsi (각시), *jibsaleum* (집사름), *ansaleum* (안사름) 'wife'
adawl (아돌) 'son'
ttawl (뚤) 'daughter'
sonji (손지) 'grandchild'
ttawlsonji (뚤손지) 'son/daughter of one's daughter'
adawlsonji (아돌손지) 'son/daughter of one's son'
seong (성) 'older brother or sister to a same-gender sibling'
asi (아시) 'younger brother or sister of same-gender sibling'
olabanim (오라바님) 'older brother to a female'
olabang (오라방) 'male sibling to a female'
nui (누이) 'female sibling of a male'
nunim (누님) 'older sister of a male'
olaebi (오래비) 'younger brother of a female' (informal)
gomo (고모) 'paternal aunt'
imo (이모) 'maternal aunt'
samchun (삼춘) 'uncle'
sawchun (ㅅ춘) 'cousin'
joke (조케) 'nephew/niece'
jawsawg (ㅈㅅ) 'grandson/granddaughter' (used by grandparents, informal)

In-Laws for a Male (Husband)

gasi-abang (가시아방) 'father-in-law, wife's father'
gasi-eomeong (가시어멍) 'mother-in-law, wife's mother'
cheo-abang (처아방) 'wife's father'
cheo-eomeong (처어멍) 'wife's mother'
cheo-nam (처남) 'wife's younger brother'
cheo-jawke (처ㅈ케) 'nephew/niece on wife's side'
maebi/maebu (매비/매부) 'brother-in-law, wife's brother'
ajumang (아주망) 'sister-in-law, brother's wife'

In-Laws for a Female (Wife)

s(s)i-abang (시/씨아방) 'father-in-law to wife'
s(s)i-eomeong (시/씨어멍) 'mother-in-law to wife'
si-nu/si-nu.ui (시누/시누의) 'husband's sister'

ajubang (아주방) 'brother-in-law, husband's brother'
seongnim (성님) 'husband's older brother's wife'
dongse (동세) 'husband's brother's wife'

In-Laws for Parents

sau (사우) 'son-in-law'
menuli (메누리) 'daughter-in-law'

3.2 Supplementary Prefixes for Kinship Terms

The following prefixes can be used to make more precise certain kinship relations (see S.-J. Song 2007).

chin- (친) 'paternal'

chin-*haleubang* (친하르방) 'paternal grandfather'
chin-*sonji* (친손지) 'grandchild from son'
chin-*samchun* (친삼춘) 'paternal uncle'
chin-*gomo* (친고모) 'paternal aunt'

dang- (당) 'paternal'

dang-*haleubang* (당하르방) 'paternal grandfather'
dang-*sonji* (당손지) 'grandchild from son'
dang-*samchun* (당삼춘) 'paternal uncle'
dang-*jawke* (당ㅈ케) 'nephew/niece from father's side'

seong- (성) 'paternal'

s**eong**-*haleubang* (성하르방) 'paternal grandfather'
s**eong**-*halmang* (성할망) 'paternal grandmother'
s**eong**-*sonji* (성손지) 'grandchild from son'

we- (웨) 'maternal'

we-*halmang* (웨할망) 'maternal grandmother'
we-*sonji* (웨손지) 'grandchild from daughter'
we-*samchun* (웨삼춘) 'maternal uncle'

daseum- (다슴) 'step'

daseum-*eomeong* (다슴어멍) 'stepmother'
daseum-*abang* (다슴아방) 'stepfather'
daseum-*adawl* (다슴아돌) 'stepson'
daseum-*ttawl* (다슴똘) 'stepdaughter'

ches- (쳇) **'oldest'** (alternates with *keun* [큰])

    ches-adawl (쳇아돌) 'first/oldest son'
    ches-ttawl (쳇똘) 'first/oldest daughter'
    ches-asi (쳇아시) 'first younger sibling'

The term *ches-* is also used in farming to denote the first agricultural product farmed in a field in a particular year; for example: *ches-gamjeo* (쳇감저) 'first crop of sweet potatoes,' *ches-jiseul* (쳇지슬) 'first crop of potatoes,' *ches-boli* (쳇보리) 'first crop of barley.'

keun (큰) **'eldest, first-born'**

    keun-abang (큰아방) 'one's father's first/eldest brother'
    keun-eomeong (큰어멍) 'the wife of one's father's eldest brother'
    keun-seong (큰성) 'first/eldest brother/sister'
    keun-ajibang (큰아지방) 'first/eldest brother-in-law'
    keun-haleubang (큰하르방) 'first/eldest brother of one's grandfather'
    keun-dongse (큰동세) 'first/eldest brother's wife'
    keun-adawl (큰아돌) 'first/eldest son'
    keun-ttawl (큰똘) 'oldest daughter'
    keun-jib (큰집) 'the house of the eldest son of a family'

ses- (셋) **'second eldest of three or more'**

    ses-olabang (셋오라방) 'second eldest brother'
    ses-abang (셋아방) 'one's father's second eldest brother'
    ses-eomeong (셋어멍) 'wife of one's father's second eldest brother'
    ses-menuli (셋메누리) 'second eldest daughter-in-law'
    ses-gomo (셋고모) 'second eldest paternal aunt'

maljes/maljas- (말젯/말잣) **'third/third eldest'** of four or more

    maljes-abang (말젯아방) 'one's father's third eldest brother'
    maljes-eomeong (말젯어멍) 'wife of one's father's third eldest brother'
    maljes-seong (말젯성) 'third eldest brother'
    maljes-we-samchun (말젯웨삼춘) 'one's mother's third eldest brother'
    maljes-imo (말젯이모) 'one's mother's third eldest sister'

jog-eun (족은) **'youngest'**

    jogeun*-adawl* (족은아돌) 'youngest son'
    jogeun*-abang* (족은아방) 'youngest (married) brother of one's father'
    jogeun*-samchun* (족은삼춘) 'youngest brother of one's father'

Certain of the above terms can be combined in various ways when the need arises (S. Oh et al. 2015, 55).

    keun-maljes*-haleubang* (큰말젯하르방) 'third brother of one's grandfather'
    ses-maljes*-haleubang* (셋말젯하르방) 'fourth brother of one's grandfather'
    jogeun-maljes*-haleubang* (족은말젯하르방) 'fifth brother of one's grandfather'

4. Other Noun Types

4.1 Compounds

Nouns can be formed by compounding two already existing nouns. (In several of the examples below, the morpheme *s* occurs between the two parts of a compound when the first part ends in a vowel; we return to this matter in section 5.2.)

Jeju-s-mal (제줏말)
Jeju-PGEN-speech
'Jeju speech'

sigge-s-nal (식겟날)
ancestor.rites-PGEN-day
'an ancestor's death anniversary'

nawmppi-s-gug (눔뻿국)
radish-PGEN-soup
'radish soup'

baleu-s-gwegi (바릇궤기)
ocean-PGEN-meat
'fish'

swe-gwegi (쉐궤기)
cow-meat
'beef'

u-s-deuleu (웃드르) 'upper field'
up-PGEN-field
'mountain village'

setang-gawlu (세탕ᄀ루)
candy-powder
'sugar'

son-geumeus (손그뭇)
hand-line
'palm line'

Compound-like nouns can also be formed by adding morphemes such as *-ge* (게) and *-dali* (다리), which were historically nouns
but now behave more like derivational affixes for words denoting
people.

-ge (게) 'person'

eob-ge (업게) 'person who takes care of a baby'
beong-ge (벙게) 'foolish person'
datang-ge/dadang-ke (다탕게/다당케) 'a person who is sly and
   talkative'
deolleong-ge (덜렁게) 'a person who is disorganized and lacking
   in concentration'

-dali (다리) 'person'

kkwe-dali (꿰다리) 'a person with a lot of tricks'
gwangjeol-dali (광절다리) 'a crazy person'
ganse-dali (간세다리) 'a lazy person'
gunyung-dali (군융다리) 'a wicked person'
molmyeong-dali (몰명다리) 'a weak and stupid person'
mongni-dali (몽니다리) 'a nasty person'

Compound-like patterns are also used to express certain diminutives
(J.-W. Ko 2011a; S.- N. Lee 1957, 58; B.-K. Koo 1999).

-egi (에기) 'baby'

song-egi (송에기) 'calf'
bing-egi (빙에기) 'chick'

-segi (세기) possibly from *egi* (에기), according to B.-K. Koo (1999, 121)

dawg-segi (독세기) 'egg' (*dawg*=chicken)
bag-segi (박세기) 'a small bowl for dipping water' (*bag*=gourd)

-sengi (셍이) 'young (animal)'[1]

mawng-sengi (뭉셍이) 'foal'
gang-sengi (강셍이) 'puppy'

---

1. The use of *ng* in association with a diminutive meaning has also been document-
   ed in Middle Korean (e.g., K.-M. Lee and Ramsey 2011, 174).

4.2 Verbal Nouns

Verbal nouns denote actions and states (table 3.1). As we will see in chapter 5, these nouns can combine with "light verbs" such as *haw-da* (ㅎ다), *na-da* (나다), and *ji-da* (지다) to create verbal expressions.

Table 3.1   Some verbal nouns

ACTIONS	STATES
gawttag (ㄱ딱) 'moving a little'	*sujil* (수질) 'motion sickness'
bunjis (분짓) 'division'	*jjokkeullag* (쪼끌락) 'smallness'
cheonggaeg (청객) 'ushering (at a funeral)'	*eojileong* (어지렁) 'mess'
buleumssi (부름씨) 'errand'	*sungag* (숭악) 'cruelty'
balmeng (발멩) 'invention'	*jawmi* (ᄌ미) 'fun'
gelhon (겔혼) 'marriage'	*gamang* (가망) 'blackness'
	jim (짐) 'steaming (of food)'
	teumeong (트멍) 'free time'

4.3 Nominalization

There are three strategies for nominalization in Jejueo.

-eum (음)[2]

ALLOMORPHY:

- *-im* after a stem that ends in *s*, *j* or *ch*
- *-um* after a stem that ends in a labial consonant
- *-m* after a stem that ends in a vowel or *l*

haw-m (ᄒᆷ) 'doing'   *sim-um* (심움) 'catching'
jus-im (줏임) 'gathering'   *sichi-m* (시침) 'washing'
daws-im (돗임) 'warmth'   *eol-m* (얾) 'coldness'
guj-im (궂임) 'badness'   *jikkeoji-m* (지꺼짐) 'happiness'

---

2. We have noted examples such as the ones below in which the nominalizer has the archaic form *-eom/am* found in Middle Korean (as well as in the continuative marker that is derived from it); see chapter 6, section 2.1.

jus-eom-jig (줏엄직)   *daws-am-jig* (돗암직)
gather-NMLZ-probability   warm-NMLZ-probability
'the likelihood of gathering (them)' 'the likelihood of it being warm'

-gi (기) (J.-h. Kim 2017, 246; see also J.-W. Ko 2011, 1, 140)

ALLOMORPHY: None.

sim-gi (심기) 'holding' *sawdab-haw-gi* (수답ㅎ기) 'washing laundry'
ib-gi (입기) 'wearing' *daws-gi* (돗기) 'warmth'

V-(eu)neun geo (V(으)는 거)

ALLOMORPHY: See chapter 8, section 1.

*Mansu-n   buleumssi haw-**neu-n**   **geo** jal haw-ju.*
Mansu-TOP errand   do-INDC-NPST.CON NMLZ well do-SE
(만순 부름씨ㅎ는 거 잘 ㅎ주)
'Mansu is good at doing errands.'

*Abang be   jjawlleu-**neu-n**   **geo** dowe-la.* (아방 베 쫄르는 거 도웨라)
father rope cut-INDC-NPST.CON NMLZ help-SE
'Help your father with the rope cutting.'

4.4 Bound Nouns

Bound nouns must be accompanied by a word or phrase that fills
out their meaning—typically either another noun or an adnominal
clause. The following bound nouns are common in Jejueo (see, e.g.,
J.-W. Ko 2011a, 114).[3]

*dawd-neu-n   **dui** (돋는 듸)* *nakkeu-l   **jung/chung***
run-INDC-NPST.CON place   fish-FUT.CON ability
'the place (I) run'   (나끌 중/충)
                                   'how to fish'

*gudum **ttamun** (구둠 따문)*   *haw-n   **cheg** (흔 책)*
dust   due.to   do-PST.CON pretending
'due to dust'   'pretending to have done (that)'

---

3. The spelling *dui* (듸) 'place' is etymological rather than phonetic; the word is
   pronounced as if it were *di*.

meog-eul   ***ttawleum*** (먹을 뜨름)   *molleu-l*   ***tawg*** (몰를 톡)
eat-FUT.CON nothing.but   not.know-FUT.CON reason
'just/only eating'   'the reason (you) don't know'

deul-eun   ***bae/ba*** (들은 배/바)   *bo-l*   ***chim***   *eus-jeo*
hear-PST.CON fact   see-FUT.CON worth not.be-SE
'the fact that (I) have heard'   (볼 침 웃저)
                                             'hardly worth seeing'

*dawl-eul-**lag*** (돌올락)   *dawl-eum-**bag*** (돌음박)
run-FUT.CON-bet   run-NMLZ-activity
'running on a bet'   'running activity'
                                             [a running game]

ga-l   ***-li*** (갈 리)
go-FUT.CON fact
'the fact that he will leave'

gyeong   *haw-l*   ***chawle/cheoli/cheole*** (경 홀 추레/처리/처레)
like.that do-FUT.CON   way
'way of doing (something) like that'

5. The Plural and Pseudo-Genitive Suffixes
5.1 The Plural

Jejueo has two plural markers:

-deol (덜) and *-ne* (네)

ALLOMORPHY: None.
USAGE: Plural marking is obligatory when a noun with a plural interpretation is accompanied by a determiner such as *i* 'this' or *geu* 'that'; otherwise, the plural marker is typically optional.

*seong-**deol*** (성덜)   *haleubang-**deol*** (하르방덜)
older.sibling-PL   grandfather-PL
'older siblings'   'grandfathers'

Only *-deol* can be used for nouns with non-human referents; *-ne* is restricted to pronouns and nouns that refer to humans.

*geu gingi-**deol*** (그 깅이덜)
that crab-PL
'those crabs'

*ga(i)-**ne*** (가(이)네)   *halmang-**ne**-ga*   *yeowag-he-ms-jeo.*
3-PL   grandmother-PL-NOM talk-do-CONT-SE
'they'   (할망네가 여왁헸저)
                                 'The grandmothers are conversing.'

On occasion, it is even possible to add *-deol* to a noun or pronoun that already carries the plural marker *-ne*.

*yecheong-**ne-deol*** (예청네덜)   *seonsuing-**ne-deol*** (선싱네덜)
married.woman-PL-PL   teacher-PL-PL
'(married) women'   'teachers'

*gaui-**ne-deol*** (가의네덜)   *neo-**ne-deol*** (너네덜)
3-PL-PL   2-PL-PL
'they'   'you (pl.)'

As was the case in Middle Korean (K.-M. Lee and Ramsey 2011, 174), *-ne* can have an "and-others" interpretation (sometimes called the "associative plural"). For instance, *Mansu-ne* (만수네) can mean 'Mansu and his family.' In patterns such as the following, *-ne* is sometimes analyzed as a possessive marker (J.-W. Ko 2011a, 145; Y.-b. Kang 2007, 55). (Korean too permits this use of *-ne*.)

*Gai neu-**ne** jib-ui   sal-ams-in-ya?* (가이 느네 집의 살았인야?)
3SG 2-PL   house-LOC live-CONT-NPST-SE
'Is s/he living in your (and your family's) house?'

*Sunja(**-ne**) ajimang-i   manawngji   gawj-eong w-as-jeo.*
Sunja(-PL)   sister.in.law-NOM pickled.garlic have-CON   come-PFV-SE
(순자(네) 아지망이 마눙지 궂엉 왓저)
'Sunja (and her family)'s sister-in-law has brought (us) pickled garlic.'

However, the real function of *-ne* here is to create an "and others" interpretation, consistent with the usual practice of pluralizing possessors related to a family member, a home, and one's country or language. Thus *neu-ne* in the first example above means 'you and others,' and *Sunja-ne* is meant to be interpreted as '*Sunja* and other family members.' For this reason, *-ne* is not allowed in patterns such as *Sunja yangji* (순자 양지) 'Sunja's face,' since a face is not something that can be jointly possessed.

5.2 The Pseudo-Genitive Suffix *-s*

ALLOMORPHY: None.

USAGE: The suffix *-s* appears in certain compounds and phrases, in the position illustrated below—between an initial word or morpheme that ends in a vowel and a second word or morpheme that begins with a consonant.

[…V]-*s*-[C…]

Called *sai-sios* (literally "in-between *s*") and dating back to Middle Korean, the morpheme is sometimes referred to as a genitive because many of the items in which it appears express a loose possessive-type relationship. We will refer to it as the "pseudo-genitive" in order to distinguish it from the full-fledged genitive suffix to be discussed in section 6.3. The following examples are from J.-W. Ko (2011a, 88–89; see also J.-W. Ko et al. 2014, 231-238).

u-s-jil (웃질)
above-PGEN-street
'overhead street'

gwi-s-bab (귓밥)
ear-PGEN-rice
'ear wax'

hwe-s-gug (횃국)
raw-PGEN-soup
'raw fish soup'

gwegi-s-jeom (궤깃점)
meat-PGEN-piece
'a piece of meat'

seo-s-kaleum (섯카름)
west-PGEN-neighborhood
'neighborhood in the west'

gawchi-s-nang (ㄱ칫낭)
chili-PGEN-tree
'chili plant'

gawle-s-chag (ㄱ렛착)
millstone-PGEN-pair
'a pair of millstones'

However, not all compounds of this type permit *sai sios*.

swe-gwegi (쉐궤기)	*swe-mag* (쉐막)
cow-meat	cow-hut
'beef'	'barn'

The pseudo-genitive suffix can also be used in combination with a locative marker to indicate a spatial association (usually location) between two things.

ssogob-ui-s-geo (쏘곱윗거)
inside-LOC-PGEN-thing
'the thing inside'

gwepang-ui-s-nalog (궤팡윗나록)
storage.room-LOC-PGEN-rice
'the rice (plants) in the storage room'

san-ui-s-nang (산윗낭)
mountain-LOC-PGEN-tree
'the trees on the mountain'

mengtengi-ye-s-paws (멩텡이엿풋)
basket-LOC-PGEN-red.bean
'the red beans in the basket'

daw-e/ye-s-bas (두엣/엿밧)
road.entry-LOC-PGEN-field
'a field that is located at the entry to the road.'

The pseudo-genitive marker is never heard as *s*. Rather, its default pronunciation is a voiceless dental stop, which has the effect of tensing a following lax obstruent. Thus *u-s-jil* (웃질) 'upper street' is pronounced as if it were *u-t-jjil*, and *gwi-s-bab* (귓밥) 'ear wax' sounds just like *gwi-t-ppab*. When the pseudo-genitive occurs in front of nasal, it is pronounced as if it were *n*: *sanui-s-nang* (산윗낭) 'trees on the mountain' is pronounced as *sanui-n-nang*.

6. Grammatical Case and Topic Markers

A variety of postnominal particles, often called "case markers," are used to identify the grammatical and semantic function of nouns and noun phrases.

6.1 Subject Marking

Subjects can be marked in a variety of ways, including by the traditional Koreanic nominative case suffix -*i* (이), which dates back to Old Korean.

-*i* (이)

> ALLOMORPHY: -*ga* (가) after a stem that ends in a vowel.
>
> USAGE: The principal function of the nominative marker is to indicate the subject.

> *Halmang-**i**   gawl-an-ya?* (할망이 굴안야?)
>
> grandma-NOM   talk-PST-SE
>
> 'Has grandmother said (that)?'

> *I   gawchi-s-nang-**i**   mujeong-haw-da.* (이 ᄀ칫낭이 무정ᄒ다)
>
> this chili-PGEN-tree-NOM health-do-SE
>
> 'This chili plant is healthy.'

> *I   banong-keul-**i**   mujeong-haw-da.* (이 바농클이 무정ᄒ다)
>
> this needle-machine-NOM durable-do-SE
>
> 'This sewing machine is durable.'

> *Mansu-**ga**   bulleumssi-haw-yeos-jeo.* (만수가 부름씨 ᄒ엿저)
>
> Mansu-NOM   errand-do-PFV-SE
>
> 'Mansu did an errand.'

> *Hawgge-**ga**   meo-n-ya?* (훅게가 먼야?)
>
> school-NOM   far-NPST-SE
>
> 'Is the school far away?'

Subjects often occur without any marker, especially in short sentences where there is no danger of misunderstanding.

Geu yecheong   *jib-ui*   *ga-s-jeo.* (그 예청 집의 갓저)

that married.woman house-DIR go-PFV-SE

'That woman has gone home.'

Yeongsu *oneol ses-adawl*   *pawl-ams-jeo.* (영수 오널 셋아돌 풀앖저)

Yeongsu today second-son sell-CONT-SE

'Yeongsu is marrying off his second son today.'

However, the nominative is called for in certain situations, such as
when the speaker wishes to highlight the referent of the subject
("s/he and only s/he").

*Mina-**ga***   *gob-ju* (미나가 곱주)

Mina-NOM pretty-SE

'Mina (not anyone else) is pretty.'

-*iseo* (이서)

A second type of subject marker is the locative particle -*iseo* (이서),
which can be used for subjects denoting a group or community (S.
Oh et al. 2015, 107; U.-T. Jung 1983, 11).

ALLOMORPHY: -*seo* after a stem that ends in a vowel. U.-T. Jung
(1983, 9) reports the use of the alternative form -*eseo* (에서).
USAGE: To mark a subject denoting a group or community.

Eotteong *u-nyeog-chib-**iseo***   *al-as-in-go?* (어떵 우녁칩이서 알앗인고?)

how   above-side-house-NOM know-PFV-NPST-SE

'How has the family from above found out (about it)?'

Uli *mawseul-**iseo*** *jal*   *he-sa-ju.* (우리 무슬이서 잘 헤사주)

1PL village-NOM   well do-OBLG-SE

'Our village must do well.'

*Si-(e)**seo***   *jil*   *menggeul-a-sa-ju.* (시 (에)서 질 멩글아사주)

village-NOM street make-LV-OBLG-SE

'The city (government) has to construct streets.'

-*la* (라)

C.-H. Kang (1983, 24–25, 40) reports that -*la* (라) could be used in
place of -*ga* by elderly speakers in rural areas as late as the 1980s.

*Neugsin-ne   seo-neo.i-**la***   *aj-an   nol-ams-in-di.*
old.person-PL three-four-NOM sit-CON play-CONT-NPST-SE
(늑신네 서너이라 앉안 놀았인디)
'Several old people are hanging out, sitting around.'

*Nuge-**la**   gyeong   gawl-eub-de-ga?* (누게라 경 긇읍데가?)
who-NOM like.that say-AH-EVI-SE
'Who said (anything) like that?'

*Al-dongne   pijengi gagsi-**la**   egi-l*
below/southern-village butcher wife-NOM baby-ACC
be-yeos-in-ge. (알동네 피젱이 각시라 에길 베엿인게)
get.pregnant-PFV-NPST-SE
'(I see that) the butcher's wife in the lower/southern part of
   the village got pregnant.'

*Neu-ne seongje-**la**   hawndui yeowag-haw-la.* (느네 성제라 훈듸 여왁ㅎ라)
2-PL   sibling-NOM together talk-do-SE
'You siblings, talk together.'

-le (레)

Y.-b. Kang (2007, 54) documents the use of *-le* as a nominative, always
with a stem that ends in a vowel.

*Sonji-**le**   Seoweol ga-n-den   haw-yeola.*
grandchild-NOM Seoul   go-NPST-CON do-SE
(손지레 서월간덴 ㅎ여라)
'S/he said that grandchild is going to go to Seoul.'

*Asi-**le**   i   jib-ui   sal-ams-jeo.* (아시레 이 집의 살았저)
younger.sibling-NOM this house-LOC live-CONT-SE
'My younger sibling is living in this house.'

6.2 Direct Object Marking

Although infrequent, an accusative case marker can be used to indicate a direct object.

-eul (을)

ALLOMORPHY: -l after a stem that ends in a vowel. The more formal variant of this morpheme, -leul, is used only occasionally (J.-W. Ko 2011a, 143).

USAGE: The primary function of the accusative marker is to indicate a direct object.

> *Uyeong-pas-dui*   *gojang-**eul** singg-eos-ju.* (우영팟듸 고장을 싱것주)
> vegetable-garden-place flower-ACC plant-PFV-SE
> 'I planted flowers in the vegetable garden.'

> *Na-**l**   dawl-ang   ga-b-seo.* (날 돌앙 갑서)
> 1SG-ACC accompany-CON go-AH-SE
> 'Please, accompany me when you go.'

> *Sili-le   gawleu-**l** dam-eula.* (시리레 ᄀ를 담으라)
> steamer-DIR flour-ACC put-SE
> 'Put the flour into the steamer.' (Y.-b. Kang 2007, 59)

6.3 Genitive

The genitive marker in Jejueo is -ui (의), which is pronounced and often spelled -i (이); see chapter 2, section 2.3. For the sake of exposition, we adopt the -i spelling here.

-i/-ui (이/의)

ALLOMORPHY:

• -e or -ye after a stem that ends in i.

USAGE: To indicate a possessor; in general, however, the possessor relation is unmarked.

> *Jib-**i**   bas-eun   eodui is-eo?* (집이 밧은 어듸 잇어?)
> house-GEN field-TOP where be-SE
> 'Where is your family's field?'

> *Si-**e/ye**-s-manung-i-la?* (시엣/옛마눙이라?)
> city-GEN-PGEN-garlic-be-SE
> 'Is it the garlic from the city?'

As we will see in section 7.1, a homophonous morpheme can also be used to mark location and direction under certain circumstances.

6.4 Dative Marking

Jejueo has at least four dative markers, whose primary function is to indicate an indirect object, typically a recipient.[4]

***-gawla* (ㄱ라)**; also spelled 곫아 (*gawl.a*)

ETYMOLOGICAL NOTE: *gawla* is derived from the verb *gawl-da* (곫다) 'to speak'; its use as a dative marker is restricted to nouns with human referents (M.-S. Kwon 2011, 21) and is possible only with verbs of speaking.

> *Gaui-**gawla** gongbui-haw-len haw-b-seo.* (가의ㄱ라 공븨ᄒ렌 흡서)
>
> 3SG-DAT   study-do-CON   do-AH-SE
>
> 'Please, tell him to study.'

The remaining three dative markers are all types of locatives built around the morpheme *dui* (듸) 'place' or the locative marker *ui* (의), which we discuss in section 7.1. The practice of using locatives to indicate indirect objects dates to Middle Korean (K.-M. Lee and Ramsey 2011, 189–190).

***-sindui* (신듸)**; also spelled 신디 (*sindi*), as we do here

ETYMOLOGICAL NOTE: *sindui* consists of the verbal root *si-* (시) 'be,' the nonpast adnominal suffix *-n* (ㄴ) and the noun *dui* (듸) 'place.' Its Middle Korean cognate was the locative noun *sondaw.i* (손디) 'place,' which also functioned as a dative marker (ibid.).

> *Geu saleum-**sindi** gawl-eub-di-ga?*
>
> that person-DAT   say-AH-EVI-SE
>
> (그 사름신디 곫읍디가?)
>
> 'Did you talk to that person?'

***-antui* (안틔)**; also spelled 안티 (*anti*), as we do here

ETYMOLOGICAL NOTE: Aspiration of the initial consonant of *dui* reflects the presence of a hidden *h* at the end of *an* 'inside'; see the discussion of this phenomenon in chapter 2, section 4.2.1.

---

4. Saltzman (2014) reports the use of *hanti*, a blend of Jejueo *anti* and Korean *hante* (한테).

I-geo   *neu-**anti** ju-ma.* (이거 느안티 주마)

this-thing 2SG-DAT give-SE

'I will give this to you.'

-apui (아픠); also spelled 아픠 (*api*), *ap.ui* (앞의) and *ap.i* (앞이)

ETYMOLOGICAL NOTE: The literal meaning of *ap* is '(in) front,' which then combines with the locative marker *-ui* (의). We use the spelling *api* when it is a dative marker and *apui* when it is a locative marker.

*Nuge-**api** ju-b-di-ga?* (누게아픠 줍디가?)

who-DAT give-AH-EVI-SE

'To whom did you give (it)?'

A second use for the dative is to indicate the possessor in patterns such as the following, which are built around an existential copula.

*Nawmppi gaui-**sindi**/**api**/**anti** sis-jeo.* (눔삐 가의신디/아픠/안티 싯저)

radish 3SG-DAT   be-SE

'S/he has the radish.'

6.5 Topic Marking

There are two apparent topic markers, *-eun* (은) and *-ilang* (이랑).

-eun (은)

ALLOMORPHY:

- *-n* (ㄴ) after a stem that ends in a vowel. Very occasionally, the variant *-neun* (는) is used in this context (J.-W. Ko 2011a, 138).

USAGE: The topic marker has two major functions: to indicate a stage-setting topic or to signal a contrast.

Stage-setting topic:

*Oneol-**eun** gwengilnal-i-u-da.* (오널은 궹일날이우다)

today-TOP Sunday-be-AH-SE

'Today is Sunday.'

Contrastive topic:

*Oneol-**eun** jawleujy-eong ani dwe-yeo.* (오널은 ᄌ르졍 아니뒈여)

today-NOM busy-CON   not become-SE

'TODAY is not possible because I'm busy (but tomorrow might
be okay).'

When it appears sentence-internally, rather than at the beginning
of a sentence, a topic-marked element can only have a contrastive
interpretation.

*Cheolsu-ga   penji-**n**   ig-eola.* (철수가 펜진 익어라)

Cheolsu-NOM letter-TOP read-SE

'I learned that Cheolsu was reading the LETTER (not something else, like a newspaper).'

-*i(l) lang* (이랑/일랑)

ALLOMORPHY:

• -*lang* (랑) after a stem that ends in a vowel or *l*

USAGE: Not well understood, but often interchangeable with
-*eun*; it appears to have a contrastive function.[5] For discussion, see
S.-D. Moon (2002) and Y.-b. Kang (2007, 61).

*Yeongsu-**lang** hawssawl il-haw-la!* (영수랑 ᄒ쏠 일ᄒ라!)

Yeongsu-TOP a.little   work-do-SE

'Youngsu (not others), work a little (please)!'

*Haleubang-**ilang** jeo-le   aj-ib-seo!* (하르방이랑 저레 앚입서!)

grandfather-TOP   there-DIR sit-AH-SE

'Grandfather (not others), sit over there!'

*Na-**lang** mawncheo awmawng-haw-k-yeo.* (나랑 ᄆ처 ᄋ뭉ᄒ켜)

1SG-TOP first   move-do-PROSP-SE

'I will move first (before others).'

---

5. J.-W. Ko (2011a, 138) treats -*ilang* as a type of subject marker. King (1994, 26)
suggests that it served as an "indicator particle" in the Korean of the seventeenth
century.

A topic marker may co-occur with a dative marker, but not with the nominative, accusative or genitive. (The form *-lang* is more common and natural than *-n* with the dative.)

*Abang-sindi-**lang** i-geo   anne-la!* (아방신디랑 이거 안네라!)
father-DAT-TOP   this-thing give-SE
'Give THIS to your FATHER!'

7. Postpositions

A large number of semantic contrasts and relations are expressed with the help of postnominal particles that are often called "postpositions."

7.1 Location and Direction

-deule/deole (드레/더레) 'to, into, toward'

ALLOMORPHY:

- *-le* (레) after a stem that ends in a vowel or *l* (S. Oh et al. 2015, 110)
- *-leule/leole* after a stem that ends in *l* and, sometimes, after a stem that ends in a vowel (J.-h. Kim 2014b, 51).
- Alternative forms include *-teule, -tile, -dile, -dele,* and *-lile* (Y.-b. Kang 2007).

*Sili-**le**   gawlu-l   dam-eula!* (시리레 ᄀᆞ를 담으라!)
steamer-DIR flour-ACC put-SE
'Put the flour into the steamer!' (ibid. Kang, 59)

*I   gawlu-**le** mul deo   biu-la!* (이 ᄀᆞ루레 물 더 비우라!)
this flour-DIR water more pour-SE
'Pour more water into this flour!' (ibid.)

*Geosseun chawm-jileum mangdegi-**le** son-eul   jeogjy-eon.*
quickly   sesame-oil   pot-DIR   hand-ACC wet-PST
(거쓴 춤지름 망데기레 손을 적견)
'(S/he) wet (her/his) hand quickly in the sesame oil pot.'
   (S. Oh et al. 2015, 110)

*I-chag-**deule** biw-a-bul-la!* (이착드레 비와불라!)
this-side-DIR pour-LV-COMPL-SE
'Pour (it) to this side!'

*Gaui-n   abang-iyeong badang-**deole** dawl-as-ju.*

3SG-TOP father-with   sea-DIR   run-PFV-SE

(가읜 아방이영 바당더레 돌앗주)

'S/he went to the sea with her/his father.'

*Hawssawl an-**teole**   aj-ila!* (ᄒᆞ쑬 안터레 앚이라!)[6]

a.little   inside-DIR sit-SE

'Sit toward the inside!'

*Yaui unyeongpas-**deole**   dawly-eo-ga-la!* (야의 우녕팟더레 ᄃᆞ려가라!)

3SG   vegetable.garden-DIR take-LV-go-SE

'Take him/her to the vegetable garden!' (based on J.-h. Kim
2014b, 51)

*Seogwipo-**leule** gibel-haw-yeon.* (서귀포르레 기벨ᄒᆞ연)

Seogwipo-DIR   contact-do-PST

'(S/he) contacted him/her in Seogwipo.' (based on J.-h. Kang
1988, 66)

-*kkawjang/kkawji* (ᄁᆞ장/ᄁᆞ지) 'until, up to'

*Yo-le-**kkawjang**-man haw-la.* (요레ᄁᆞ장만 ᄒᆞ라)

point-DIR-until-only do-SE

'Do it only up to this point.'

*Joyeongge-lo dawli-**kkawjang** ga-s-jeo.* (조영게로 ᄃᆞ리ᄁᆞ장 갓저)

bicycle-INST bridge-DIR   go-PFV-SE

'(I) went to the bridge by bicycle.'

-*ui/i* (의/이) 'in, at'

ALLOMORPHY:

• -*e* after a stem that ends in *i*, as in *si-e* (시에) 'to/in the city,' and
  possibly after a stem ending in *l* according to Y.-H. Park (1960,
  1988), as in *jeol-e* (절에) 'to/in the temple.'[7]

---

6. The aspiration in the first consonant of -*teole* reflects a hidden *h* at the end of *an*;
   see chapter 2, section 4.2.1.

7. Y.-H. Park (1960, 1988) reports use of the allomorph -*ye* (예) after a stem ending
   in a vowel of any type: *gwi-ye* (귀예) 'in the ear,' *nae-ye* (내예) 'to/in the river' and
   che-ye (체예) 'in the sieve.'

USAGE: Marks a location for stative verbs and direction for action verbs; also used for time.

*Yecheong   sangbang-**ui**   si-n-ya?* (예청 상방의 신야?)
married.woman living.room-LOC be-NPST-SE
'Is the (married)woman in the living room?'

*Seong   badang-**ui** sy-eo?* (성 바당의 셔?)
older.sibling sea-LOC   be-SE
'Is my older sibling at the sea?'

*Jeongji-**e**   ga-ms-in-ya?* (정지에 갊인야?)
kitchen-DIR go-CONT-NPST-SE
'Are you going to the kitchen?'

*Bam-**ui**   na-denggi-deul   mal-la.* (밤의 나뎅기들 말라)
night-LOC out-wander.around-NMLZ not.do-SE
'Do not wander around at night.' (J.-h. Kim 2014b, 45)

It is no accident that this suffix is homophonous with the genitive marker (section 6.3) as this form had the same two functions in Middle Korean (I. Lee and Ramsey 2000, 291; K.-M. Lee and Ramsey 2011, 189). We distinguish between them here by using the spelling *-i* for the genitive and *-ui* for the locative.

-uiseo/iseo (의서/이서) 'at, in'

ALLOMORPHY:

• *-seo* (서) after a stem ending in a vowel, and sometimes even after a stem ending in a consonant, as in *uli jib-seo* (우리집서) 'in our house.'

USAGE: Used primarily to denote the place where an action occurs (see S.-D. Moon 1987).

*Hawgge-**seo** gongbui-haw-ge.* (훅게서 공븨ᄒ게)
school-LOC   study-do-SE
'Let's study at school.'

*Ga-ne badang-**uiseo** hui-eoms-jeo.* (가네 바당의서 희없저)
3-PL   sea-LOC   swim-CONT-SE
'They are swimming in the sea.'

*Abang ap-**uiseo**   musigeo haw-yeoms-in-ya?*
father front-LOC what   do-CONT-NPST-SE
(아방 앞의서 무시거 ㅎ였인야?)
'What are you doing in front of father?'

Location and direction are also often expressed with the help of
bound nouns that may themselves be accompanied by a postposition.

*Bas-**dui**   dawl-ams-u-da.* (밧듸 돌앖우다)
field-place run-CONT-AH-SE
'I am going to the field.'

*Gonengi jeo   nang **al-le***   *sis-jeo.* (고넹이 저 낭 알레 싯저)
cat   that tree   under-LOC be-SE
'The cat is under that tree.'

*Gawlgaebi jeo   nang **u-ui***   *sis-jeo.* (골개비 저 낭 우의 싯저)
frog   that tree   top-LOC be-SE
'The frog is on that tree.'

*Malchug   jeo   nang **du-ui***   *sis-jeo.* (말축 저 낭 두의 싯저)
grasshopper that tree   behind-LOC be-SE
'The grasshopper is behind that tree.'

*Jungi   jeo   nang **jawkkaws-dui** sis-jeo.* (중이 저 낭 ㅈ꼇듸 싯저)
mouse that tree   nearby-place be-SE
'The mouse is near that tree.'

*Bingegi jeo   nang **yawp-ui** sis-jeo.* (빙에기 저 낭 욮의 싯저)
chick   that tree   next-LOC be-SE
'The chick is next to that tree.'

*Songegi jeo   nang **ap-ui***   *sis-jeo.* (송에기 저 낭 앞의 싯저)
calf   that tree   front-LOC be-SE
'The calf is in front of that tree.'

*Eomeong **ap-deole** sa-la.* (어멍 앞더레 사라)
mother   front-DIR stand-SE
'Stand in front of (your) mother.'

*Gudeul **sogob-seo**   musigeo sichi-men?* (구들 소곱서 무시거 시치멘?)

room   inside-LOC what   wash-SE

'What are you washing in the room?'

7.2 Source

-butteo/-buteo/-buteom (부떠/부터/부텀) 'from'[8]

*Oneol-**butteo**-n   jeoseul deul-eos-in-ge.* (오널부떤 저슬 들엇인게)

today-from-TOP winter enter-PFV-NPST-SE

'(I see that) it is winter from today.'

*Neu-**buteom** haw-la.* (느부텀 ᄒ라)

2SG-from   do-SE

'You go first!'

A source interpretation can also be expressed with the help of the *-antiseo* (안티서), *-apiseo* (아피서), or *-sindiseo* (신디서) when the referent of the noun is human.

*Penji   eomeong-**anti-seo**/**api-seo**   w-as-in-ya?*

green.onion mother-DAT-LOC/DAT-LOC come-PFV-NPST-SE

(펜지 어멍안티서/아피서 왓인야?)

'Has the letter come from (your) mother?'

*I   don-eun   seong-**sindi-seo**   w-as-ju.* (이 돈은 성신디서 왓주)

this money-TOP older.sibling-DAT-LOC come-PFV-SE

'This money came from my older sibling.'

7.3 Comitative, Conjunctive, Disjunctive

Comitative markers have two basic functions in Jejueo. On the one hand, they can express the relationship of togetherness normally conveyed by the preposition *with* in English. On the other hand, when they conjoin two nouns, they can fulfill the coordinating function associated with English *and*.

---

8. J.-h. Kim (2014b, 35) claims that the older generation uses the form *-buteo* more whereas the younger generation prefers *-butteo*.

-*iyeong* (이영) **'with, and'**

ALLOMORPHY:

• -*yeong* after a stem ending in a vowel

*Gaui-n   eomeong-**iyeong** sawdab-haw-yeoms-u-ge.*
3SG-TOP mother-with   laundry-do-CONT-AH-SE
(가읜 어멍이영 〻답ᄒ였우게)
'S/he is doing the laundry with his/her mom.'

*Na-**yeong** dawlbengi sim-ge.* (나영 돌벵이 심게)
1SG-with   snail   gather-SE
'Let's gather snails together (lit. with me)!'

-*gwang* (광) **'with, and'**

ALLOMORPHY:

• -*wang* after a stem ending in a vowel (sometimes)

*Jiseul-**gwang** dawgsegi* (지슬광 독세기)
potato-with   egg
'potatoes and eggs'

*Na-n   neu-**wang/gwang** gawjji   sunul-euk-yeo.*
1SG-TOP 2SG-with   together exchange.work-PROSP-SE
(난 느왕/광 ᄀ찌 수눌으켜)
'I will exchange work with you.' (U.-T. Jung 1983, 28)

*Jeo   aui-deol-**gwang** hawndui babjuli   sim-ula.*
that kid-PL-with   together dragonfly catch-SE
(저 아의덜광 ᄒ듸 밥주리 심우라)
'Catch dragonflies together with those kids.'

-*hawgo/hawgog* (ᄒ고/ᄒ곡) **'with, and'**

*Na-n   abang-**hawgo/hawgog** gawjji   chogi   ta-k-yeo.*
1SG-TOP father-with   together mushroom pick-PROSP-SE
(난 아방ᄒ고/아방ᄒ곡 ᄀ찌 초기 타켜)
'I will pick mushrooms with my father.'

*Nang-**hawgo** gojang hawssawl singgeu-la.* (낭흐고 고장 흐쌀 싱그라)

tree-and   flower little   plant-SE

'Please plant some trees and flowers.'

-ina (이나) 'or, just'

ALLOMORPHY: *-na* after a vowel.

*gai-**na** yai-**na*** (가이나 야이나)

3SG-or 3SG-or

'either that one or this one'

*Gwegi-**na** gawj-eong o-la!* (궤기나 궂엉 오라!)

meat-just have-CON come-SE

'Bring just meat!'

7.4 Instrument, Cause

-eulo (으로) 'with' (instrument)

ALLOMORPHY:

• *-lo* after a stem ending in a vowel or *l*

*Boli-**lo***   *tteog menggeul-ju.* (보리로 떡 멩글주)

barley-INST cake make-SE

'We make a cake with barley.'

*Makke-**lo***   *kkwe*   *ppaws-ila.* (마께로 꿰 뽓이라)

wooden.bat-INST sesame.seed crush-SE

'Crush the sesame seeds with the (wooden) bat.'

-ttamun(e) (따문(에)) 'because of'

Na-n   *aui-deol-**ttamun**(e) sawdab mos*   *haw-yeon-ge.*

1SG-TOP child-PL-because   laundry cannot do-PST-EMPH

(난 아의덜 따문(에) ᄉ답 못 ᄒ연게)

'I couldn't do the laundry because of the children.'

-e (에) 'because of, due to'

Don   *beol-m-e*   *duly-eon.* (돈 벌에 두련)

money earn-NMLZ-due.to go.crazy-PST

'She has gone crazy making money.' (based on J.-h. Kang 1987, 525)

Gawlu gawl-m-e   *jichy-eon.* (ㄱ루 곯에 지쳔)

flour   grind-NMLZ-because tired-PST

'Because of grinding flour, I got tired.'

Geu hanui-bawleum-e   *gamjeo-s-jul*   *mawn*

that northern-wind-because sweet.potato-PGEN-stem all

bul-ly-eo-na-bi-s-jeo. (그 하늬ㅂ름에 감젓줄 몬 불려나빗저)

blow-PASS-LV-come.out-COMPL-PFV-SE

'All the sweet potato stems were blown away because of the
   northern wind.'

7.5 Comparative

-bodan (보단)/ bodam (보담) 'than'

*Mansu-ga seong-**bodan***   *yawmang-ji-n*   *geo*

Mansu-NOM older.brother-than sharpness-be-NPST NMLZ

dalm-a. (만수가 성보단 ㅇ망진 거 닮아)

seem-SE

'It looks like Mansu is more bold and clever than his older
   brother.'

-chulug (추룩) 'like'

*Neu-**chulug** ganse   haw-min sawlchi-n-da.* (느추룩 간세ㅎ민 술친다)

2SG-like   laziness do-CON   put.on.weight-NPST-SE

'If (you) are lazy like you are, you will put on weight.'

deo (더) 'more'

*Yugji-le   ga-jen   haw-min gongbui **deo**   hayeong he-sa-n-da.*

mainland-DIR go-CON do-CON   study   more a.lot   do-OBLG-NPST-SE

(육지레 가젠 ㅎ민 공븨 더 하영 헤산다)

'You need to study more if you want to go to the mainland.'

deol (덜) 'less'

*Yaui **deol** seollu-n   seng-i-yeo.* (야의 덜 설룬 셍이여)

3SG   less   sad-NPST.CON appearance-be-SE

'This kid seems less sad.'

-gawti/gawchi/gawjji (ᄀᆯ이/ᄀ치/ᄀ찌) 'alike, similar to'[9]

*Mansu-**gawti** buleumssi jal haw-neun aui-ga eos-jeo.*
Mansu-like errand well do-NPST.CON child-NOM not.be-SE
(만수ᄀᆯ이 부름씨 잘 ᄒ는 아의가 엇저)
'There is no child who can do an errand well like Mansu.'

-isa (이사) 'unlike others, just' (contrastive)

ALLOMORPHY:

• -sa after a stem ending in a vowel.

*Gasi-abang-**isa*** *buje-nan-ge* (가시아방이사 부제난게)
wife-father-unlike.others rich-CON-EMPH
'Because my father-in-law is rich, unlike others.'

*Na-**sa*** *jiseul kkab chuli-ju.* (나사 지슬깝 추리주)
1SG-unlike.others potato price pay-SE
'As for *me*, I will pay for the potatoes.'

*Ije-**sa*** *jeongji-seo yeowag haw-yeoms-jeo.*
now-just kitchen-LOC conversation do-CONT-SE
(이제사 정지서 여왁 ᄒ엾저)
'Now they are talking in the kitchen.'

When *-isa* appears on a direct object, it gives an interpretation in which an entire action (making traditional cloth in the example below) is placed in contrast.

*Menggeul-man haw-yeos-ju, galos-**sa*** *pawl-a-bw-as-eo.*
make-only do-PFV-SE galos-just sell-LV-try-PFV-SE
(멩글만 ᄒ엿주 갈옷사 풀아봣어)
'In contrast to selling *galos*, we only made it.' (*galos* is a traditional cloth.)

---

9. This word is derived from the root *gawt-* (ᄀᆯ) 'be alike, similar.' Its etymological spelling would therefore be *gawt.i* (ᄀᆯ이).

-jillung (질룽) 'most'

*Yaui **jillung** gobdeulag-haw-n-ge.* (야의 질룽 곱들락ᄒ운게)
3SG   most   beautiful-do-NPST-SE
'(I see that) this kid is the most beautiful.'

-mani (만이 or 마니) 'as much as, as many as'

*Olabang-**mani**   haw-la.* (오라방만이 ᄒ라)
older.brother-as.much do-SE
'Do as much as your older brother.'

*Cheolsu seong-**mani**   ji-n-ge.* (철수 성만이 진게)
Cheolsu older.brother-as.much tall-NPST-SE
'(I see that) Cheolsu is as tall as his older brother.'

-nyang (냥) 'in accordance with' (often used with a sarcastic connotation)

*Neu mawm-**nyang**   haw-la.* (느 몸냥 ᄒ라)
2SG wish-accordance do-SE
'Do as you wish.'

*Mansu haw-neu-n   **nyang**   haw-la.*
Mansu do-INDC-NPST.CON accordance do-SE
(만수 ᄒ는 냥 ᄒ라)
'Do it together in accordance with the way Mansu does it.'

7.6 Quantity, Scope, and Focus

-aulla (아울라) 'even'

*Bojegi-**aulla**   ga-bul-eon?* (보제기아울라 가불언?)
fisherman-even go-COMPL-PST
'Even the fisherman has left?'

-bekk-i (베끼 or 벢이) 'except, other than' (requires an accompanying negated verb)

*Seonsuing-**bekk-i**   haw-l   saleum-i   eus-da.*
teacher-except-LOC do-FUT.CON person-NOM not.be-SE
(선싱벢이 훌 사름이 읏다)
'No one can do this except the teacher.'

-do (도) 'also, as well, too, even'

> *Eomeong-do gobdag-haw-n-ge.* (어멍도 곱닥흔게)
> mother-too   beautiful-do-NPST-SE
> '(I see that) Mother is also beautiful.'

> *Ttawl-deol-do   mag yawmang-ji-n-ge.* (뚤덜도 막 으망진게)
> daughter-PL-even very smart-be-NPST-SE
> '(I see that) the daughters are very smart too.'

-ilageune (이라근에) 'X and only X' (primarily used in imperatives)

> ALLOMORPHY:

> • *-lageun(e)* after a stem ending in a vowel or *l*

> *Cheolsu-lageun(e) i-dui-seo   il   haw-la.*
> Cheolsu-only   this-place-LOC work do-SE
> (철수라근(에) 이듸서 일 흐라)
> 'Only Cheolsu, you work here.'

S. Oh et al. (2015) note that the function of *-ilageun* overlaps with
that of the topic marker *-ilang*.

-ilangmalang (이랑마랑) 'anything but, far from, not at all'

> ALLOMORPHY:

> • *-langmalang* (랑마랑) after a stem ending in a vowel or *l*

> *Gongbui-langmalang, Cheolsu buleumssi he-ms-jeo.*
> study-far.from   Cheolsu errand   do-CONT-SE
> (공븨랑마랑 철수 부름씨헸저)
> 'Far from studying, Cheolsu is doing an errand.'

-ilado (이라도) 'at least'

> ALLOMORPHY:

> • *-lado* (라도) after a stem ending in a vowel

> *Jiseul-ilado   hawkkawm chi-ju.* (지슬이라도 흐끔 치주)
> potato-at.least a.little   steam-SE
> 'You should have steamed some potatoes at least.'

-jjili (찌리) 'among, by themselves'

*Inyeog-ne-**jjili**   ig-ju.* (이녁네찌리 익주)
self-PL-among   do-SE
'You should read it among yourselves.'

*Jinyeog-ne-deol-**jjili*** *haw-yeo-sa-ju.* (지녁네덜찌리 ᄒ여사주)
self-PL-PL-among   do-LV-OBLG-SE
'They must do (it) among themselves.'

-jjum (쯤) 'approximately'

*Nang   yeol   bon-**jjum*** (낭 열 본쯤)
tree   ten   CLAS-approximately
'about ten seedlings'

-man (만) 'only, just'

*Jawbum-**man***   *awj-eong*   *o-la.* (줍움만 웆엉 오라)
chopsticks-only bring-CON come-SE
'Bring only the chopsticks.'

*Hawn   beon-**man***   *sawdab   haw-ge.* (ᄒ 번만 ᄉ답ᄒ게)
one   time-only laundry do-SE
'Let's do the laundry just once.'

-nyangeulo (냥으로) 'alone, by oneself'

*Gongbui-n   neu-**nyang-eulo*** *he-sa-n-da.* (공븬 느냥으로 헤산다)
study-TOP   2SG-accord-by   do-OBLG-NPST-SE
'You must study by yourself (of your accord).'

-sseog (썩) 'each'

*Hawna-**sseog*** *te.u-b-seo.* (ᄒ나썩 테웁서)
one-each   distribute-AH-SE
'Please distribute (them) one at a time.'

Numerals, Deictics, and Pronouns

1. Introduction

In this chapter, we continue our discussion of Jejueo nouns by considering their use with numerals and with deictics, and by examining various types of pronoun-like expressions.

2. Numerals

2.1 Cardinal Numbers

Jejueo has two series of cardinal numbers, one easily traceable to Middle Korean and the other to Chinese (table 4.1). The Koreanic numbers one through four have a somewhat different form when they are used with a following noun or classifier.

hawn gae (흔 개)	'one thing'
du gae (두 개)	'two things'
sui gae (싀 개)	'three things'
nui gae (늬 개)	'four things'

In principle, the Koreanic numbers are used only up to 99, but we have found that some older speakers mix Chinese and Koreanic numbers for quantities of 100 or more. In the following examples, the first part of the number (*beg* '100' or *cheon* '1000') is Chinese and the second part is Koreanic.

Table 4.1   Koreanic and Chinese numbers in Jejueo

KOREANIC	CHINESE	MEANING
hawna (호나)	*il* (일)	'one'
dul/du.i (둘/두이)	*i* (이)	'two'
swis/seoi (쉿/서이)	*sawm/sam* (솜/삼)	'three'
nuis/neoi (닛/너이)	*saw* (ᄉ)	'four'
dasaws (다솟)	*o* (오)	'five'
yawsaws (오솟)	*yug* (육)	'six'
ilgob (일곱)	*chil* (칠)	'seven'
yawdawb (오돕)	*pal* (팔)	'eight'
aob (아옵)	*gu* (구)	'nine'
yeol (열)	*sib* (십)	'ten'
sumul (수물)	*i-sib* (이십)	'twenty'
seoleun/seolleun/seolheun (서른/설른/설흔)	*sawm-sib* (솜십)	'thirty'
ma.eun (마은)	*saw-sib* (ᄉ십)	'forty'
swin (쉰)	*o-sib* (오십)	'fifty'
yeswin (예쉰)	*yug-sib* (육십)	'sixty'
ileun/illeun/ilheun (이른/일른/일흔)	*chil-sib* (칠십)	'seventy'
yawdeun (오든)	*pal-sib* (팔십)	'eighty'
a.eun/aheun (아은/아흔)	*gu-sib* (구십)	'ninety'
	beg (벡)	'one hundred'
	cheon (천)	'one thousand'

beg hawna (벡 호나) '101'   *beg dul* (벡 둘) '102'
beg suis (벡 쉿) '103'   *beg nuis* (벡 닛) '104'
i-beg yeol nuis (이벡 열닛) '214'   *cheon sumul dasaws* (천 수물 다솟)
                                     '1025'

2.2 Ordinal Numerals

Ordinal numbers are created by adding the suffix *-che/cha* (체/차) to the corresponding Koreanic cardinal number. (The one exception here is *cheos-che* (첫체) 'first,' which is suppletive.)

cheos-che	(첫체)	'first'
dul-che	(둘체)	'second'
suis-che	(쉿체)	'third'
nuis-che	(닛체)	'fourth'
dasaws-che	(다솟체)	'fifth'
yawsaws-che	(오솟체)	'sixth'
ilgob-che	(일곱체)	'seventh'

yawdawb-che	(으듭체)	'eighth'
aob-che	(아옵체)	'ninth'
yeol-che	(열체)	'tenth'

Use of Numerals in the Expression of Time

Koreanic numbers are used to express the hour when talking about time and periods of time.

hawn *si* (흔시)	**du** *sigan* (두 시간)
one o'clock	two hour
'one o'clock'	'two hours'

In contrast, Chinese numbers are used for minutes and seconds.

hawn si   **sib** *bun* (흔시 십분)
one   o'clock 10 minute
'ten minutes after one'

For periods of twenty hours or longer, both Koreanic and Chinese numbers can be used.

Koreanic:	Chinese:
sumu *sigan* (수무 시간)	**i-sib** *sigan* (이십 시간)
twenty hour	two-ten hour
'twenty hours'	'twenty hours'

Months, Days, and Weeks

Chinese numbers are used to name the first ten months of the year. (The names for November and December have number-based and non-number-based variants.)[1]

il-*weol* (일월)	January [lunar calendar: *jeong-weol* (정월), *sae-dawl* (새둘)]
i-*weol* (이월)	February [lunar calendar: *yeongdeung-dawl* (영등둘)]
sam-*weol* (삼월)	March

---

1. The months of January, July, August, and November are pronounced *illweol, chillweol, pallweol,* and *sibillweol,* respectively, with doubling of the *l*; see chapter 2, section 4.2.2.

***saw**-weol* (ᄉᆞ월)	April
***o**-weol* (오월)	May
***yu**-weol* (유월)	June
***chil**-weol* (칠월)	July
***pal**-weol* (팔월)	August
***gu**-weol* (구월)	September
***si**-weol* (시월)	October
***sibil**-weol* (십일월)	November [lunar calendar: *dongji-s-dawl* (동짓돌)]
***sibi**-weol* (십이월)	December [lunar calendar: *saws-dawl* (소돌)]

Some older speakers express days of the month based on the lunar calendar. In this system, the first nine days of the month begin with the morpheme *chaw* (ᄎᆞ) 'beginning,' followed by the appropriate Koreanic number. Days 10 through 19 begin with *yeol* (열), and days 20 through 29 with *sumu* (수무). [A common variant of *sumu* is *seumu* (스무).] The word *geumum* (그뭄) is used for day 30.

The Lunar Calendar—Days of the Month

***chaw**-hawlu* (ᄎᆞ ᄒᆞ루)	1st day
***chaw**-iteul* (ᄎᆞ이틀)	2nd
***chaw**-saw(h)eul* (ᄎᆞ ᄉᆞ을/흘)	3rd
***chaw**-na(h)eul* (ᄎᆞ나을/흘)	4th
***chaw**-das.swe* (ᄎᆞ닷쉐)	5th
***chaw**-yaws.swe* (ᄎᆞ 옷쉐)	6th
***chaw**-illwe* (ᄎᆞ일뤠)	7th
***chaw**-yawdeule* (ᄎᆞ ᄋᆞ드레)	8th
***chaw**-aheule/**chaw**-a.eule* (ᄎᆞ아흐레/ᄎᆞ아으레)	9th
***yeol**-heul* (열흘)	10th
***yeol**-hawlu* (열ᄒᆞ루)	11th
***yeol**-iteul* (열이틀)	12th
***yeol**-saw(h)eul* (열ᄉᆞ을/흘)	13th
***yeol**-na(h)eul* (열나을/흘)	14th
***yeol**-das.swe, boleum* (열닷쉐, 보름)	15th
***yeol**-yaws.swe* (열 옷쉐)	16th
***yeol**-illwe* (열일뤠)	17th
***yeol**-yawdeule* (열 ᄋᆞ드레)	18th
***yeol**-aheule/**yeol**-a.eule* (열아흐레/열아으레)	19th
sumu (수무)	20th
***sumu**-hawlu* (수무ᄒᆞ루)	21st
***sumu**-iteul* (수무이틀)	22nd

sumu-saw(h)eul (수무ᄉ을/흘)	23rd
sumu-na(h)eul (수무나을/흘)	24th
sumu-das.swe (수무닷쉐)	25th
sumu-yaws.swe (수무웃쉐)	26th
sumu-illwe (수무일뤠)	27th
sumu-yawdeule (수무ᄋ드레)	28th
sumu-aheule/sumu-a.eule (수무아흐레/수무아으레)	29th
geumum (그뭄)	30th ('last day')

A: *Oneol meteul-go?* (오널 메틀고?)

today what.date-SE

'What date is it today?'

B: *Oneol **chaw-das.swe**-masseum.* (오널 츠닷쉐마씀)

today beginning-fifth.day-AH.SE

'Today is the 5th.'

*Oneol **geumum**-masseum.* (오널 그뭄마씀)

today last.day-AH.SE

'Today is *geumum*.'

A: *Geu Yeongsu abang sigge   eoneuje-go?*

that Yeongsu father   memorial.service when-SE

(그 영수 아방 식게 어느제고?)

'When is Yeongsu's father's memorial service day?'

B: *Dongji-s-dawl   **sumu-aheule**-u-da.*

winter.solstice-PGEN-month twenty-nine-AH-SE

(동짓돌 수무아흐레우다)

'It is November 29th.'

*Sam-weol   **chaw-yeos.swe**-i-lgeo-u-da.* (삼월 츠웃쉐일거우다)

three-month beginning-sixth.day-be-FUT-AH-SE

'It could be March 6th.'

In contrast to months and days of the month, the days of the week are not based on numerals.

weol-yoil (월요일)	Monday [pronounced *weollyoil*]
hwa-yoil (화요일)	Tuesday
su-yoil (수요일)	Wednesday
mog-yoil (목요일)	Thursday
geum-yoil (금요일)	Friday
ban-gwengil (반궿일)	Saturday
gwengil (궿일)	Sunday

3. Classifiers (Counters) and Units of Measurement

Numerals are usually used with a "classifier" or "counter" that is compatible with the accompanying noun. The numeral + classifier complex follows the noun with which it is associated; in cases where the number is ordinal, *che* (체) is added to the classifier.

*nang hawn **jae*** (낭 흔 재)   *nang du **jae**   che* (낭 두 재체)

tree   one   CLAS   tree   two CLAS ORD

'one tree'   'the second tree'

3.1 Common Classifiers

A variety of classifiers are available for use with nouns that are accompanied by a numeral or other quantity-denoting word. The generic classifier *gae* (개) can be used with most inanimate nouns; however, a more specialized classifier is often employed, depending on the type of referent. The following examples are from S.-r. Kim (2008), J.-W. Ko (2011a), and P.-h. Hyun et al. (2009), as well as from various consultants.

be/keoli/keolli (베/커리/컬리) for shoes, footwear

*sin   ilgob   **be*** (신 일곱 베)

shoes seven CLAS

'seven pairs of shoes'

bis (빗) for pieces of *sili-tteog* (rice cake), or loaves of *sangwe-tteog* (bread made from flour or barley)

*sangwe-tteog   hawn **bis*** (상웨떡 흔 빗)

sangwe-rice.cake one   CLAS

'a loaf of *sangwe-tteog*'

bon (본) for seedlings, trees

*Mikkang-nang hawn yeol **bon**-jjum   singg-eos-jeo*

tangerine-tree about ten CLAS-about plant-PFV-SE

(미깡낭 ᄒᆞᆫ 열 본쯤 싱것저)

'(I) planted about ten tangerine seedlings.'

bul (불) for sets of clothing

*os   hawn **bul*** (옷 ᄒᆞᆫ 불)

cloth one   CLAS

'one set of clothing'

*galjungi du **bul*** (갈중이 두 불)

galjungi two CLAS

'two sets of *galjungi*' (traditional work clothing)

cheog (척) for ships/boats

*te.u hawn **cheog*** (테우 ᄒᆞᆫ 척)

boat one   CLAS

'one boat'

gogji (곡지) for musical pieces

*nolle hawn **gogji*** (놀레 ᄒᆞᆫ 곡지)

song one   CLAS

'one song'

gab (갑) for packs

*hwagwag hawn **gab*** (화곽 ᄒᆞᆫ 갑)

match   one CLAS

'a pack of matches'

gwag/kkwag (곽/꽉) for boxes/packs

*dambae hawn **gwag/kkwag*** (담배 ᄒᆞᆫ 곽/꽉)

cigarette one   CLAS

'a pack of cigarettes'

jae (재) **for trees**

    *nang hawn **jae*** (낭 혼 재)

    tree   one   CLAS

    'one tree'

jali (자리) **for pairs of pigs, dogs, or chickens**

    *dosegi du **jali*** (도세기 두 자리)

    pig   two CLAS

    'two pairs of pigs'

jawlog (즈록) **for cigarettes, rice cakes, and other cylinder-shaped objects**

    *yeobcho   hawn **jawlog*** (엽초 혼 즈록)

    cigarette one   CLAS

    'one (hand-rolled) cigarette'

    *tteog hawn **jawlog*** (떡 혼 즈록)

    cake one   CLAS

    'one (cylinder-shaped) rice cake'

jeob (접) **for a bundle of 120 pieces of dried seaweed**

    *meyeog   hawn **jeob*** (메역 혼 접)

    seaweed one   CLAS

    'one bundle of dried seaweed'

juje (주제) **for rain, showers, wind** (used only with *hawn* 'one' or *du-eo* 'about two')

    *sswenegi du-eo   **juje*** (쒜네기 두어 주제)

    shower   two-about CLAS

    'about two rounds of showers'

    *bawlawm hawn **juje*** (ᄇᆞ롬 혼 주제)

    wind   one   CLAS

    'one round of wind'

keoli/geoli (커리/거리) **for houses**

> *jib   du   **keoli*** (집 두 커리)
>
> house two CLAS
>
> 'two houses'

mawli (무리) **for animals**

> *swe   du   **mawli*** (쉐 두 무리)
>
> cow two CLAS
>
> 'two cows'

meng (멩) **for people**

> *hawgseng   hawn   **meng*** (흑셍 흔 멩)
>
> student   one   CLAS
>
> 'one student'

mus (뭇) **for bundles of fish (10 fish)**

> *baleu-s-gwegi   hawn   **mus*** (바릇궤기 흔 뭇)
>
> sea-PGEN-meat one   CLAS
>
> 'one bundle of fish'

nang (낭) **for sheets of dried seaweed**

> *meyeog   hawn   **nang*** (메역 흔 낭)
>
> seaweed one   CLAS
>
> 'one sheet of dried seaweed'

pani (파니) **for a section/patch**

> *jiseul   hawn   **pani*** (지슬 흔 파니)
>
> potato one   CLAS
>
> 'one patch of potatoes'

pegi (페기) **for heads of cabbage or kimchi**

> *bechi   sui   **pegi*** (베치 싀 페기)
>
> cabbage three CLAS
>
> 'three heads of cabbage'

tawllae (톨래) **for thread**

> *ssil   du   tawllae* (씰 두 톨래)
>
> thread two CLAS
>
> 'two rolls of thread'

3.2 Units of Measurement

A variety of counters are used for the measurement of weight, size, distance, and mass. Many of the following examples are drawn from work by S.-r. Kim (2008), P.-h. Hyun et al. (2009), and J.-W. Ko (2011a), as well as from information provided by our consultants.

Units of Weight

geun (근) **for the weight of meat and produce** (1 *geun*= 600 g)

> *meyeog   nui/neo **geun*** (메역 늬/너 근)
>
> seaweed   four   MEAS
>
> 'four *geun* of seaweed'

ching/cheung (칭/층) **for the weight of meat and produce** (1 *cheung*= 100 *geun*)

> *dosegi hawn **ching/cheung*** (도세기 혼 칭/층)
>
> pig   one   MEAS
>
> 'one *cheung* of pig'

> *meyeog   hawn **ching/cheung*** (메역 혼 칭/층)
>
> seaweed one   MEAS
>
> 'one *cheung* of seaweed'

don (돈) **for the weight of gold and silver**

> *geum seog   **don*** (금 석 돈)
>
> gold   three MEAS
>
> 'three *don* of gold'

Units of Size and Distance

cham (참) **for distance** (1 *cham*≈ 2 km)

> *du-eo   **cham** dwe-n   dui* (두어 참 뒌 듸)
>
> two-about MEAS become-NPST.CON place
>
> 'a place about two *cham* away'

chi (치) **for measuring cloth** (5 cm)

> *gwangmog   du   chi* (광목 두 치)
> cotton.cloth two MEAS
> 'two *chi* of cotton cloth' (10 cm of cotton cloth)

ja (자) **for measuring cloth** (50 cm or 10 *chi*)

> *Geu gwangmog   mes   ja?* (그 광목 멧자?)   *Hawn ja.* (흔 자)
> that cotton.cloth how.many MEAS   one   MEAS
> 'How many *ja* is that cotton cloth?'   'One *ja*.'

jeog/jig (적/직) **a bite, a sip, a spoonful**

> *gaeyeog   hawn jeog/jig* (개역 흔 적/직)
> gaeyeog one   MEAS
> 'a sip of *gaeyeog*' (a beverage made from powdered grain)

> *mawmawl-beombeog   hawn jeog/jig* (ᄆᆞᆯ범벅 흔 적/직)
> buckwheat-beombeog one   MEAS
> [also *mawmul* (ᄆᆞᆯ)]
> 'a spoonful of buckwheat *beombeog*' (food made from buck-
>   wheat flower and hot water)

> *Jiseul   hawn jeog/jig* (지슬 흔 적/직)
> potato one   MEAS
> 'a bite of potato'

mun (문) **for rubber shoes**

> *Mes   mun sin-eoms-in-i?* (멧 문 신없인이?)   *Sumul-hawn mun.*
> which MEAS wear-CONT-NPST-SE   twenty-one   MEAS
> 'What shoe size do you wear?'   (수물 흔 문)
>   'size twenty-one *mun*'

ppom (뽐) **the stretch of a hand**

> *I   gwangmog   mes   ppom-i-go?*   *Yeol ppom.* (열 뽐)
> this cotton.cloth how.many MEAS-be-SE   ten MEAS
> (이 광목 멧 뽐이고?)   'Ten hands-width'
> 'How many *ppom* is this cotton cloth?'

*Mul-gwegi hawn   du-eo   **ppom** dwe-n   geo*
water-meat approximately two-about MEAS   become-NPST.CON thing
sim-un   geo   dalm-a. (물궤기 혼 두어 뽐 뒌 거 심운 거 닮아)
catch-NPST.CON NMLZ seem-SE
'It looks like that (they) caught a fish that is about two *ppom*.'

majigi/maljigi (마지기/말지기) **for farmland** (397–496 m^2)

*bas   hawn **majigi*** (밧 혼 마지기)
field one   CLAS
'one *majigi* of field'

Units of Mass Involving Bundles and Packs

bali (바리) **for loads that can be carried by a pack animal**

*jideulkeo hawn **bali*** (지들커 혼 바리)
firewood one   MEAS
'one *bali* of firewood'

dan (단) **for produce**

*manong sui   **dan*** (마농 싀 단)
garlic   three MEAS
'three bundles of garlic'

jawlle/jawlli (졸레/졸리) **bundle/bunch (needles, firewood)**

*nang du **jawlle*** (낭 두 졸레)
tree   two MEAS
'two bundles of firewood'

jul (줄) **for a set of 10 eggs**

*dawgsegi hawn **jul*** (둑세기 혼 줄)
egg   one   MEAS
'one pack of eggs'

kkwemi (꿰미) **for a set of 10 fish**

*ogdom hawn **kkwemi*** (옥돔 혼 꿰미)
tile.fish one   MEAS
'a pack of tilefish'

mus (뭇) **for harvested barley or a bundle of 10 fish** (1 *mus*=one armful)

chol hawn ***mus*** (촐 흔 뭇)

hay   one   MEAS

'one armful of hay'

pan (판) **for a set of 30 eggs**

dawgsegi hawn ***pan*** (독세기 흔 판)

egg   one   MEAS

'one crate of eggs' (30 eggs)

Units for Measuring Grains and Alcohol

hawb/hob (흡/홉) **for grains** (calculated in a square wooden bowl called a *hobsali*)

yu   *sui*   ***hawb*** (유 싀 흡)

perilla.seed three MEAS

'three *hob* of perilla seeds' (perilla is a plant belonging to the mint family)

dwe (뒈 = *seung/sing* (승/싱)) **for grains** (calculated in a square wooden bowl called a *dwesbag*)

yu   *yeol* ***dwe*** (유 열 뒈) (*daedu* 1 *mal*)

perilla.seed ten MEAS

'ten *dwe* of perilla seeds'

dweagsegi (뒈악세기) **for grains** (calculated in a wooden bowl called a *dweagsegi*)

yu   *hawn* ***dweagsegi*** (유 흔 뒈악세기)

perilla.seed one   MEAS

'one *dweagsegi* of perilla seeds'

chungi/chuni/chun (충이/추니/춘) **for alcohol** (calculated in a ceramic bottle called a *chungi*)

sul   *hawn* ***chungi*** (술 흔 충이)

alcohol one   MEAS

'one *chungi* of alcohol'

gamengi (가멩이) **for grains, salt, fertilizer, potatoes, etc.** (calculated in a woven straw bag called a *gamengi*)

yu   *hawn **gamengi*** (유 혼 가멩이)

perilla.seed one   MEAS

'one *gamengi* of perilla seeds'

Table 4.2   Some units of measurement

1 *hop* = 0.18 liters
4 *hop* = *soseung* 1 *dwe* = 1 *dweagsegi* (.72 liters)
10 *hop* = *daeseung* 1 *dwe* (1.8 liters)
daeseung 4 *dwe* = *soseung* 10 *dwe* = *sodu* 1 *mal* (7.2 liters)
sodu 1 *mal* = 0.1 *gamengi* (7.2 liters)
daedu 1 *mal* = 0.1 *seom* (18 liters)
1 *chungi* = *daeseung* 10 *dwe* (18 liters)
1 *gamengi* = *daedu* 5 *mal* = *sodu* 10 *mal* (72 liters)
10 *gwan* = 1 *gamengi* = 40 kg (including the weight of the container)

Source: S.-r. Kim (2008, 15–19) and S.-J. Kim (2014, 63, 155–156).

gwan (관) **for produce such as tangerines, potatoes, and sweet potatoes** (1 *gwan* = 3.75 kg)

*mikkang   hawn **gwan*** (미깡 혼 관)

tangerine one   MEAS

'one *gwan* of tangerines'

mal (말) **for measuring grains** (1 *mal* = 7.2 liters)

On Jeju Island, *neog dwe* (넉 뒈) '4 *dwe*' is equivalent to 1 *mal*. On the Korean mainland, *yeol dwe* (열 뒈) '10 *dwe*' is equivalent to 1 *mal*. Jeju Islanders use the terms *sodu hawn mal* (소두 혼 말) and *daedu hawn mal* (대두 혼 말), respectively, for these measures (based on S.-r. Kim 2004, 24; S.-J. Kim 2014, 156).

yu   *hawn **mal*** (유 혼 말)

perilla.seed one   MEAS

'one *mal* of perilla seeds'

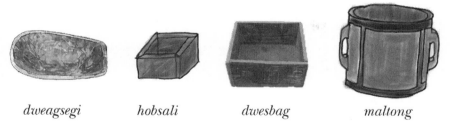

dweagsegi   *hobsali*   *dwesbag*   *maltong*

Figure 4.1   Traditional measuring containers (based on S.-J. Kim 2016, 53 & 231)

seom/seog (섬/석) **for grains** (1 *seom= sodu* 15 *mal= daedu* 6 *mal*; S.-r. Kim, 2004, p. 24)

*ssawl hawn **seom*** (쌀 흔 섬)

rice   one   MEAS

'one *seom* of rice'

4. Deixis

Jejueo makes extensive use of deixis, both in its determiner system and in its pronoun system (see section 5). There are four deictic determiners.

i/yo (이/요)	'this': near the speaker
geu (그)	'that': near the addressee or absent from sight
jeo (저)	'that': distant from both speaker and addressee
jyo (죠)	'that': emphatic form of *jeo,* very distant from both speaker and addressee

To emphasize a greater distance, speakers tend to lengthen the vowel sound in *jeo* and *jyo.*

4.1 Person and Object Deixis

A major function of deictic determiners is to indicate the location of a person or object with respect to the speaker.

I   jijibai-n   nuge-go? (이 지집아인 누게고?)

this girl-TOP who-SE

'Who is this girl?'

Geu *jijibai-do neu beos-i-ga?* (그 지집아이도 느 벗이가?)
that girl-too 2SG friend-be-SE
'Is that girl too your friend?'

Jeo *sawnai-gwang* ***jyo*** *jijibai-n gawjji   w-as-eola.*
that (young)man-with that girl-TOP together come-PFV-SE
(저 ᄉ나이광 죠 지집아인 ᄀ찌 왓어라)
'That guy has come together with that girl over there.'

4.2 Spatial Deixis

Deictic determiners can be used in conjunction with location-denoting bound nouns such as *dui* (듸) 'place,' *chag* (착) 'side,' *le* (레) 'direction toward,' and *pen* (펜) 'side' to express spatial position with respect to the speaker.

Yo-dui   *sa-ng   is-ib-seo!* (요듸 상 잇입서!)
this-place stand-CON be-AH-SE
'(You'd) better stand here for now!'

Geu-dui   *musigeo is-u-gwa?* (그듸 무시거 잇우꽈?)
that-place what   be-AH-SE
'What is there?'

Jeo-dui   *ga-ng   bo-b-seo!* (저듸 강 봅서!)
that-place go-CON see-AH-SE
'Go there and check!'

Abang-eun ***geu-le***   *dawl-an-ge.* (아방은 그레 돌안게)
father-TOP   that-DIR run-PST-SE
'(I saw) father going that way.'

*I-**chag**-deole aj-ila!* (이착더레 앚이라!)
this-side-DIR sit-SE
'Sit to this side!'

*I-**pen**-deole awmawng-haw-la!* (이펜더레 ᄋ뭉ᄒ라!)
this-side-DIR move-do-SE
'Come to this side!'

4.3 Temporal Deixis

A parallel strategy is used for the expression of temporal deixis, this time with the help of bound nouns denoting time-related concepts, including *sawsi* (ᄉᆞ시) 'time,' *gawli* (ᄀᆞ리) 'moment,' and *je* (제) 'time.' (The latter form is pronounced *jje* after a word that ends in *l* or *n*.)

> *Geu **sawsi**-n   bonggeu-l   ge   eus-eos-ju.* (그 ᄉᆞ신 봉글 게 읏엇주)
> that time-TOP gather-FUT.CON thing not.be-PFV-SE
> 'There wasn't anything to gather at that time.'

> *Geu **gawli**-n   eodui gob-eub-di-ga?* (그 ᄀᆞ린 어듸 곱읍디가?)
> that time-TOP where hide-AH-EVI-SE
> 'Where did you hide in those times?'

> *duli-n   **je*** (두린 제)
> young-PST.CON time
> 'the time when I was young'

> *bulleumssi haw-l   **je*** (부름씨 홀 제)
> errand   do-FUT.CON time
> 'the time when s/he will do an errand'

The following are fixed expressions that can no longer be broken into their component parts.

> *geujige* (그지게) 'the day before yesterday'
> *geukkeujige* (그끄지게) / *geugeujige* (그그지게) 'three days ago';
>   also *geujig asisnal* (그직 아싯날)
> *geuleuhe* (그르헤) 'two years ago'
> *geukkeuleuhe* (그끄르헤) / *geugeuleuhe* (그그르헤) 'three years ago'

5. Personal Pronouns and Their Equivalents

Jejueo lacks the type of fully developed pronoun system typical of European languages, particularly in the case of third-person pronouns.

5.1 First Person

Jejueo has just two first-person pronouns: *na/nae* (나/내) for the singular and *uli* or *uli-deol* (우리(덜)) for the plural.

Na *gob-as-jeo.* (나 곱앗저)
1SG hide-PFV-SE
'I hid.'

Na*-ga*   *bas-dui*   *ga-k-u-da.* (나가 밧듸 가쿠다)
1SG-NOM field.place go-PROSP-AH-SE
'I will go to the field.'

Nae *haw-jeo.* (내 ㅎ저)
1SG do-SE
'I will do (it).' (P.-h. Hyun 1977b, 242)

Uli *mawn gawchi   sawdab haw-lgeo-ju.* (우리 ㅁㄴ ㄱ치 ㅅ답ㅎ거주)
1PL all   together laundry do-FUT-SE
'We will all do the laundry together.'

Uli-deol*-eun mawn gawti*   *ga-lgeo-ju.* (우리덜은 ㅁㄴ 곹이 갈거주)
1PL-PL-TOP   all   together go-FUT-SE
'We are going all together.'

5.2 Second Person

An overt second-person pronoun is not used when addressing an
older person. However, various forms can be used to address a
younger person. The two most basic are *neu/ni* (느/니) and *ji* (지),
which can be pluralized as *neu-ne(-deol)* (느네(덜)) and *ji-ne(-deol)* (지
네(덜)), respectively.

Neu *eodui si-n-i?* (느 어듸 신이?)
2SG where be-NPST-SE
'Where are you?'

Neu*-ga*   *haw-la!* (느가 ㅎ라!)
2SG-NOM do-SE
'You do (it)!'

Neu-ne(-deol)*-eun i-dui*   *si-la.* (느네(덜)은 이듸 시라)
2-PL-PL-TOP   this-place be-SE
'You guys, stay here.'

Ji-n   *musigeo*   *sa-ms-eo?* (진 무시거 샀어?)

2SG-TOP which.thing buy-CONT-SE

'What are you buying?'

Ji-n   *musa mulkkuleog ai*   *meog-eon?* (진 무사 물꾸럭 아이 먹언?)

2SG-TOP why   octopus   not eat-PST

'Why didn't you eat octopus?'

Ji-n   *nuge-la?* (진 누게라?)

2SG-TOP who-SE

'Who are you?'

The form *neu* is used primarily for addressing younger individuals and very close friends or siblings, as well as people of lower social status. The *ji* form is used to address younger individuals in a more respectful manner. (As we will see in section 6, *ji* can also be used as a third-person reflexive pronoun.)

Another strategy for referring to an addressee makes use of the forms *inyeog* (이녁) or *jinyeog* (지녁), which can also be used as reflexive pronouns (see section 6). The corresponding plural is formed by adding either *ne* or *ne-deol* (Y.-b. Kang 2007, 47–48).

Jinyeog-eun *nuge-la?* (지녁은 누게라?)

2SG-TOP   who-SE

'Who are you?'

Inyeog-ne-n *musa w-an?* (이녁넨 무사 완?)

2-PL-TOP   why   come-PST

'Why did you (pl.) come here?'

Inyeog-ne-deol-eun *musa w-an?* (이녁네덜은 무사 완?)

2-PL-PL-TOP   why   come-PST

'Why did you (pl.) come here?'

5.3 Third Person

There are no third-person pronouns *per se* in Jejueo. Instead, a phrase created by contracting a deictic determiner and the noun *aui* (아의) 'person' is used to indicate reference to a previously mentioned third party.

yai/yaui (야이/야의) 'this person' (informal) [from *i aui*]

jai/jaui (자이/자의) 'that person'; 'he/she' (informal), for a
    person who is present [from *jeo aui*].

gai/gaui (가이/가의) 'he/she' (informal), for a person who is
    not present [from *geu aui*]

Gai *nang singg-eos-eon-ge.* (가이 낭 싱것언게)

3SG   tree   plant-PFV-PST-SE

'(I saw that) s/he had planted a tree.'

Jai *na   adeol-i-la.* (자이 나 아덜이라)

3SG   1SG   son-be-SE

'He is my son.'

These forms can be pluralized, with possible further contraction, by
adding *ne* (네) or *ne-deol* (네덜).

Ga(i)-ne-*sindi   deul-eo-bo-la.* (가(이)네신디 들어보라)

3-PL-DAT   ask-LV-try-SE

'Ask them a question.'

Ja(i)-ne-deol *eodeule dawl-ams-in-i?* (자이네덜 어드레 돌았인이?)

3-PL-PL   where   run-CONT-NPST-SE

'Where are they going?'

Ya(i)-ne *nuge?* (야(이)네 누게?)

3-PL   who

'Who are these folks?'

Ja(i)-ne *nuge?* (자(이)네 누게?)

3-PL   who

'Who are those folks (who are present here)?'

Ga(i)-ne *nuge?* (가(이)네 누게?)

3-PL   who

'Who are those folks (who are not present here)?'

Another set of pronoun-like items is used for third parties who
are younger than the speaker or have a lower social rank (J.-W. Ko
2011a, 122; Y.-b. Kang 2007, 48).

inmi/ilmi (인미/일미) for a person near the speaker
jeonmi/jeolmi (전미/절미) for a person distant from both speaker
    and addressee
geunmi/geulmi (근미/글미) for a person who is not present

Inmi *na-l   jawdeul-ly-eoms-u-ge.* (인미 날 ᄌᆞ들렸우게)

3SG   1SG-ACC worry-CAUS-CONT-AH-SE

'S/he is worrying me.'

Jeolmi-*l eotteong haw-ko?* (절밀 어떵 ᄒᆞ코?)

3SG-ACC how   do-SE

'What can I do with him/her?'

Geulmi-*n eoduile gob-an?* (글민 어듸레 곱안?)

3SG-TOP   where   hide-PST

'Where did s/he hide?

6. Other Types of Pronouns

6.1 Reflexives and Reciprocals

The principal reflexive pronouns used in Jejueo are listed in table 4.3.

Table 4.3   Reflexive pronouns in Jejueo

SINGULAR	PLURAL
inyeog (이녁)	*inyeog-ne(-deol)* (이녁네(덜))
jinyeog (지녁)	*jinyeog-ne(-deol)* (지녁네(덜))
ji (지)	*ji-ne(-deol)* (지네(덜))

Gai-n **inyeog**-*man senggag-haw-ju.* (가인 이녁만 셍각ᄒᆞ주)

3SG-TOP self-only   think-do-SE

'S/he thinks about only herself/himself.'

Gai-n **jinyeog** *honcha-man buleumssi haw-yeon-ge.*

3SG-TOP self   alone-only   errand   do-PST-SE

(가인 지녁 혼차만 부름씨 ᄒᆞ연게)

'S/he did the errand all by herself/himself.'

These pronouns can have second-person and third-person referents
only; a first-person referent is expressed in a more roundabout way,
by the phrase *nyang-eulo* 'of one's own accord.'

I-geo   ***inyeog/jinyeog****-i haw-yeos-eo?* (이거 이녁/지녁이 ᄒ엿어?)
this-thing 2SG-NOM   do-PFV-SE
'Did you do this thing?'

The reflexive form *ji* can be used as a subject for purposes of contrastive emphasis.

Ji*-ga   haw-yeo-sa-ju.* (지가 ᄒ여사주)
self-NOM do-LV-OBLG-SE
'S/he has to do it herself/himself.'

Ji*-n   jal   meog-ju-ge.* (진 잘 먹주게)
self-TOP well eat-SE-EMPH
'S/he herself/himself eats well.'

Reciprocality can be expressed by using *seolo-deol* (서로덜).

Neu-ne-n ***seolo-deol***   *mengsim-he-sa-n-da.* (느넨 서로덜 멩심헤산다)
2-PL-TOP each.other-PL care-do-OBLG-NPST-SE
'You should be good to each other.'

6.2 Interrogative Pronouns

Jejueo has the interrogative pronouns listed below.

nuge (누게)	'who'
musin (무신)	'which'
musigeo/musingeo (무시거/무신거)	'what' (lit. 'which thing')
eodeule/eodui(le) (어드레/어듸(레))	'(to) where'
eoneuje (어느제)	'when'
musa (무사)	'why'
eotteong (어떵)	'how'
eolme (얼메)	'how much/how many'
mes (멧)	'how many/which/what'
meteul (메틀)	'what date/how many days'

Oneol ***meteul****-i-go?* (오널 메틀이고?)
today what.date-be-SE
'What date is it today?'

*Oneol **musin**-nal?* (오널 무신날?)

today   which-day

'What day is it today?'/'What's the occasion today?'

*Neu-ne eomeong **eodui** si-n-i?* (느네 어멍 어듸 신이?)

2-PL   mother   where be-NPST-SE

'Where is your mother?'

*I-geo-n   **musigeo**?* (이건 무시거?)

this-thing-TOP what

'What is this?'

Eodeule *dawl-ams-eo?* (어드레 돌앖어?)

where   run-CONT-SE

'Where are you going?'

*Jai-n   **musa** gob-an?* (자인 무사 곱안?)

3SG-TOP why   hide-PST

'Why did (s)he hide?'

***Nuge**-yeong gingi meog-eon-di?* (누게영 깅이 먹언디?)

who-with   crab   eat-PST-SE

'Who did (you) eat crabs with?'

*Geu yecheong   **nuge**-kkwa/kkwang?* (그 예청 누게꽈/꽝?)

that married.woman who-SE

'Who is that woman?'

Eotteong *senggy-eos-eon-i?* (어떵 셍곗언이?)

how   look.like-PFV-PST-SE

'What did (s/he) look like?'

*Neu-n   **eoneuje** awmawng-haw-jen?* (는 어느제 ᄋ몽ᄒ젠?)

2SG-TOP when   move-do-PROSP.SE

'When do you want to leave (move)?'

*Jai **musa** gyeong   we-yeoms-in-i?* (자이 무사 경 웨엾인이?)

3SG why   like.that shout-CONT-NPST-SE

'Why is s/he shouting like that?'

Interrogative pronouns may also be used as indefinite pronouns
with the sense of "some X" or "any X."

Nuge   *is-eo?* (누게 잇어?)

anyone be-SE

'Is anyone here?'

Nuge   *sungteol-eos-jeo.* (누게 숭털엇저)

someone imitate-PST-SE

'(I) imitated someone.'

Neu-do **musigeo**   *haw-yeo-sa-lgeo-n-di.* (느도 무시거 ㅎ여살건디)

2SG-too something do-LV-OBLG-FUT-NPST-SE

'You should do something too.'

Eodui   *ga-ng*   *nol-ge.* (어듸 강 놀게)

somewhere go-CON hang.out-SE

'Let's go somewhere to hang out.'

5

Verbs

1. Introduction

Verbs in Jejueo consist of a root, followed by one or more suffixes that mark a variety of grammatical contrasts, including voice, causation, aspect, modality, tense, evidentiality, deference, sentence type, and formality, all of which we discuss in detail in chapters 6 through 8.

> *Mansu jeb-**hy-eos-eo**.* (만수 젭혓어)
> Mansu catch-PASS-PFV-SE
> 'Mansu got caught.'

> *Halmang   sawdab haw-**yeos-ik-eun-ga**?* (할망 ᄉ답ᄒ엿이큰가?)
> grandmother laundry do-PFV-PROSP-NPST-SE
> 'Could grandmother have finished doing the laundry (right now)?'

> *Ga-ne dolegi dunggeuly-**eoms-eon-ge**.* (가네 도레기 둥글렸언게)
> 3-PL   top   roll-CONT-PST-SE
> '(I saw) them rolling the top.'

In discussing the internal structure of verbs, we will use the term "stem" to refer to the form to which a suffix attaches. Thus in the second example above, the root *haw-* serves as the stem for *-yeos, haw-yeos* is the stem for *-ik*, and so on.

Our focus in this chapter is on the basic verb types found in Jejueo and their interaction with phenomena such as causativization, passivization, negation, and adverbial modification.

2. Types of Verbs

There are several classes of verbs in Jejueo, each with its own properties and uses.

2.1 Action Verbs and Descriptive Verbs

Whereas action verbs denote dynamic events, descriptive (or adjectival) verbs are used to express states and properties. In the examples in table 5.1, verbs are presented in their most basic "dictionary" form, which is marked by the suffix -da (다).

Table 5.1   Action verbs and descriptive verbs

ACTION VERBS	DESCRIPTIVE VERBS
meog-da (먹다) 'eat'	daws-da (돗다) '(be) warm'
beli-da (베리다) 'see'	beochi-da (버치다) '(be) heavy, difficult'
gawd-da (곧다) 'speak'	eol-da (얼다) '(be) cold'
ttawli-da (뜨리다) 'hit'	yallub-da (얄룹다) '(be) thin'
ta-da (타다) 'pick'	hulg-da (흙다) '(be) big, thick'
ka-da (카다) 'mix/burn'	jil-da (질다) '(be) long'
te.u-da (테우다) 'distribute'	bawdi-da (ᄇ디다) '(be) close'
dekki-da (데끼다) 'throw'	jjawlleu-da (쫄르다) '(be) short'

2.2 Copulas

The verb i-da (이다) 'be' and its negative counterpart ani-da (아니다) 'not be' are used to express the relationship of identity. Unlike other verbs, i-da cannot stand alone; it must always cliticize to a noun. (There is no such constraint on ani-da.)

I-geo-n   galos-i-yeo. (이건 갈옷이여)

this-thing-TOP galos-be-SE

'These are work clothes.' [galos are persimmon-dyed traditional work clothes]

Geo-n   mulkkuleog **ani-ju**. (건 물꾸럭 아니주)

thing-TOP octopus   not.be-SE

'That thing isn't an octopus.'

I-dui-n   *sangbang-i-yeo.* (이딘 상방이여)
this-place-TOP living.room-be-SE
'This is a living room.'

The copula is not overtly expressed in the present tense when it occurs after a stem that ends in a vowel.

Yai illeum Sunja-la. (야이 일름 순자라)
3SG name Sunja-SE
'Her name is Sunja.'

Nuge-kkwa? (누게꽈?)
who-SE
'Who are you?'

Moreover, it is absent in the following patterns, regardless of whether the stem ends in a vowel or a consonant.

I-geo-n   *musigeo?* (이건 무시거?)
this-thing-TOP what
'What is this?'

Oneol meteul-go? (오널 메틀고?)
today what.date-SE
'What date is it today?'

I-geo   *te.u?* (이거 테우?)
this-thing boat
'Is this a boat?'

I-geo   *mulkkuleog?* (이거 물꾸럭?)
this-thing octopus
'Is this an octopus?'

I-dui-ga   *sangbang.* (이듸가 상방)
this-place-NOM living.room
'This place is the living room.'

In order to express occurrence or location in a particular place or time (a second function of copulas in European languages),

Jejueo uses a different verb, which has several variants: *sis-da* (싯다), which does not permit inflection, *is-da* (잇다), and *si-da* (시다),[1] along with the negative form *eus-da/eos-da* (읏다/엇다).

> *Asi*   *jeongji-e*   ***sis****-jeo/****is****-eo/****sy****-eo.*
> younger.sibling kitchen-LOC   be-SE/be-SE/be-SE
> (아시 정지에 싯저/잇어/셔)
> '(My) younger sibling is in the kitchen.'

> *Olabang*   *jeongji-e*   ***eus****-jeo.* (오라방 정지에 읏저)
> older.brother kitchen-LOC not.be-SE
> '(My) older brother is not in the kitchen.'

2.3 Auxiliary Verbs

Jejueo also has various auxiliary verbs, including several identical to Korean because of their shared Middle Korean origin, which attach to a preceding verb stem with the help of the linking vowel *-eo*.

-eo (어)

> USAGE: Linking vowel.
> ALLOMORPHY:
>
> • *-a* (vowel harmony; see chapter 2, section 4.2.4)
> • either Ø or *-yeo* after a stem ending in *e* or *ae*: *me-* (메) or *me-yeo* (메여) 'pull'
> • Ø after a stem ending in *a*: *ka* (카) 'burn'
> • *-yeo* (or, less commonly, *-ya*) after a stem ending in *i* or *aw*: *haw-yeo* (ᄒᆞ여) or *haw-ya* (ᄒᆞ야) 'do'

Auxiliary verbs modulate the meaning of the clause's main verb in a variety of ways.

anne-da **(안네다) lit. 'give':** used for an action that benefits someone of higher social status

> *Abang-sindi geyeog haw-yeo-****anne****-la!* (아방신디 게역 ᄒᆞ여안네라!)
> father-DAT   geyeog do-LV-give-SE
> 'Make *geyeog* for father!' (*geyeog* is a drink made with roasted grain powder)

---

1. The roots *(i)si-* ((이)시) and *is* (잇) are found in Middle Korean as well (K.-M. Lee & Ramsey 2011, 200).

bi-da (비다) **completive** (semantically similar to *bul-da* below)

PRONUNCIATION NOTE: In the examples below, the perfective suffix *-eos* can be contracted to *-s*.

Mansu eomeong sawdab haw-yeoms-(i)gwante na-n
Mansu mother laundry do-CONT-CON   1SG-TOP
*naw-a-**bi**-(eo)s-jeo.* (만수 어멍 ㅅ답ᄒ엾(이)관테 난 나와빗저)
come.out-LV-COMPL-PFV-SE
'Because Mansu's mother was doing the laundry, I came out.'

*Jiseul   mawn sichy-eo-**bi**-(eo)s-jeo.* (지슬 ᄆ 시쳐빗(비엇)저)
potato all   wash-LV-COMPL-PFV-SE
'(I) washed all the potatoes.'

*Gai-ne beos   eodeule   dawl-a-**bi**-(eo)s-jeo*
3-PL   friend somewhere run-LV-COMPL-PFV-SE
(가이네 벗 어드레 돌아빗(비엇)저.)
'Their friend went off to somewhere.'

*I-geo   uli sawchun-i   as-a-**bi**-n-da.* (이거 우리 ㅅ춘이 앗아빈다)
this-thing 1PL cousin-NOM take-LV-COMPL-NPST-SE
'Our cousin may take this away.'

bo-da (보다) **'try'** (lit. **'see'**)
*Ssawl gwe-w-a-**bo**-la.* (쏠 궤와보라)
rice   boil-CAUS-LV-try-SE
'Try to boil the rice.'

*I-dui-seo   jideuly-eo-**bo**-la.* (이듸서 지들려보라)
this-place-LOC wait-LV-try-SE
'Try to wait here.'

bul-da (불다) lit. **'throw out; do completely':** indicates an event that yields a complete result (similar to *bi-da* above)
*Nang gai-ga   mawn singg-eo-**bul**-eos-jeo.* (낭 가이가 ᄆ 싱거불엇저)
tree   3SG-NOM all   plant-LV-COMPL-PFV-SE
'S/he planted all the trees.'

*Nawmppi nuge-ga   mawn dekky-eo-**bul**-eos-jeo.*

radish   someone-NOM all   throw-LV-COMPL-PFV-SE

(놈삐 누게가 몬 데껴불엇저)

'Someone threw away all the radish.'

*Geu heobeog   sichy-eo-**bul**-la.* (그 허벅 시쳐불라)

that water.jug wash-LV-COMPL-SE

'Wash that water jug completely!'

deul-da (들다) lit. 'enter': indicates a change of state

*Jjawl-a-**deul**-eos-jeo.* (쫄아들엇저)

narrow-LV-enter-PFV-SE

'(It) became narrow.'

do-da (도다) lit. 'give': request to a friend or younger person to carry out an action for the benefit of the speaker; *do-da* appears only with the imperative suffix *-la*

*Geu jiseul   sichy-eong na-sindi **do**-la.* (그 지슬 시청 나신디 도라)

that potato wash-CONT 1SG-DAT   give-SE

'Wash that potato and give it to me.'

*Na dugji   hawssawl nuleutt-eo-**do**-la.* (나 둑지 흣쏠 누르떠도라)

1SG shoulder a.little   press-LV-give-SE

'(Please) massage my shoulders a little.'

ga-da (가다) lit. 'go': indicates a change that is underway

*Mul-i   ssa-**ga**-nan   yap-ams-u-ge.*

water-NOM ebb-go-CON shallow-CONT-AH-SE

(물이 싸가난 얖앖우게; also spelled 야팖우게)

'(It) is becoming shallow because the tide is going out.'

*Nal-i   daws-a-**ga**-nan,   bas-deule ga-bw-a-sa-k-yeo.*

day-NOM warm-LV-go-CON field-DIR   go-see-LV-OBLIG-PROSP-SE

(날이 둣아가난 밧드레 가봐사켜)

'Because the day is becoming warm, I should go to the field and check (it).'

*Mansu mulkkuleog hayeong sim-eo-jy-eo-**ga**-nan*   *mag*

Mansu octopus   a.lot   catch-LV-become-LV-go-CON very

jikkeojy-eon. (만수 물꾸럭 하영 심어져가난 막 지꺼젼)

happy-PST

'Mansu was very happy because he was starting to catch more
   and more octopus.'

ji-da (지다) lit. **'become, be':** change of state

*Nuil-eun   mag eol-eo-**ji**-k-yeo.* (늴은 막 얼어지켜)

tomorrow-TOP very cold-LV-become-PROSP-SE

'(It looks like that) it will become very cold tomorrow.'

*Il   hayeong he-nonan   jug-eo-**ji**-k-yeo.* (일 하영 헤노난 죽어지켜)

work a.lot   do-because die-LV-become-PROSP-SE

'I will become close to dying because I work a lot.'

ji-da (지다) **'can, be able to'**

*Neu mulkkuleog sim-eo-**ji**-neu-n-ya?* (느 물꾸럭 심어지는야?)

2SG octopus   catch-LV-ABIL-INDC-NPST-SE

'Can you catch an octopus?'

*Abang san-dam   haw-yeo-**ji**-neu-n-ga?* (아방 산담ᄒ여지는가?)

father grave-stone.fence do-LV-ABIL-INDC-NPST-SE

'Can father build a grave stone-fence?'

*Jegi   dawl-eumin eomeong michy-eo-**ji**-lgeo-yeo.*

quickly run-if   mother catch.up-LV-ABIL-FUT-SE

(제기 돌으민 어멍 미쳐질거여)

'If (you) run fast, (you) will be able to catch up with mother.'

*Sunja chogi   ta-**ji**-n-da.* (순자 초기 타진다)

Sunja mushroom pick-ABIL-NPST-SE

'Sunja can pick mushrooms.'

*Neu chawlle   menggeul-a-**jy**-eo?* (느 출레 멩글아져?)

2SG side.dish make-LV-ABIL-SE

'Can you make side dishes?'

I-geo   *singg-eo-**ji**-k-eollang*   *gawj-eong ga-la.*

this-thing plant-LV-ABIL-PROSP-CON take-CON go-SE

(이거 싱거지컬랑 궂엉 가라)

'If you can plant this, take (it).'

ju-da (주다) lit. 'give': used for an action that benefits the speaker or someone of lower social status

Geu-geo   *na-sindi as-a-**ju**-b-seo.* (그거 나신디 앗아줍서)

that-thing 1SG-DAT   take-LV-give-AH-SE

'(Please) pass me that.'

Geu jiseul   *sichy-eo-**ju**-eos-jeo.* (그 지슬 시쳐주엇저)

that potato wash-LV-give-PFV-SE

'I washed that potato (for him/her).'

Na dugji   *hawssawl nuleutt-eo-**ju**-b-seo.* (나 둑지 흥쏠 누르떠줍서)

1SG shoulder a.little   press-LV-give-AH-SE

'(Please) massage my shoulder a little.'

na-da (나다) lit. 'used to': indicates habituality in the past

ALLOMORPHY: *la-* (라) after the copula *i-*.

*Gingi hayeong sim-eo-**na**-s-jeo.* (깅이 하영 심어낫저)

crab   a.lot   catch-LV-HAB-PFV-SE

'I used to catch a lot of crabs.'

Na-ga   *sigge-mengjil*   *mawn chawlly-eo-**na**-s-jeo.*

1SG-NOM ancestral.rites-holiday all   prepare-LV-HAB-PFV-SE

(나가 식게멩질 문 출려낫저)

'I used to prepare all the memorial services for the ancestors.'

Na-ga   *seonsuing-i-**la**-s-jeo.* (나가 선싱이랏저)[2]

1SG-NOM teacher-be-HAB-PFV-SE

'I used to be a teacher.'

---

2. We have also observed the following form, whose analysis is not yet clear. *seonsuing-i-**la-na**-s-jeo.* (선싱이라낫저) 'I used to be a teacher.'

sa-da (사다) 'must'

> *Mansu hawgge ga-**sa**-n-da.* (만수 흑게 가산다)
>
> Mansu school   go-OBLG-NPST-SE
>
> 'Mansu must go to school.'

> *Na-ga   buleumssi haw-yeo-**sa**-ju-ge.* (나가 부름씨 ᄒ여사주게)
>
> 1SG-TOP errand   do-LV-OBLG-SE-EMPH
>
> 'I should do an errand.'

> *Gongbui-n neu-nyang-eulo he-**sa**-n-da.* (공븬 느냥으로 헤산다)
>
> study-TOP   2SG-accord-with do-OBLG-NPST-SE
>
> 'You must study by yourself (of your own accord).'

> *Nal daws-a-ga-nan,   bas-deule ga-bw-a-**sa**-k-yeo.*
>
> day warm-LV-go-CON field-DIR   go-see-LV-OBLG-PROSP-SE
>
> (날 돗아가난, 밧드레 가봐사켜)
>
> 'Because the day is becoming warm, I should go and check the
>   field.'

> *Beg bul   awj-eong illwe   sal-a-**sa**   haw-yeo.*
>
> 100 dollars have-CON one.week live-LV-OBLG do-SE
>
> (벡불 웇엉 일뤠 살아사 ᄒ여)
>
> 'I have to live for a week on 100 dollars.'

> *Neu-ga   menal mul jil-eo-w-a-**sa**   haw-n-da.*
>
> 2SG-NOM daily water draw-LV-come-LV-OBLG do-NPST-SE
>
> (느가 메날 물 질어와사 ᄒ다)
>
> 'You have to draw water every day.'

2.4 "Light" Verbs

Many action and descriptive verbs are created by combining a so-
called light verb with a noun that denotes either an action or a state.
The most commonly used light verb is *haw-da* (ᄒ다) 'do.' When inflected for aspect, the root for *haw-da* has the alternative form *he:*
***haw**-yeos-eo* (ᄒ엿어) or ***he**-s-eo* (헷어) for 'did' and ***haw**-yeoms-eo* (ᄒ엾어)
or ***he**-ms-eo* (헴어) for 'be doing.'

haw-da (ᄒ다) lit. 'do'

Combination with a noun denoting an action:

gongbui-haw-da (공븨ᄒ다)
study-do-SE
'study'

geojisgal-haw-da (거짓갈ᄒ다)
lie-do-SE
'tell a lie'

buleumssi-haw-da (부름씨ᄒ다)
errand-do-SE
'run an errand'

chulyeom-haw-da (추렴ᄒ다)
slaughter-do-SE
'kill animals (cows and pigs for eating)'

Combination with a noun denoting a state:

gobdag-haw-da (곱닥ᄒ다)
beauty-do-SE
'be pretty'

nogolog-haw-da (노고록ᄒ다)
satisfied-do-SE
'be satisfied/relaxed/composed'

nolang-haw-da (노랑ᄒ다)
yellow-do-SE
'be yellow'

dawlkolawm-haw-da (돌코롬ᄒ다)
sweetness-do-SE
'be sweet'

majig-haw-da (마직ᄒ다)
propriety-do-SE
'be proper/right'

kkawjjing-haw-da (끄찡ᄒ다)
sameness-do-SE
'be the same'

Geudeul-i   mag dawsdaws-haw-yeos-jeo. (구들이 막 돗돗ᄒ엿저)
room-NOM very warm-do-PFV-SE
'The room is very warm.'

Mag nawlssag-haw-n-ge. (막 눌싹ᄒ게)
very fatigue-do-NPST-SE
'(I) am very tired.'

At least two other verbs fulfill a similar function: *ji-da* (지다) for property-denoting nouns and *nae(u)-da* (내(우)다) for action-denoting nouns.

ji-da (지다) lit. 'be, become'

jawmi-ji-da (주미지다)
interest-be-SE
'be interesting'

sawl-ji-da (술지다)
flesh-be-SE
'be fat'

yawmang-ji-da (으망지다)
sharpness-be-SE
'be bold and clever'

ppon-ji-da (뽄지다)
style-be-SE
'be stylish'

nae(u)-da (내(우)다) lit. 'arise, bring out'

*Jaui-ne jeong   haw-dang hawnkkeus **nae-u**-n-da.*
3-PL   like.that do-CON   big.trouble arise-CAUS-NPST-SE
(자의네 정 ᄒ당 훈꿋내운다)
'They will cause big trouble if they keep behaving like that.'

*Teumeong-**nae**-eong eomeong chib-ui-do   ga-ng   bo-gog   haw-la.*
gap-bring.out-CON mother house-DIR-too go-CON see-CON do-SE
(트멍내엉 어멍 칩의도 강 보곡 ᄒ라)
'Make some free time and go to your mother's house to check on her.'

2.5 Nominalized Verbs

Jejueo makes quite extensive use of "nominalized sentences" in which the verb carries the nominalizer *-eum* (or one of its allomorphs); see chapter 3, section 4.3. This pattern seems to be especially common in *wh* questions and exclamations that make reference to an ongoing state or event (Y.-G. Han 1984).

*Neu musigeo haw-**m**?* (느 무시거 홈?)
2SG what   do-NMLZ
'What are you doing?'

*Neu musigeo sim-**um**?* (느 무시거 심움?)
2SG what   catch-NMLZ
'What are you catching?'

*Na chawlle   menggeul-**m**.* (나 출레 멩귬)
1SG side.dishes make-NMLZ
'I am making side dishes.'

The nominal status of these sentences is confirmed by the fact that they can occur with a copula (plus sentence ender) or with particles that are normally found just with nouns.

With a copula:

Musa yeong   daws-im-i-la? (무사 영 돗임이라?)
why   like.this warm-NMLZ-be-SE
'Why is it warm like this?' (Y.-G. Han 1984, 232)

Musigeo haw-m-i-la? (무시거 홈이라?)
what   do-NMLZ-be-SE
'What are you doing?' (ibid.)

Jib-deule   dawl-eum-i-u-da. (집드레 돌음이우다) [root = *dawd-*]
home-DIR run-NMLZ-be-AH-SE
'I am going home.'

With a particle normally used with nouns:

I   gangsengi yeong-do   akkaw-um-do!
this puppy   like.this-even cute-NMLZ-SE
(이 강셍이 영도 아꾸움도!) [root = *akkawb*]
'What a cute puppy!'

Nal-do   yeong   daws-im-gwang! (날도 영 돗임광)
day-even like.this warm-NMLZ-SE
'What a warm day!'

3. Causatives

Jejueo uses two major strategies for expressing causation, one involving suffixation and the other making use of a separate verb with a causative meaning.

3.1 Suffixal Causatives

A small number of verbs of Middle Korean provenance can be causativized by adding a suffix to their root. This suffix has a variety of allomorphs, also dating back to Middle Korean, whose choice cannot be predicted by general rule. Moreover, as the examples in table 5.2 help illustrate, addition of the suffix can trigger umlaut in the root; see chapter 2, section 4.2.6.

Table 5.2 Causatives formed by suffixes

Suffix	Base verb	After causativization
-i(u) (이(우))	*meog-da* (먹다) eat-SE	*meg-i(u)-da* (메이(우)다) 'make eat' eat-CAUS-SE
	na-da (나다) come.out-SE	*nae(u)-da* (내(우)다) 'bring out' bring.out.CAUS-SE 'bring out/arise'
-hi(u) (히(우))	*sseog-da* (썩다) heartbroken-SE	*sseg-hi(u)-da* (쎅히(우)다) 'make heartbroken' heartbroken-CAUS-SE
	bawlg-da (붉다) bright-SE	*bawlg-hi(u)-da* (붉히(우)다) 'brighten' bright-CAUS-SE
-li(u) (리(우))	*nawl-da* (놀다) fly-SE	*nawl-li(u)-da* (놀리(우)다) 'make fly' fly-CAUS-SE
	al-da (알다) know-SE	*al-li(u)-da* (알리(우)다) 'inform, report' know-CAUS-SE
-gi(u) (기(우))	*beos-da* (벗다) undress-SE	*bes-gi(u)-da* (벳기(우)다) 'undress' undress-CAUS-SE
-gu(u) (구(우))	*dod-da* (돋다) erupt-SE	*dod-gu(u)-da* (돋구(우)다) 'provoke' erupt-CAUS-SE
-chu(u) (추(우))	*nawj-da* (낮다) low-SE	*nawj-chu(u)-da* (낮추(우)다) 'make low' low-CAUS-SE
-ji(u) (지(우))	*nug-da* (눅다) lie-SE	*nug-ji(u)-da* (눅지(우)다) 'lay down' lie-CAUS-SE
	sim-da (심다) hold-SE	*sim-ji(u)-da* (심지(우)다) 'make hold' hold-CAUS-SE
	aj-da (앉다) sit-SE	*aj-ji(u)-da* (앉지(우)다) 'make sit' sit-CAUS-SE
-u (우)	*gwe-da* (궤다) boil	*gwe-u-da* (궤우다) 'make boil' boil-CAUS-SE

Aui   eomeong ap-ui   aj-ji-la! (아의 어멍 앞의 앉지라!)
child mother front-LOC sit-CAUS-SE
'Make the child sit in front of (his/her) mom!'

Asi-ga   *yeon-eul u-teule nawl-**ly**-eos-jeo.*
younger.brother-NOM kite-ACC up-DIR fly-CAUS-PFV-SE
(아시가 연을 우트레 눌럿저)[3]
'Younger brother flew the kite high.'

*Eomeong-i   adeol dos-gwegi meg-**i**-men.* (어멍이 아덜 돗궤기 멕이멘)
mother-NOM son   pig-meat eat-CAUS-SE
'Mother is feeding (her) son pork.'

*Pungche-l   al-leole   nawj-**chu**-ju-ge.* (풍첼 알러레 늦추주게)
wind.break-ACC below-DIR low-CAUS-SE-EMPH
'You'd better lower the wind break.'

3.2 Verbal Causatives

A second and highly productive strategy for causativization involves
two steps: adding the suffix *-ge* (게), *-gesili* (-게시리), or *-eulen* (으렌)
to the verb that is to be causativized, and combining the result with
the verb *haw-da* (ᄒ다) or *siki-da* (시키다). Whereas *-len* can occur with
either *haw-da* or *siki-da*, *-ge* and *-gesili* typically occur with *haw-da*.

*Abang-i   ses-ttawl   jib-deule   dawd-**ge(sili)** **haw**-yeos-jeo.*
father-NOM second-daughter house-DIR run-CON   do-PFV-SE
(아방이 셋뚤 집드레 돋게(시리) ᄒ엿저)
'Father made his second daughter go home.'

*Eomeong-i   na   mul   jil-eo-o-**len**   **siky**-eos-jeo.*
mother-NOM 1SG water draw-LV-come-CON order-PFV-SE
(어멍이 나 물 질어오렌 시켯저)
'Mother made me draw water.'

*Bas-dui   ga-**len**   **siky**-eos-jeo.* (밧듸 가렌 시켯저)
field-place go-CON order-PFV-SE
'I ordered (him/her) to go to the field.'

*Aui   mulkkuleog meog-**ge(sili)** **haw**-la.* (아의 물꾸럭 먹게(시리) ᄒ라)
child octopus   eat-CON   do-SE
'Let the child eat octopus.'

---

3. The aspiration at the beginning of *teule* reflects the presence of a hidden *h* at the
    end of *u* in Middle Korean (K.-M. Lee & Ramsey 2011, 183).

Where there is a choice between the suffixal causative and the verbal causative, the former expresses a more direct type of causation.

Suffixal Causative:

Aui gwegi meg-i-la.
child meat eat-CAUS-SE
(아의 궤기 멕이라)
'Feed the kid meat.'

Aui nug-ji-la. (아의 눅지라)
child lie.down-CAUS-SE
'Lie the kid down.'

Verbal Causative:

Aui gwegi meog-ge haw-la.
child meat eat-CON do-SE
(아의 궤기 먹게 ㅎ라)
'Make/let the kid eat meat.'

Aui nug-ge   haw-la.
child lie.down-CON do-SE
(아의 눅게 ㅎ라)
'Make/let the kid lie down.'

4. Passivization

There are at least two parallel strategies for expressing a passive meaning in Jejueo, one involving suffixation and the other relying on a special auxiliary verb.

4.1 Suffixation Strategy

A relatively small set of verbs is passivized with the help of a suffix that attaches to their root. As the examples below help illustrate, the allomorphs of this suffix are homophonous with a subset of the allomorphs of the morphological causative (section 3.1) and trigger umlaut under the same conditions (hence *meog-da* 'eat,' but *meg-hi-da* 'be eaten'). The verbs in the examples below are all Middle Korean in origin (like the passive suffixes themselves) and are therefore very similar to Korean.

-i (이)	*joch-i-da* (좇이다)	*chug-i-da* (축이다)
	chase-PASS-SE	wet-PASS-SE
	'be chased'	'be wetted'
-hi (히)	*meg-hi-da* (멕히다)	*jeb-hi-da* (젭히다)
	eat-PASS-SE	catch-PASS-SE
	'be eaten'	'be caught'

-li (리)	*dawl-li-da* (둘리다)	*pawl-li-da* (풀리다)
	hang-PASS-SE	sell-PASS-SE
	'be hung'	'be sold'
	deul-li-da (들리다)	*yawl-li-da* (율리다)
	hear-PASS-SE	open-PASS-SE
	'be heard'	'be opened'
-gi (기)	*gawm-gi-da* (곱기다)	*en-gi-da* (엔기다)
	close-PASS-SE	hug-PASS-SE
	'be closed'	'be hugged'

Dodognom-i jeb-hy-eos-eo. (도둑놈이 젭혓어)
thief-NOM   catch-PASS-PFV-SE
'The thief got caught.'

Mawn   pawl-ly-eos-jeo. (몬 풀럿저)
everything sell-PASS-PFV-SE
'Everything got sold.'

4.2 Auxiliary Verb Strategy

A second strategy for forming a passive makes use of the bound auxiliary verb *-ji-da* (지다). In its most basic use, *-ji-da* combines with an intransitive verb to create an inchoative meaning similar to English "become" or "turn into"; see section 2.3 above.

daws-a-ji-da (돗아지다)   *gwe-yeo-ji-da* (궤여지다)
warm-LV-become-SE   boil-LV-become-SE
'become warm'   'become boiled'

When *-ji-da* combines with a transitive verb, the result is a passive meaning.

Joyeongge golangchang-deule bag-a-jy-eos-jeo.
bicycle   ditch-DIR   hit-LV-AUX-PFV-SE
(조영게 고랑창드레 박아젓저)
'A bicycle got bumped into the ditch.'

*Chawlle   da   menggeul-a-**jy**-eos-jeo.* (출레 다 멩글아젓저)
side.dish all make-LV-AUX-PFV-SE
'The side dishes are all made.'

5. Negation

There are three basic negators in Jejueo: *an/ani* (안/아니) 'not,' *ai* (아
이) 'not,' and *mos* (못) 'cannot.' Each can occur in a "short-negation"
pattern and a "long-negation" pattern.

5.1 Short Negation

In cases of short negation, the negator directly precedes the verb.

*Na-n   badang-i **an/ani/ai** ga-k-yeo.* (난 바당이 안/아니/아이 가켜)
1SG-TOP sea-to   not   go-PROSP-SE
'I am not going to the sea.'

*Neu **an/ani** sawl-ji-n-ge.* (느 안/아니 술진게)
2SG not   fat-be-NPST-SE
'(I see that) you're not fat.'

*Eomeong oneol pojang **mos**   jjawlleu-k-en.*
mother   today curtain cannot cut-PROSP-SE
(어멍 오널 포장 못 쫄르켄)
'Mother said she can't cut the curtain today.'

When the verbal expression consists of a verbal noun and the light
verb *haw-da*, the negator may often precede or follow the noun (S.-D.
Moon 1999a, 16-17).

***Ani** gobdag haw-da.*	*Gobdag **ani** haw-da.* (곱닥 아니ᄒ다)
not pretty do-SE	pretty not do-SE
(아니 곱닥ᄒ다)	'S/he is not beautiful.'
'S/he is not beautiful.'	
***Ani** nolang haw-da.*	*Nolang **ani** haw-da.* (노랑 아니ᄒ다)
not yellow do-SE	yellow not do-SE
(아니 노랑ᄒ다)	'It is not yellow.'
'It is not yellow.'	

Ani *yewag* *haw-yeos-jeo.*   *Yewag* *ani* *haw-yeos-jeo.*

not talk   do-PFV-SE   talk   not do-PFV-SE

(아니 예왁 ᄒᆞ엿저)   (예왁 아니 ᄒᆞ엿저)

'I didn't talk.'   'I didn't talk.'

The forms *ani* and *ai* also function as negative copulas.

Geo   *mulkkuleog* **ani/ai**. (거 물꾸럭 아니/아이)

thing octopus   not.be

'That thing isn't an octopus.'/'Is that not an octopus?'

I-geo   *na-geo*   **ani**. (이거 나거 아니)

this-thing 1SG-thing not.be

'This is not mine.'/'Isn't it mine?'

5.2 Long Negation

In long negation, *an/ani/ai* and *mos* combine with *haw-da,* forming a complex unit that can then negate the preceding verb. That verb in turn must carry a nominalizing suffix, usually *-ji* (지) or its accusative-marked counterpart *-jil* (질).

-ji (지)

ALLOMORPHY:

• *-(eu)ji* after a stem that ends in a velar consonant
• *-(i)ji* after a stem that ends in *s, j,* or *ch*
• *-(u)ji* after a stem that ends in a labial consonant. In the case of certain verbs, such as *dab-* 'build,' use of the allomorph *-uji* is accompanied by deletion of the stem-final *b* (see chapter 2, section 4.1.8). Speakers therefore have a choice between *dab-ji* and *da-uji.*

I s*angbang-eun*   *neolleu-ji*   **ani haw**-da.

this living.room-TOP spacious-NMLZ not do-SE

(이 상방은 널르지 아니ᄒᆞ다)

'The living room is not spacious.'

Geo-n   *gob-ji*   **ani haw**-n-ge. (건 곱지 아니 ᄒᆞᆫ게)

that-TOP pretty-NMLZ not do-NPST-SE

'(I see) that is not beautiful.'

*Mansu-n   nang geuchi-**ji** **ani** **haw**-yeos-jeo.*
Mansu-TOP   tree   cut-NMLZ not do-PFV-SE
(만순 낭 그치지 아니ᄒᆞᆼ엿저)
'Mansu didn't cut down the trees.'

*Dawgmawleub ap-anonan, bas-dui-l   ga-**ji-l**   **mos***
knee   hurt-CON   field-place-ACC go-NMLZ-ACC cannot
he-ms-jeo. (둑ᄆᆞ릅 아파노난 밧딜 가질 못 햿저)
do-CONT-SE

'(I) haven't been able to go to the field because my knee
  hurts.'

*Kong-do   gwe-u-**ji**   **mos**   haw-yeo?* (콩도 궤우지 못 ᄒᆞ여?)
bean-even boil-CAUS-NMLZ cannot do-SE
'Can't you even boil beans?'

*Na dam   dab-**ji**   **mos**   haw-yeo.* (나 담 답지 못ᄒᆞ여)
1SG stone.fence build-NMLZ cannot do-SE
[alternative form: *da-**uji*** (다우지)]
'I can't build a stone fence.'

*Geu-dui   gob-ji-**ji**   **mal**-la.* (그듸 곱지지 말라)
that-place hide-CAUS-NMLZ not.do-SE
'Don't hide it there.'

As the following examples help illustrate, the negated verb may
on occasion carry a suffix other than *-ji*; see also S.-J. Song (2007,
937) and S.-D. Moon (1999a).[4]

*Na-n   duli-n   ttae ssaw-eo-bo-**do**   **ani** haw-yeos-jeo.*
1SG-TOP young-NPST.CON time fight-LV-try-even not do-PFV-SE
(난 두린 때 싸워보도 아니 ᄒᆞᆼ엿저)
'I didn't even fight in my childhood.'

---

4. The verbal suffix *-deol/deul* in the final three examples below is an evident
   cognate of Middle Korean *-dol*, which had a similar function (e.g., I. Lee &
   Ramsey 2000, 299).

*Yeongsu-n   bas-dui-do   ga-**deol** **ani** haw-yeos-jeo.*
Yeongsu-TOP field-place-even go-NMLZ not do-PFV-SE
(영순 밧듸도 가덜 아니 ᄒᆞ엿저)
'Yeongsu didn't even go to the field.'

*Haleubang dumbi-do meog-**deol mos**   he-ms-jeo.*
grandfather tofu-even eat-NMLZ cannot do-CONT-SE
(하르방 둠비도 먹덜 못 헸저)
'Grandfather cannot even eat tofu.'

*Bam-ui   na-denggi-**deul**   **mal-la**.* (밤의 나뎅기들 말라)
night-LOC out-wander.around-NMLZ not.do-SE
'Do not wander around at night.' (J.-h. Kim 2014, 45)

Long negation is less common than short negation (S.-D. Moon 1999a, 47) in everyday conversations, and is sometimes associated with special semantic effects, such as the expression of the speaker's opinion or the description of a situation that is in some way unusual.

5.3 Other Negation Patterns

Inherently Negative Verbs

Three verbs in Jejueo are inherently negative. The first is *molleu-da* (몰르다) 'not know,' corresponding to *al-da* (알다) 'know.'

*Na-n   gaui **molleu**-k-u-da.* (난 가의 몰르쿠다)
1SG-TOP 3SG   not.know-PROSP-AH-SE
'I don't know him/her.'

A second inherently negative verb is *eus-da/eos-da* (읏다/엇다) 'not be, not have,' corresponding to the triplet *sis-da* (싯다), *is-da* (잇다) and *si-da* (시다).

*Gaui-n   jwe-n   ge   **eus**-da.* (가읜 쮄 게 읏다)
3SG-TOP hold-NPST.CON thing not.have-SE
'S/he has no possessions.'

*Mansu-n   bunsi   **eus**-in   aui-yeo.*
Mansu-TOP maturity not.have-NPST.CON child-SE
(만순 분시 웃인 아의여)
'Mansu is an immature child.'

The third verb of this type is *mal-da* (말다), which has two quite different uses. On the one hand, it can be used with the meaning of 'not want.'

*Gingi **mal**-da.* (깅이 말다)
crab   not.want-SE
'I don't want the crab.'

*Amu-geos-do   **mal-as**-jeo.* (아무것도 말앗저)
any-thing-even not.want-PFV-SE
'(I said) I didn't want anything.'

On the other hand, *mal-da* can also be used to negate imperatives and propositives, as described in the next subsection.
A striking feature of *mal-da* and *eus-da/eos-da* is that they can also be used as a way of saying no in response to a question. (*Mal-da* can be used in this way only for action verbs.)

Gingi sim-uk-a? (깅이 심우카?)	***Ma**-u-da.* (마우다) or	***Mal**-da.* (말다)
crab catch-PROSP-SE	not.do-AH-SE	not.do-SE
'Shall we catch crab?	'No.'	'No.'

Nal mag daws-an?	***Eos**-u-da.* (엇우다) or	***Eos**-da.* (엇다)
day very warm-PST	not.be-AH-SE	not.be-SE
(날 막 돗안?)	'No.'	'No.'
'Is the weather very warm?'		

Gai jile k-eo?	***Eos**-u-da.* (엇우다) or	***Eos**-da.* (엇다)
3SG height tall-SE	not.be-AH-SE	not.be-SE
(가이 지레 커?)	'No.'	'No.'
'Is s/he tall?		

Negating Imperatives and Propositives

Imperatives and propositives are negated by *mal-da* (말다).

Nawm-sindi gawd-ji   ***mal-ge!*** (눔신디 귿지 말게!)
other-DAT   tell-NMLZ   not.do-SE
'Let's not talk to others!'

Sawdab-ilang haw-ji   ***mal-ju.*** (ᄉ답이랑 ᄒ지 말주)
laundry-TOP   do-NMLZ not.do-SE
'Let's not do the laundry!'

Jawdeul-ji   ***mal-la!*** (ᄌ들지 말라!)
worry-NMLZ   not.do-SE
'Don't worry!'

Negative Polarity Items

The word *amu* (아무), in combination with the suffix *-do* (도), creates a "negative polarity item" that requires a negative in the same clause.

Amu-do *sawdab* **an**   *haw-yeos-in-ge.* (아무도 ᄉ답 안 ᄒ엿인게)
any-even laundry not do-PFV-NPST-SE
'(I see that) nobody did the laundry.'

Amu-geos-do   ***ani/ai*** *dekky-eos-jeo.* (아무것도 아니/아이 데꼇저)
any-thing-even not   throw-PFV-SE
'I didn't throw anything away.'

Amu-chung-do   **an** *he-s-in-ge.* (아무충도 안 헷인게)
any-damage-even not do-PFV-NPST-SE
'(I see that) nothing has been damaged.'

A variety of other expressions also require an accompanying negative, including *hawssawldo* (ᄒ쓸도) 'even a bit,' *ameng* (아멩) 'even, however much,' *sengsil/sengsim* (셍실/셍심) 'ever,' *do* (도) 'even,' *geudas* (그닷) 'much at all,' *hawneosi* (ᄒ엇이) 'so much,' *yeong* (영) 'at all,' *nawsi* (ᄂ시) 'at all,' *dangchwe* (당췌) 'at all,' and *bekki* (벡이) 'except.'

Gai-n   **hawssawl-do** *awmawng* **an** *he-ms-jeo.*
3SG-TOP little.bit-even move   not do-CONT-SE
(가인 ㅎ쑬도 ㅇ뭉 안했저)
'S/he doesn't move a bit.'

Ameng *gawl-a-do*   *na-n*   **molleu-k-yeo.** (아멩 곬아도 난 몰르켜)
whatever talk-LV-even 1SG-TOP not.know-PROSP-SE
'However much you talk (to me), I don't understand.'

O-l   *jeoseul-eun* **hawneosi** *eol-ji*   **an**
come-PROSP.CON winter-TOP so.much   cold-NMLZ not
haw-n-den   *haw-yeola.* (올 저슬은 ㅎ엇이 얼지 안 ㅎ덴 ㅎ여라)
do-NPST-CON   do-SE
'(It was said that) the coming winter will not be so cold.'

Neu-ne asi-n   **dangchwe** *dawl-eum-bag*   **mos**
2-PL   younger.sibling-TOP at.all   run-NMLZ-activity cannot
haw-yeo? (느네 아신 당췌 돌음박 못 ㅎ여?)
do-SE
'Is your younger sibling that bad at running?'

*Mansu mulkkuleog-***bekki** *ai*   *sim-eo?* (만수 물꾸럭 벡이 아이 심어?)
Mansu octopus-except   not catch-SE
'Does Mansu catch only octopus?'

Geu bibali-n **gyeong** *il*   **an** *haw-n-da-ge.*
that girl-TOP like.that work not do-NPST-SE-EMPH
(그 비바린 경 일 안 ㅎ다게)
'That girl doesn't work (much) like that.'

Halmang-eun   *ses-ttawl-ne*   *jib-ui*   **nawsi ani**
grandmother-TOP second-daughter-PL house-DIR at.all   not
ga-ms-jeo. (할망은 셋똘네집의 ㄴ시 아니 갔저)
go-CONT-SE
'Grandmother doesn't go to (her) second daughter's house
    at all.'

6. Adverbs

Adverbs make up a very diverse class of items in Jejueo, in terms of both their form and the type of meaning they express. We will describe a few of the more common types here; see K.-S. Moon (2006) for a detailed study, on which we draw here.

6.1 Derived Adverbs

A large number of manner adverbs are derived from descriptive verbs with the help of the suffixes *-ge* (게) and *-i* (이). (*-hi* and *-li* are allomorphs of *-i*.)

-ge (게)

bawdige (부디게) 'closely'

bonggeushawge (봉굿ᄒ게) 'fully (rounded)'

bulnage (불나게) 'hurriedly'

dawndawnhawge (돈돈ᄒ게) 'firmly'

geumchaghawge (금착ᄒ게) 'surprisingly'

gobongdoege (고봉되게) 'fully'

jage (자게) 'quickly' (also, *jegi* 제기)

ppawjjaghawge (뽀짝ᄒ게) 'tightly'

-i/-hi/-li (이/히/리)

bawjilani/bawjilanhi (부지란이/부지란히) 'diligently'

bingsagi/bingsegi (빙삭이/빙섹이) 'gently' (smile)

han.geolhi/han.geolli (한걸히/한걸리) 'freely'

hawneosi (ᄒ엇이) 'so much'

hwaleuleughi (화르륵히) 'quickly'

inchigi (인칙이) 'earlier'

isikkengi (이시껭이) 'for a long time'

jogeumani/jogeumanhi (조그만이/조그만히) 'moderately'

kawkawlhi/kawlkawlli (ᄏ콜히/콜콜리) 'neatly'

ogosengi (오고셍이) 'quietly, carefully (so as not to damage, disrupt, or disturb), motionless, still'

ssawlhi (쏠히) 'slowly, smoothly'

-lagi/legi (락이/렉이)

hetteullagi/hetteullegi (헤뜰락이/헤뜰렉이) 'losing balance'

heullagi/heullegi (흘락이/흘렉이) 'loosely'

jalagi/jalegi (자락이/자렉이) 'largely, suddenly'

mawnggeullagi (몽글락이) 'round and slippery objects slipping from the hand'

6.2 Other Types of Adverbs

At least two other major classes of adverbs can be identified.

Adverbs Expressing Extent and Amount

daejagi (대작이) 'thickly (covered with a substance such as glue)'
dege (데게) 'very'
geoja (거자) 'almost'
geonjum (건줌) 'nearly, almost'
geujalag (그자락) 'that much'
godeug (고득) 'fully'
gyeong(do) (경(도)) 'very, much'
hawkkom (ᄒ꾸) 'a little, a bit'
hawmateumin (ᄒ마트민) 'nearly, almost'
hawmchi (ᄒ치) 'altogether'
hawssawl (ᄒ쓸) 'a little'
hayeong (하영) 'many, much'
kawmkawmi (콤콤이) 'in detail'
mag (막) 'just, very, a lot'
sawmppag (ᄉᆞᆷ빡) 'fully'

Adverbs Expressing Time- and Speed-Related Concepts

ajeog (아적) 'still'
bawlsseo(la) (ᄇᆞᆯ써(라)) 'already'
duleongcheongi (두렁청이) 'all of a sudden'
eodugeogbolgag (어둑억볼각) 'always'
eolpeus (얼풋) 'all of a sudden'
gawja (ᄀᆞ자) 'still'
gaws (ᄀᆞᆺ) 'soon, just now'
gawsse (ᄀᆞ쎄) 'now, a second ago'
geolssagjige (걸싹지게) 'quickly'
geosseun (거쓴) 'quickly'
geuja (그자) 'always'
geujesa (그제사) 'just then'
godeulbe (고들베) 'continuously, frequently'
hawngsang (ᄒᆞ상) 'always'
hawnjeo (ᄒᆞᆫ저) 'in a hurry, fast, quickly'
hawnjine (ᄒᆞᆫ지네) 'always, frequently'
hwag (확) 'at once'
ije (이제) 'now'
ijesa (이제사) 'just now'
iljjigengi (일찍엥이) 'rather early'

isdang (잇당) 'later'
jangheulelo (장흐레로) 'continuously'
jawju (즈주) 'frequently, often'
jegi (제기) 'quickly'
jugjang (죽장) 'throughout, all the time'
mileus (미릇) 'early'
naenang (내낭) 'throughout, all the time'
neujigengi (느직엥이) 'rather late'
neulyang (느량) 'always'
ole (오레) 'long time'
yejeome (예점에) 'always'

Many of these adverbs (*ole, ije, geujesa, jawju, godeug*, and so on) bear an obvious similarity to their Korean counterparts, thanks to a shared resemblance to their Middle Korean cognates (*olae, ije, geujeza, jawjo, gawdeug*, respectively).

6

Aspect, Modality, and Tense

1. Introduction

As noted in the previous chapter, the morphological structure of Jejueo verbs can be described with reference to a template consisting of a root followed by a series of slots, each of which accommodates suffixes expressing particular types of grammatical information. The next section of this chapter focuses on contrasts involving aspect, modality, tense, and evidentiality. Section 3 describes a variety of nonsuffixal strategies for expressing these sorts of notions.

2. Aspect, Modality, and Tense

The first slot after the root is reserved for the expression of voice or causation, as discussed in the previous chapter (sections 3 and 4). The next four slots are devoted to the expression of aspect, modality, and tense, which occur after the verb root in that order, consistent with the typological generalization proposed by Van Valin & Polla (1997, 40ff.). A final slot is available to host a connective (in the case of a dependent clause) or a sentence ender, whose choice depends in part on the preceding suffixes. We examine these items in detail in chapters 7 and 8.

V-Pass/Caus-**Aspect-Aspect-Modality-Tense**(-Connective/
Sentence Ender)

Although rare, there are patterns in which all four slots associated with aspect, modality, and tense are simultaneously filled.

*Geu-dui   ga-ng   bo-nan   meog-**eoms-eos-ik-eun**-ge.*

that-place go-CON see-CON eat-CONT-PFV-PROSP-NPST-SE

(그듸 강 보난, 먹었엇이큰게)

'When you went to see that place, (s/he) must have been
  eating.'

We will proceed from "the inside out," considering the morphemes listed below in their order of proximity to the verb root.

V - *Aspect - Aspect - Modality - Tense*

-eoms	-eos	-(eu)neu	-eun
		-euk	-eon
			-eul

2.1 Slot 1: The Continuative Aspect

The first aspectual slot is reserved for the suffix *-eoms*, whose primary
function is to indicate that an event is conceptualized as ongoing or
"in progress" relative to a particular point in time—a classic function
of an aspectual category that is variously called "continuative," "du-
rative," "imperfective," and "progressive." For the sake of exposition,
we will use the term "continuative" (CONT), with the understanding
that this label is meant to be descriptive and does not imply any particular theoretical perspective on aspect (e.g., Comrie 1976; Dahl
1985).

-eoms (엄)

ALLOMORPHY:

- *-ams* (vowel harmony; see chapter 2, section 4.2.4)
- either *-ms* or *-yeoms* after a stem ending in *e* or *ae*: *gwe-ms-eo* (궦
  어) or *gwe-yeoms-eo* (궤없어) 'is boiling'
- *-ms* after a stem ending in *a*: *ka-ms-eo* (깒어) 'is burning'
- *-yeoms* (or, less commonly, *-yams*) after a stem ending in *i* or *aw*:
  haw-yeoms-eo (ㅎ없어) or *haw-yams-eo* (ㅎ앖어) 'is doing'

USAGE: Marks an ongoing event when used with an action-
denoting verb. In the absence of indications to the contrary, that
event is given a nonpast interpretation (including, possibly, a future
interpretation).

*Gawlgaebi chawj-**ams**-eo.* (굴개비 춫앖어)

frog   search-CONT-SE

'(S/he) is looking for the frog.'

*Hawgge-deule dawl-**ams**-eo.* (훅게드레 돌앖어)

school-DIR   run-CONT-SE

'S/he is running to school.'

*Yeongsu mulkkuleog sim-**eoms**-eo.* (영수 물꾸럭 심없어)

Yeongsu octopus   catch-CONT-SE

'Yeongsu is catching an octopus.'

*Seong   nuilmoli   Seoweol ga-**ms**-jeo.*

older.sibling day.after.tomorrow Seoul   go-CONT-SE

(성 닐모리 서월 값저)

'My older sibling is going to Seoul the day after tomorrow.'

*Nuil   musigeo he-**ms**-in-i?* (닐 무시거 헸인이?)

tomorrow what   do-CONT-NPST-SE

'What are you doing tomorrow?'

*Eomeong menal   gingi sim-**eoms**-jeo.* (어멍 메날 깅이 심없저)

mother   everyday crabs catch-CONT-SE

'Mother is catching crabs every day.'

When *-eoms* appears on a descriptive verb, it adds an inchoative element to the verb's meaning.

*Nawj-**ams**-jeo.* (놎앖저)

low-CONT-SE

'(It) is getting low.'

*Daws-**ams**-jeo.* (돗앖저)

warm-CONT-SE

'(It) is becoming warm.'

*Jip-**eoms**-jeo.* (지펎저, also spelled 짚없저)

deep-CONT-SE

'(It) is becoming deep.'

The phonology of *-eoms* calls for special attention. Its unusual coda (*-ms*) reflects its likely origin as a combination of the Middle Korean nominalizer *-eom* and the existential verb *si-da* (P.-h. Hyun 1976, 36; J.-h. Kang 1987, 531; J.-r. Hong 1993,103), which fused into a continuative marker, as suggested by various scholars, including J.-h. Kim (2014a) and S. Oh et al. (2016).

When followed by a syllable that begins with a vowel, the *s* of the continuative marker is of course heard at the beginning of that syllable, consistent with the general phonotactic practice (see chapter 2, sections 2.4 and 3).

> *Dekky-**eoms**-eo.* (데꼈어) pronounced *dekkyeom.seo*
>
> throw-CONT-SE
>
> 'S/he is throwing (it) away.'

When a following sentence ender begins with a consonant, the *s* is not directly pronounced. However, it can trigger tensing in the consonant, as happens in the case of *-jeo* and *-ji*, for instance. (As noted in chapter 2, section 4.1.3, tensing of a lax consonant after an *s* is widespread in Koreanic phonology.)

> *Dekky-**eoms**-jeo.* (데꼈저) pronounced *dekkyeom.**jjeo***
>
> throw-CONT-SE
>
> 'S/he is throwing (it) away.'

> *Dekky-**eoms**-ji?* (데꼈지?) pronounced *dekkyeom.**jji***
>
> throw-CONT-SE
>
> 'S/he is throwing (it) away, right?'

Interestingly, there is no tensing in the case of the sentence enders *-ga* and *-dia*. As we will see in chapter 7 (sections 2.1 and 2.2), this contrast is correlated with an independently required distinction between two classes of sentence enders.

> *Dekky-**eoms**-ga?* (데꼈가?) pronounced *dekkyeom.**ga***, not ***kka***
>
> throw-CONT-SE
>
> 'Is s/he throwing (it) away?'

We will write the continuative marker in these patterns as *-eom* (엄) rather than *-eoms* (엤), with the understanding that there is just one continuative morpheme and that the *-eom* allomorph shows up only in certain restricted contexts, such as before the sentence ender *-ga* and *-dia*.[1]

The *-eom* variant of the continuative marker is also associated with the appearance of an excrescent (etymologically unmotivated) *n* in front of a connective or sentence ender that begins with *i* or *y*.

Musigeo singg-eom-n-i? (무시거 싱겸니?)
what   plant-CONT-EXC-SE
'What is s/he planting?'

Nang ssa-m-n-ye. (낭 쌈네)
tree   cut.down-CONT-EXC-SE
'Look, s/he is cutting down a tree (with a saw).'

Malchug   chawj-am-n-ya? (말축 촟암냐?)
Grasshopper look.for-CONT-EXC-SE
'Is s/he looking for grasshoppers?'

Haleubang mulkkuleog sim-eom-n-yen   deul-eola.
grandfather octopus   catch-CONT-EXC-CON ask-SE
(하르방 물꾸럭 심엄녠 들어라)
'S/he asked whether grandfather is catching an octopus.'

The occurrence of *n* in these patterns is reminiscent of the phenomenon of *n* insertion in compounds, discussed in chapter 2, section 4.1.6. As far as we can tell, no suffix other than *-eom* triggers this effect. Thus, there is no excrescent *n* after the perfective marker in the following examples.

*Malchug   chawj-**as-ya**?* (말축 촟앗야?)
grasshopper find-PFV-SE
'Did s/he find grasshoppers?'

*Musigeo singg-**eos-i**?* (무시거 싱것이?)
what   plant-PFV-SE
'What did s/he plant?'

---

1. We do not preclude the possibility that *-(eo)m* in these patterns is a nominalizer, as it was in Middle Korean.

2.2 Slot 2: The Perfective Aspect

The second aspectual slot is reserved for the suffix *-eos*, which has a range of related uses.

-eos (엇)

ALLOMORPHY:

- *-as* (vowel harmony; see chapter 2, section 4.2.4)
- either *-s* or *-yeos* after a stem ending in *e* or *ae*: *gwe-s-jeo* (궷저) or *gwe-yeos-jeo* (궤엿저) 'boiled'
- *-s* after a stem ending in *a*: *ka-s-jeo* (캇저) 'burned'
- *-yeos* (or less commonly *-yas*) after a stem ending in *i* or *aw*: *haw-yeos-jeo* (ㅎ엿저) or *haw-yas-jeo* (ㅎ얏저) 'did'

USAGE: Following Hyun (1976, 145), we believe that *-eos* is best characterized as a perfective marker that presents an event seen in its entirety (Comrie 1976, 18). Like perfective markers in general (Dahl 2014, 19), *-eos* is very commonly used with action verbs to refer to past events.

*Gawse dekky-**eos**-jeo.* (ᄀ세 데꼇저)
scissors throw-PFV-SE
'S/he threw away the scissors.'

*Jiseul pa-**s**-jeo.* (지슬 팟저)
potato dig-PFV-SE
'S/he dug potatoes.'

*Cheolsu mom gawm-**as**-jeo.* (철수 몸 ᄀ맛저)
Cheolsu body wash-PFV-SE
'Cheolsu washed (his) body.'

*Nalle   geoduw-**as**-jeo.* (날레 거두왓저) [root = *geodub-*]
dried.grains collect-PFV-SE
'S/he gathered/harvested the grain.'

As a perfective marker, *-eos* is not restricted to events in the past. It can also be used to express events in the nonpast, including even the future, as long as they are conceptualized in their entirety. At least two such uses can be identified in Jejueo. The first involves a hypothetical event in the future, as exemplified below.

*Beos-deol-i   hayeong w-**as**-imin   joh-euk-yeo.*
friend-PL-NOM many   come-PFV-CON good-PROSP-SE
(벗덜이 하영 왓이민 좋으켜)
'It would be nice if many friends came.'

*Badang-deole mawncheo dawl-**as**-ima.* (바당더레 몬처 돌앗이마)
sea-DIR   first   run-PFV-SE
'I will have run to the sea first.'

The second involves a type of imperative pattern in which the addressee is urged to promptly complete an action.

*Neu-man ga-**s**-ila!* (느만 갓이라!)
2SG-only go-PFV-SE
'Go (and get there) alone (first)!'

*Neu mawncheo meog-**eos**-ila!* (느 몬처 먹엇이라!)
2SG first   eat-PFV-SE
'Finish eating first!'

Turning now to descriptive verbs, we find a varied set of interpretations. One particularly interesting interpretation arises in patterns such as the following, where the perfective can refer not only to a past situation, but also to a current state that contrasts with a previous situation.

Perfective (implied comparison):

*Neu yangji mag gobdag-haw-**yeos**-jeo.* (느 양지 막 곱닥ᄒ엿저)
2SG face   very beauty-do-PFV-SE
'Your face is very pretty (compared to the way it was).'

Nonperfective (no comparison):

Neu yangji mag gobdag-haw-da. (느 양지 막 곱닥ᄒ다)
2SG face   very beauty-do-SE
'Your face is very pretty.'

Perfective (implied comparison):

*Nal mag eol-**eos**-jeo.* (날 막 얼엇저)

day   very   cold-PFV-SE

'It is very cold (compared to before).'

Nonperfective (no comparison):

Nal mag eol-da. (날 막 얼다)

day   very   cold-SE

'It is cold (I feel it).'

2.3 Slot 3: Modality

The third slot in the inflectional template for the Jejueo verb accommodates two markers of modality. The first of these expresses a range of future-related meanings including prediction, conjecture, and intention. We will treat this class of meanings as instances of a "prospective" modality (PROSP).

-euk (윽)

ALLOMORPHY:

- *-ik* after a stem that ends in *s*, *j*, or *ch*
- *-uk* after a stem that ends in a labial consonant
- *-k* after a stem that ends in a vowel or *l*

USAGE: With a first-person subject, *-euk* indicates a future intention; in other cases, it typically has a conjectural interpretation. [As the examples below help illustrate, *-k* is pronounced (and written in Hangeul) as part of the morpheme that follows it.]

First-person subject:

*Nawmppi dekki-**k**-yeo.* (눔삐 데끼켜)

radish   throw-PROSP-SE

'I will throw away the radish.'

*Jaeyeol sim-**uk**-yeo.* (재열 심우켜)

cicada catch-PROSP-SE

'I will catch cicadas.'

*Seonsuing-anti bingtteog   anne-**k**-yeo.* (선싱안티 빙떡 안네켜)
teacher-DAT   buckwheat.roll give-PROSP-SE
'I will give the teacher a buckwheat roll.'

*Geu gingi na-ga   jab-**uk**-yeo.* (그 깅이 나가 잡우켜)
that crab   1SG-NOM catch-PROSP-SE
'I will catch that crab.'

*Na-n   mikkang   an/ani te.u-**k**-yeo.* (난 미깡 안/아니 테우켜)
1SG-TOP tangerine not   distribute-PROSP-SE
'I'm not going to distribute tangerines.'

*Na-ga   gawl-a-bo-**k**-u-da.* (나가 골아보쿠다)
1SG-NOM speak-LV-try-PROSP-AH-SE
'I'll try to speak (to him/her).'

*Bawleum keu-ge   bul-**k**-eun-ge.* (부름 크게 불큰게)
wind   big-ADV blow-PROSP-NPST-SE
'(It looks to me like) there will be a strong wind.'

Non-first-person subject:

*Gai bi-n   geo   jal   mul-**k**-eun-ge.* (가이 빈 거 잘 물큰게)
3SG borrow-PFV.CON thing well pay.back-PROSP-NPST-SE
'(It looks like) s/he will pay back the thing that s/he
   borrowed.'

*Neu-ga jal-do   haw-**k**-yeo.* (느가 잘도 ㅎ켜)
you-TOP well-too do-PROSP-SE
'(I don't think) you will do well.'

*Gai jile-ga   keu-**k**-eul-a.* (가이 지레가 크클아)
3SG height-NOM grow-PROSP-FUT-SE
'It seems that s/he will grow tall.'

J.-r. Hong (1993, 17) suggests that *-euk* may have come from the
Mongolian future-denoting noun *qu* (e.g., Hsiao 2013). Support for
this idea comes from its co-occurrence in some patterns with the

segment *y*, which might be interpreted as a contracted relic of the copula *i-* 'be' (P.-h. Hyun 1974, 96; Y.-J. Jung 1983, 319).[2]

> *Buleumssi haw-**k**-**y**-eo.* (부름씨 ᄒ켜)
>
> errand   do-PROSP-be-SE
>
> 'I will do the errand.'

However, it is also worth noting that the use of *-euk* with other sentence enders shows no sign of the copula's presence. (If there were a copula in the example below, the verb would be pronounced *haw-k-y-u-da.*)

> *Buleumssi haw-**k**-u-da.* (부름씨 ᄒ쿠다)
>
> errand   do-PROS-AH-SE.
>
> 'I will do the errand.'

We take no position here on the etymology of *-euk.*

A second modality marker signals a realis interpretation.

–(eu)neu ((으)ㄴ)

ALLOMORPHY:

- *-(i)neu* after a stem that ends in *s*, *j*, or *ch*
- *-(u)neu* after a stem that ends in a labial consonant
- *-neu* after a stem ending in a vowel or *l* (which then deletes)

USAGE: When attached to a bare stem, *-(eu)neu* signals a fact or a habitual action in the nonpast, complementing the semantic range of the irrealis *-euk.*[3] It is always accompanied by the nonpast suffix *-(eu)n*; see section 2.4.1 for further discussion.

Action verbs:

> *Menal   badang-deule dawd-**neu-n**-ya?* (메날 바당드레 돋는야?)
>
> everyday sea-DIR   run-INDC-NPST-SE
>
> 'Does s/he run to the sea every day?'

---

2. Unlike most time-related inflectional suffixes, *-euk* can be directly followed by only a very small number of clause-ending morphemes, most notably *-yeo* and *-yen* (see chapters 7 and 8).

3. *-(eu)neu* can be traced to Middle Korean *-naw* (ᄂ), whose function was to mark the indicative (realis) mood (Martin 1992, 716; K. M. Lee & Ramsey 2011, 210).

*Nuge-ga   kong gaw-**neu-n**-i?* (누게가 콩 ᄀᆞ는이?) [root=*gawl-*]
who-NOM bean grind-INDC-NPST-SE
'Who grinds beans?'

*Geu nongbani dosegi jillu-**neu-n**-ye.* (그 농바니 도세기 질루는예)
that farmer   pig   raise-INDC-NPST-SE
'That farmer raises pigs.'

*Neu menal   mom gawm-(**u**)**neu-n**-ya?* (느 메날 몸 ᄀᆞ우는야?)
2SG everyday body wash-INDC-NPST-SE
'Do (you) bathe every day?

*Mansu-n   musa menal   badang-ui-man dawd-**neu-n**-go?*
Mansu-TOP why   every day sea-DIR-only   run-INDC-NPST-SE
(만순 무사 메날 바당의만 돋는고?)
'Why does Mansu run only to the sea every day?'

*Seongje-n   hawgge ga-**neu-n**-ga?* (성젠 훅게 가는가?)
sibling-TOP school go-INDC-NPST-SE
'Do the siblings go to school?'

Descriptive verbs:

*Geu gudeul mag daws-(**i**)**neu-n**-ye.* (그 구들 막 ᄃᆞᆺ(이)는예)
that room   very warm-INDC-NPST-SE
'That room is very warm.'

*Geu gudeul mag daws-(**i**)**neu-n**-ya?* (그 구들 막 ᄃᆞᆺ(이)는야?)
that room   very warm-INDC-NPST-SE
'Is that room very warm?'

*I   bul   an ssa-min,   eodug-**euneu-n**-ga?*
this light not turn.on-CON dark-INDC-NPST-SE
(이 불 안 싸민, 어둑으는가?)
'If (I) don't turn this light on, would it be dark?'

2.4 Slot 4: Tense

The fourth and final time-related inflectional slot is the locus for tense-marking morphemes. Jejueo appears to have a tense system based on a three-way contrast involving nonpast, past, and future.

2.4.1 The Nonpast

The default tense interpretation in Jejueo is "nonpast," which occurs in the absence of any explicit marking of tense.

Jiseul   meog-ju. (지슬 먹주)

potato eat-SE

'S/he eats potatoes.' / 'You should have eaten potatoes.'[4]

Mansu jegi   dawd-na. (만수 제기 돋나)

Mansu   quickly   run-SE

'Mansu runs fast.'

Na-ga jiseul   dekki-jeo. (나가 지슬 데끼저)

I-NOM potato throw-SE

'I will throw away the potato.'

Jaeyeol sim-eoms-eo. (재열 심없어)

cicada catch-CONT-SE

'S/he is catching the cicada.'

The nonpast can also be marked overtly by the suffix *-eun.*

-eun (은)

ALLOMORPHY:

- *-in* after a stem that ends in *s, j,* or *ch*
- *-un* after a stem that ends in a labial consonant (optional)
- *-n* after a stem that ends in a vowel or *l,* which is then deleted

USAGE: When added to a bare stem, *-eun* signals a fact or a habitual action in the nonpast.

---

4. The "should have" interpretation seems to be tied to the presence of the sentence ender *-ju.*

Action verbs:

*Cheolsu dos-gwegi meog-**eun**-da.* (철수 돗궤기 먹은다)
Cheolsu pig-meat eat-NPST-SE
'Cheolsu eats pork.'

*Bojegi-n   menal gaekkaws-deule dawl-**eun**-da.*
fisherman-TOP daily   seashore-DIR   run-NPST-SE
(보제긴 메날 개껏드레 둘은다)
'The fisherman runs to the seashore every day.'

*Sunja musigeo   jal   chawj-**in**-da.* (순자 무시거 잘 촛인다)
Sunja something well find-NPST-SE
'Sunja finds things well.'

*Seong   menal   mom gawm-**un**-da.* (성 메날 몸 곱운다)
older.sibling every day body wash-NPST-SE
'(My) older sibling bathes every day.'

It is even possible to use *-eun* on a verb denoting a future event.

*Geu nongbani nuil   jang-ui   ga-**n**-da.* (그 농바니 닐 장의 간다)
that farmer   tomorrow market-DIR go-NPST-SE
'(I conjecture that) the farmer will go to the market
    tomorrow.'/'The farmer would go to the market
    tomorrow.'/'(Don't worry,) the farmer will go to the market
    tomorrow.'

The suffix can also be used with descriptive verbs or a copula.

Descriptive verbs:

*Seongsanpo badang-eun mag jip-**un**-da.*
Seongsanpo sea-TOP   very deep-NPST-SE
(성산포 바당은 막 지푼다/짚운다)
'The sea at Seongsanpo is very deep.'

Malchug-i-n-da. (말축인다)
grasshopper-be-NPST-SE
'It must be a grasshopper.'

*I   sin-eun   jog-**eun**-ga?* (이 신은 족은가?)

this shoe-TOP small-NPST-SE

'Are these shoes small?'

*I   gudeul-eun eotteong yeong   daws-**in**-go?*

this room-TOP   why   like.this warm-NPST-SE

(이 구들은 어떵 영 돗인고?)

'How come this room is this warm?'

*I   moje-n   musa yeong   keu-**n**-i?* (이 모젠 무사 영 큰이?)

this hat-TOP   why   like.this big-NPST-SE

'Why is this hat so big like this?'

-eun versus *-(eu)neu-n*

The forms *-eun* and *-(eu)neu-n* are in complementary distribution when they combine with the bare stem of an action verb or a descriptive verb: only *-eun* can occur with the sentence ender *-da*, while only *-(eu)neu-n* can appear with *-ye, -di, -ya, -i, -ga,* and *-go*.

eun-da:

*Jiseul   meog-**eun-da**.* (지슬 먹은다)

potato eat-NPST-SE

'S/he eats potatoes.'

neu-n-ye/di/ya/i/ga/go:

*Jiseul   meog-**neu-n-ye**.* (지슬 먹는예)

potato eat-INDC-NPST-SE

'S/he eats potatoes.'

*Jiseul   meog-**neu-n-di**.* (지슬 먹는디)

potato eat-INDC-NPST-SE

'S/he eats potatoes.'

*Jiseul   meog-**neu-n-ya**?* (지슬 먹는야?)

potato eat-INDC-NPST-SE

'Does s/he eat potatoes?'

*Musigeo meog-**neu-n-i**?* (무시거 먹는이?)

what   eat-INDC-NPST-SE

'What does s/he eat?'

*Musigeo meog-**neu-n-go**?* (무시거 먹는고?)

what   eat-INDC-NPST-SE

'What does s/he eat?'

*Jiseul   meog-**neu-n-ga**?* (지슬 먹는가?)

potato eat-INDC-NPST-SE

'(I wonder whether) s/he eats potatoes.'

However, if the stem is inflected for aspect, both *-eun* and *-(eu) neu-n* are possible regardless of whether the sentence ender is *-da, -ye, -di, -ya, -i, -ga,* or *-go*. This results in intriguing semantic contrasts. As illustrated in the following pairs of sentences, *-(eu)neu* implies a longer-lasting and hence more certain state of affairs (Y.-J. Ko 2007, 102; see also C.-H. Woo 2005 and D.-Y. Moon 2004).

-eun (short-term situation):

*Bang daws-**in**-ye.* (방 돗인예)

room warm-NPST-SE

'The room is hot (right now).'

-(eu)neu-n (long-term tendency):

*Bang daws-**(i)neu-n**-ye.* (방 돗이는예)

room warm-INDC-NPST-SE

'The room is (generally) hot.'

-eun (short-term situation):

*Geu dui   jiseul-eun guj-**in**-ya?* (그 듸 지슬은 궂인야?)

that place potato-TOP bad-NPST-SE

'Are the potatoes from that place bad (currently)?'

-(eu)neu-n (permanent state):

*Geu dui   jiseul-eun guj-**ineu-n**-ya?* (그 듸 지슬은 궂이는야?)

that place potato-TOP bad-INDC-NPST-SE

'Are the potatoes from that place (always) bad?'

A parallel contrast can be observed in action verbs. (Recall that *-in* and *-ineu-n* are the allomorphs of *-eun* and *-(eu)neu-n* that appear after a stem ending in *s*.)

> *-eun* (single event):
>
> *Haleubang   yawdawb-si-e,   bab   meog-eos-**in**-ga?*
>
> grandfather eight-hour-at meal eat-PFV-NPST-SE
>
> (하르방 ᄋᆞ돕시에 밥 먹엇인가?)
>
> 'Did grandfather eat a meal or not at 8:00?'/'I wonder whether grandfather ate at 8:00.'
>
> *-(eu)neu-n* (habit):
>
> *Haleubang   yawdawb-si-e   bab   meog-eos-**ineu-n**-ga?*
>
> grandfather eight-time-at meal eat-PFV-INDC-NPST-SE
>
> (하르방 ᄋᆞ돕시에 밥 먹엇이는가?)
>
> 'Has grandfather (usually) finished eating his meal by 8:00?'/ 'I wonder whether grandfather would have (usually) finished eating by 8:00.'
>
> *-eun* (ongoing event):
>
> *Abang   cheg   ig-eoms-**in**-ye.* (아방 첵 익엄신예)
>
> father book read-CONT-NPST-SE
>
> 'Father is reading the book (right now).'
>
> *-(eu)neu-n* (habit):
>
> *Abang   cheg   ig-eoms-**ineu-n**-ye.* (아방 첵 익엄시는예)
>
> father book read-CONT-INDC-NPST-SE
>
> 'Father is (usually in the middle of) reading a book (when his children get home).'

(Y.-j. Ko 2007 offers further examples and a somewhat different analysis.)

Is *-(eu)neun* a single morpheme?

Because *-(eu)neu* must always be accompanied by *-n*, Jejueo speakers may well think of *-(eu)neun* as a single suffix in at least some contexts. Nonetheless, for the sake of exposition, we will treat *-(eu)neu* as a separate morpheme that is associated with the third slot in the verbal inflectional template, filling out the pattern of suffixal morphology as follows.

$$V\text{-}Aspect\text{-}Aspect\text{-}Modality\text{-}Tense$$

-eoms	-eos	-(eu)neu	-eun
		-euk	-eon
			-eul

One advantage of this analysis is that it sheds light on an otherwise curious fact about *-euk*. As illustrated below, *-euk* is able to co-occur with each of the three tense markers associated with the fourth slot in our template.

With *-eun*:

*Chawlle   jal   menggeul-**k-eun**-ge.* (출레 잘 멩글큰게)
side.dishes well make-PROSP-NPST-SE
'(It appears that s/he) will make side dishes well.'

With *-eon*:

*Jawnyag meog-**(eu)k-eon**, jegi   jib-deule o-la.*
dinner   eat-PROSP-PST   quickly home-DIR come-SE
(즈냑 먹컨/먹으컨, 제기 집드레 오라)
'If you wanted to eat dinner, come home quickly.'

With *-eul*:

*Na-ga   gawlgaebi sim-**uk-eul**-a.* (나가 골개비 심우클아)
1SG-NOM frog   catch-PROSP-FUT-SE
'I will catch the frog.'

Crucially, though, *-euk* cannot occur with *-(eu)neu-n*. The likely reason is simple: the two share the same inflectional slot and can therefore not both occur on the same verb.

2.4.2 The Past

The past tense is marked by the suffix *-eon*.

-eon (언)

ALLOMORPHY:

- *-an* (vowel harmony; see chapter 2, section 4.2.4)
- either *-n* or *-yeon* after a stem ending in *e* or *ae*: *gwe-n* (궨) or *gwe-yeon* (궤연) 'boiled'
- *-n* after a stem ending in *a*: *ka-n* (칸) 'burned'
- *-yeon* after a stem ending in *i* or *aw*: *haw-yeon* (ᄒ연) 'did'

USAGE: Because the perfective suffix *-eos* (see section 2.2) is often associated with the expression of events that are already complete, its range of uses overlaps to some degree with that of *-eon*. For example, when used on a verb that denotes an instantaneous action or a longer-term activity with an easily imagined end point, *-eon* signals a past event, just as *-eos* does.

> *Jiseul pa-n.* (지슬 판)
> potato dig-PST
> '(I) dug potatoes.'

> *Mulkkuleog sim-eon.* (물꾸럭 심언)
> octopus catch-PST
> '(I) caught an octopus.'

> *Pojang geuchy-a-bul-eon.* (포장 그챠불언)
> curtain cut-LV-COMPL-PST
> '(I) cut away the curtain.'

> *Cheolsu-ne abang eonchinag jug-eon.* (철수네 아방 언치낙 죽언)
> Cheolsu-PL father last.night die-PST
> 'Cheolsu's father died last night.'

Moreover, as in the case of *-eos*, the use of *-eon* with a descriptive verb can express a present state that contrasts with a previous situation.

> *Neu yangji-n mag gobdag-haw-yeon.* (느 양진 막 곱닥ᄒ연)
> 2SG face-TOP very beauty-do-PST
> 'Your face is very pretty (compared to the past).'

*Nal mag eol-**eon**.* (날 막 얼언)

day very cold-PST

'It is very cold (compared to before).'

-eos versus *-eon*

The use and distribution of *-eos* and *-eon* differ in several respects. One very obvious difference involves their relative position: *-eos* occurs in the inflectional slot to the left of the modality marker *-euk*, whereas *-eon* occurs to its right.

*Joban   meog-**eos-ik-eon**-ga?* (조반 먹엇이컨가?)

breakfast eat-PFV-PROSP-PST-SE

'Would s/he have eaten breakfast (by now)?'

As noted previously, work on typology suggests that these positions are normally associated with aspect and tense, respectively.

Other differences involve matters of usage. For one thing, *-eon* cannot express hypothetical events unless it is accompanied by the prospective marker *-euk*, as in the following example.

*Jawnyag meog-**(eu)k-eon**, jegi   jib-deule   o-la.*

dinner   eat-PROSP-PST   quickly home-DIR come-SE

(조냑 먹컨/먹으컨, 제기 집드레 오라)

'If you wanted to eat dinner, come home quickly.'

There is no such restriction on *-eos*, as illustrated in the following example repeated from section 2.2. (The past tense marker *-eon* cannot occur with *-eumin* 'if.')

*Beos-deol-i   hayeong w-**as**-imin   joh-euk-yeo.*

friend-PL-NOM many   come-PFV-CON good-PROSP-SE

(벗덜이 하영 왓이민 좋으켜)

'It would be nice if many friends came.'

The perfective also differs from *-eon* in being able to occur in imperatives.

*Neu mawncheo meog-**eos**-ila!* (느 모처 먹엇이라!)

2SG first   eat-PFV-SE

'Finish eating first!'

In addition, unlike *-eos, -eon* is able to occur without a sentence ender, as in many of the examples above. Moreover, as we will see in the next chapter, the type of sentence enders and connectives with which *-eon* does occur are almost completely different from those that are used with *-eos*.

2.4.3 The Future

The future can be marked by the suffix *-eul*, in the fourth inflectional slot.

-eul (을)

ALLOMORPHY:

- *-il* after a stem that ends in *s, j,* or *ch*
- *-ul* after a stem that ends in a labial consonant (optional)
- *-l* after a stem that ends in a vowel or *l*, which is then deleted

USAGE: The suffix *-eul* yields a variety of future-related interpretations. A future-like interpretation is especially obvious with first- and second-person subjects.

> *I-geo   neu-ga   meog-eul-la?* (이거 느가 먹을라?)
> this-thing 2SG-NOM eat-FUT-SE
> 'Will you eat this?'

> *Neu-ga   gingi sim-ul-la?* (느가 깅이 심울라?)
> 2SG-NOM crab catch-FUT-SE
> 'Will you catch some crabs?'

> *Neu-ga   bas ga-l-la?* (느가 밧 갈라?)
> 2SG-NOM field plow-FUT-SE
> 'Will you plow the field?'

> *Nuil-eun   unyeongpas   ga-l-dia?* (닐은 우녕팟 갈디아?)[5]
> tomorrow-TOP vegetable.garden go-FUT-SE
> 'Do you want to go to the vegetable garden tomorrow?' (asking about the addressee's intention)

In some cases, *-eul* appears with the prospective marker *-euk*, which occurs in the immediately preceding inflectional slot.

---

5. *-euldia/eultia* (을디아/을티아) is often pronounced *-euldya/eultya* (을댜/을탸).

*Na-ga songegi chawj-**ik-eul**-a.* (나가 송에기 춫이클아)
1SG-NOM calf find-PROSP-FUT-SE
'I will find the calf.'

*Na-ga nang-gaji ssa-**k-eul**-a.* (나가 낭가지 싸클아)
1SG-NOM tree-branch saw-PROSP-FUT-SE
'I will cut the branch off (with a saw).'

*Neu penji ig-**euk-eul**-a?* (느 펜지 익으클아?)
2SG letter read-PROSP-FUT-SE
'Do you want to read the letter?'

*Mansu Seoweol ga-**k-eul**-ala.* (만수 서월 가클아라)
Mansu Seoul go-PROSP-FUT-SE
'(I sensed that) Mansu would go to Seoul.'

Some younger speakers even use this pattern without a sentence ender.

*Na-ga hawgge-deule dawl-**euk-eul**.* (나가 흑게드레 돌으클)
I-NOM school-DIR run-PROSP-FUT
'I will run to school.'

*Na-ga jawg-**euk-eul**.* (나가 죽으클)
I-NOM write-PROSP-FUT
'I will write (it).'

A very common pattern in speakers of all ages involves the use of *-eul* with the nominalizer *geo* (literally 'thing').

*Ga-**lgeo**-u-da.* (갈거우다)
go-FUT-AH-SE
'I'll go.'/'I'm gonna go.'

*Na-ga ill-eo-bu-n don chawj-**ilgeo**-yeo.*
1SG-TOP lose-LV-COMPL-NPST.CON money find-FUT-SE
(나가 일러분 돈 춫일거여)
'I will find the lost money.'

Haleubang-i   *uli asi-anti*   *ibul*   *deokk-eo-ju-**lgeo**.*
grandfather-NOM 1PL younger.sibling-DAT blanket cover-LV-give-FUT
(하르방이 우리 아시안티 이불 더꺼줄거)
'Grandfather will cover our younger sibling with a blanket.'

Malchug   *sim-**ulgeo**?* (말축 심울거?)
grasshopper catch-FUT
'Are you going to catch a grasshopper?'/'Do you want to catch
  a grasshopper?'

I-geo   *guj-**ilgeo**-la.* (이거 궂일거라)
this-thing bad-FUT-SE
'This thing may be bad.'

Nel-eun   *bas*   *ga-**lgeo**-yeo.* (넬은 밧 갈거여) [root = *gal-*]
tomorrow-TOP field plow-FUT-SE
'(I) will plow the field tomorrow.'

Although we assume that grammaticalization has forged *-eul*
and *geo* into a single complex marker that we have glossed simply as
"future" (FUT), there are at least two reasons to think that *geo* has retained some of its original nominal status.

First, we find patterns such as the following in which *geo* is followed by the nonpast marker *-(eu)n*, whose occurrence entails the
presence of a verb.

Halmang   *jiseul*   *meog-eoms-**ilgeo**-n-ga?* (할망 지슬 먹었일건가?)
Grandmother potato eat-CONT-FUT-NPST-SE
'Would grandmother be eating potatoes?'

The "missing" verb here can only be the copula *i-da*, which is not
overtly expressed when added to a noun stem, such as *geo*, that ends
in a vowel (see chapter 5, section 2.2).

Second, as illustrated in the examples below, the *-eulgeo* pattern
can be negated by adding the negative copula *ani-da*.

Meog-eulgeo *ani-(u)-kkwa.* (먹을거 아니 (우)꽈?)
eat-FUT   not.be-(AH)-SE
'You should have eaten (why didn't you?).'

*Ga-lgeo **ani**-(u)-kkwa.* (갈거 아니 (우)꽈)

go-FUT not.be-(AH)-SE

'You should have gone (why didn't you?).'

-eul versus *-euk*

Because we cannot directly know the future, the expression of futurity is inexorably tied up with conjecture, intention, and volition (Dahl 1985, 103). As a result, this use of *-eul* overlaps significantly with the expressive range of the prospective suffix *-euk*. The following two patterns are thus very similar in meaning.

*Halmang gingi meog-eoms-**ilgeo**-n-ga?* (할망 깅이 먹없일건가?)

grandmother crab eat-CONT-FUT-NPST-SE

'Could grandmother be eating crabs (right now)?'

*Halmang gingi meog-eoms-**ik**-eun-ga?* (할망 깅이 먹없이큰가?)

grandmother crab eat-CONT-PROSP-NPST-SE

'Could grandmother be eating crabs (right now)?'

However, there are also differences between the two markers. One such difference can be seen in the following contrast.

*Buleumssi haw-**k**-u-da.* (부름씨 ᄒ쿠다)

errand do-PROSP-AH-SE

'I'll do the errand.'

*Buleumssi haw-**lgeo**-u-da.* (부름씨 홀거우다)

errand do-FUT-AH-SE

'I'll do the errand.' / 'I am going to do the errand.'

In a context where a mother is urging her son to do something, a response containing *-eulgeo* suggests that he had previously decided to do so and perhaps had even got started. In contrast, a response with *-euk* indicates that he has decided on the spot to comply with his mother's request. The use of *-euk* to indicate a promise can also be seen in patterns such as the following.

*Jil gawl-a-ju-min, kkab haw-**k**-u-da.* (질 굴아주민 깝 ᄒ쿠다)

way tell-LV-give-CON price do-PROSP-AH-SE

'If you tell me the way, I will reward you.' (based on Dahl 2000, 790)

Several uses of *-eul* confirm that it is able to refer to a future time without implying intentionality, conjecture, or volitionality. For instance, in response to a question such as "What time does the game begin tomorrow?" one can respond with the purely factual information that it will begin at 3:00 by using *-eulgeo*.

> Q: *Nuil   mes-si-e   gongchallag haw-lgeo-la?*
>   tomorrow what-time-at soccer   do-FUT-SE
>   (닐 멧시에 공찰락 훌거라?)
>   'What time does the soccer game begin tomorrow?'

> A: *Nuil   se-si-e   haw-lgeo-yeo.* (닐 세시에 훌거여)
>   Tomorrow three-time-at do-FUT-SE
>   '(It) will begin at 3:00.'

The prospective suffix *-euk* cannot be used in this context.

Two other contexts that require *-eul* are typically associated with a future tense in other languages (Dahl 2000). An example of each follows.

> Q: *I   chogi   meog-eumin eotteong haw-lgeo-n-go?*
>   This mushroom eat-CON   how   do-FUT-NPST-SE
>   (이 초기 먹으민 어떵 훌 건고?)
>   'What will happen if (I) eat this mushroom?'

> A: *Jug-eulgeo-yeo.* (죽을거여)
>   die-FUT-SE
>   '(You) will die.' (based on Dahl 2000, 789)

> *Mag jawmi-ji-n   mal   deul-eos-in-di,   neu-do*
> Very fun.be-NPST.CON speech hear-PFV-NPST-CON 2SG-too
> *deul-eumin us-eo-ji-lgeo-yeo.*
> hear-CON   laugh-LV-become-FUT-SE
> (막 주미진 말 들엇인디, 느도 들으민 웃어질거여)
> 'I heard a very funny story, and if you hear it, you will laugh too.' (based on Dahl 2000, 793)

For a more general discussion of the contrast between *-eulgeo* and *-euk*, see J.-r. Hong (1993).

2.5 Temporal Combinations

Certain of the time-related markers that we have been considering can co-occur, creating intricate semantic effects. Here are some examples, including a few that appeared earlier in this chapter.

-eoms + *-eos* (엇 + 엇)

The combination of the continuative suffix *-eoms* with the perfective suffix *-eos* is used to describe an unfolding event in the past.

*Dam daw-**ams-eos**-ju-ge.* (담 다았엇주게) [verb root = *dab-*]

wall   build-CONT-PFV-SE-EMPH

'S/he was (in the middle of) building a wall.'

-eoms + *-eon* (엇 + 언)

A similar interpretation arises when *-eoms* occurs with *-eon*.

*Ga-ne dolegi dunggeul-ly-**eoms-eon**-ge.* (가네 도레기 둥글렀언게)

3-PL   top   roll-CAUS-CONT-PST-SE

'(I saw that) they were (in the middle of) rolling the top.'

-eoms + *-eun* (엇 + 은)

The use of *-eoms* with the nonpast suffix *-eun* gives a present progressive interpretation. (Because *-eun* follows a suffix ending in *s*, it has the allomorph *-in* in this pattern.)

*Musa yeong jolaw-**ams-in**-go?* (무사 영 조라았인고?) [root = *jolab-*]

why   so   sleepy-CONT-NPST-SE

'Why am I so sleepy?'

*Gawja sawdab haw-**yeoms-in**-ya?* (ᄀ자 ᄉ답 ᄒ였인야?)

still   laundry do-CONT-NPST-SE

'Are you still doing the laundry?'

*Eomeong melcheos   geoly-**eoms-in**-ge.* (어멍 멜첫 거렀인게)

mother   pickled.anchovy scoop-CONT-NPST-SE

'Mother is scooping up pickled anchovy.'

-eoms + *-euk* (없 + 옥)

Combination of the continuative suffix with the prospective marker *-euk* yields a future progressive meaning. (*-euk* is represented here by the allomorph *-ik*, because the preceding suffix ends in *s*.)

> *Na jiseul meog-**eoms-ik**-yeo.* (나 지슬 먹없이켜)
>
> 1SG potato eat-CONT-PROSP-SE
>
> 'I will be eating potatoes.'

-eoms + *-(eu)neun* (없 + (으)는)

Combination of the continuative marker with the indicative nonpast marker *-(eu)neu-n*, signals a habitual ongoing event.

> *Ga-ng bo-min, halmang   joban   meog-**eoms-ineu-n**-ga?*
>
> go-CON see-CON grandmother breakfast eat-CONT-INDC-NPST-SE
>
> (강보민, 할망 조반 먹없이는가?)
>
> 'When s/he gets there, is grandmother (usually in the middle of) eating breakfast?'

-eos + *-eos* (엇 + 엇)

A double perfective marker signals a past event that was either habitual or occurred prior to a stipulated point of time in the past.

> *Yeosnal-e-n   jo-pab   meog-**eos-eos**-ju.* (엿날엔 조팝 먹엇엇주)
>
> old.days-at-TOP millet-rice eat-PFV-PFV-SE
>
> '(We) used to eat millet rice in the old days.'

> *Geu ttae-n   gai-ga   penji gob-jy-**eos-eos**-ju.*
>
> that time-TOP 3SG-NOM letter hide-CAUS-PFV-PFV-SE
>
> (그 땐 가이가 펜지 곱졋엇주)
>
> 'At that time, he had (already) hidden the letter.'

We assume that the two instances of *-eos* share the same second slot in the verb's inflectional template.

-eos + *-eun* (엇 + 은)

The combination of *-eos* and *-eun* (represented by the allomorph *-in*) gives an interpretation in which a past event has current relevance.

I-geo   *bew-**as-in**-dido*   *ij-a-bul-eos-jeo.*
this-thing learn-PFV-NPST-CON forget-LV-COMPL-PFV-SE
(이거 베왓인디도 잊아불엇저)
'Although I have learned this, I have completely forgotten.'

*Bab meog-**eos-in**-dido be-ga*   *gawll-an-ge.*
food eat-PFV-NPST-CON stomach-NOM hunger-PST-EMPH
(밥 먹엇인디도 베가 굴란게)
'Even though I had a meal, I got hungry.'

-eos + -eon

The perfective marker can co-occur with the past-tense suffix, yielding an interpretation in which the event is complete in the past, before its effects are observed.

Seong-eun   *unyeongpas-deule*   *dawl-**as-eon**-ge.*
older.sibling-TOP vegetable.garden-DIR run-PFV-PST-SE
(성은 우녕팟드레 돌앗언게)
'(I noticed that) my older sibling had gone to the vegetable garden.'

-eos + -euk

Combination of the perfective suffix *-eos* with *-euk* (whose allomorph here is *-ik*) can yield two interpretations: it can have a future perfective meaning (especially with a first-person subject), or it can express a conjecture about the future completion of an event.

*Gawse chawj-**as-ik**-yeo.* (ㄱ세 춫앗이켜)
scissors find-PFV-PROSP-SE
'I will have found the scissors.'/'S/he should have found the scissors (by now).'

-eos + -(eu)neu-n (엇 + (으)는)

Combination of the perfective suffix *-eos* with the indicative nonpast marker *-(eu)neu-n* indicates a habitual event that is seen as complete from the perspective of the present moment.

*Ga-ng bo-min, halmang   joban   meog-**eos-ineu-n**-ga?*
go-CON see-CON grandmother breakfast eat-PFV-INDC-NPST-SE
(강보민, 할망 조반 먹엇이는가?)

'When you get there, is grandmother (usually) finished
    eating?'

-euk + -eun

Occurrence of the conjectural marker *-euk* with the nonpast
suffix *-eun* and the sentence ender *-ge* expresses the speaker's conjecture about a likely future event, based on a current observation.

*Chawlle   jal   menggeul-**k-eun**-ge.* (출레 잘 멩글큰게)
side.dishes well make-PROSP-NPST-SE
'(It appears that) s/he may make side dishes well.'

*Dosegi-do jillu-**k-eun**-ge.* (도세기도 질루큰게)
pig-too   raise-PROSP-NPST-SE
'(It looks like) s/he may raise pigs too.'

*Ttawl-i   chawj-**ik-eun**-ge.* (똘이 촞이큰게)
daughter-NOM look.for-PROSP-NPST-SE
'(It seems that) your daughter may be looking for you.'

-euk + -eon

The combination *-(eu)k* and *-eon* expresses a hypothetical desire.

*Jawnyag meog-**(eu)k-eon**, jegi   jib-deule   o-la.*
dinner   eat-PROSP-PST   quickly home-DIR come-SE
(자냑 먹컨/먹으컨, 제기 집드레 오라)
'If you wanted to eat dinner, come home quickly.'

-euk + -eul

The co-occurrence of *-euk* and *-eul* yields an intention interpretation with a first- or second-person subject, but a conjectural interpretation in other cases. See also chapter 6, section 2.4.3.

*Na-ga   cheg   gob-ji-**k-eul**-a.* (나가 첵 곱지클아)
1SG-NOM book hide-CAUS-PROSP-FUT-SE
'I will hide the book.'

*Na-ga   nang ssa-**k-eul**-a.* (나가 낭 싸클아)

1SG-NOM tree   saw-PROSP-FUT-SE

'I will cut the tree down (with a saw).'

*Neu cheg   ig-**euk-eul**-a?* (느 첵 익으클아?)

2SG book read-PROSP-FUT-SE

'Do you want to read a book?'

*Mansu awmong-haw-**k-eul**-ala.* (만수 으몽ᄒ클아라)

Mansu move-do-PROSP-FUT-SE

'(I sensed that) Mansu would move.'

It is also possible to have more than two time-related suffixes on the same verb. The first two examples below are from N.-D. Lee (1982, 13, 25).

*Sawdab haw-**yeoms-ik-eun**-ga?* (ᄉ답ᄒ없이큰가?)

laundry do-CONT-PROSP-NPST-SE

'Would s/he be doing the laundry (right now)?'

*Gingi hawncha mawn sim-**eos-ik-eun**-ya?* (깅이 훈차 먼 심엇이큰야?)

crab alone   all   catch-PFV-PROSP-NPST-SE

'(Do you think) s/he may have caught all the crabs by herself/ himself?'

*Geomjil me-**yeoms-eos-eos**-ju.* (검질 메엾엇엇주)

weed   pull-CONT-PFV-PFV-SE

'S/he had been pulling weeds.'

*Mikkang gojang ta-**ms-eos-eon**.* (미깡 고장 탒엇언)

tangerine flower pick-CONT-PFV-PST

'S/he had been picking tangerine flowers.'

*Joban   meog-**eos-ik-eon**-ga.* (조반 먹엇이컨가)

breakfast eat-PFV-PROSP-PST-SE

'S/he would have eaten breakfast (by now).'

See chapter 6, section 2, for an example involving four time-related suffixes.

2.6 Summary

In sum, as a first approximation, there appear to be four inflectional slots devoted to the expression of temporality in Jejueo. The first two are for aspectual suffixes—the continuative marker *-eoms* and perfective suffix *-eos*. The third slot hosts the indicative and prospective markers [*-(eu)neu* and *-euk*], which we treat as instantiations of modality because of their association with intention, conjecture, and certainty, and the fourth is reserved for a three-way tense contrast involving *-eun, -eon,* and *-eul.*

V–Aspect–Aspect-Modality–Tense

-eoms	*-eos*	*-(eu)neu*	*-eun*
		-euk	*-eon*
			-eul

Under the right conditions, each suffix in the template is able to select any of the suffixes to its right to be the next morpheme in the verbal complex, regardless of the slot in which it occurs. Thus, *-eoms* can be immediately followed by *-eos* in slot 2, or by *-(eu)neu* (*-ineu*) or *-euk* (*-ik*) in slot 3, or by a tense marker in slot 4, or even by just a sentence ender. (We discuss the relationship between sentence enders and verbal inflection in the next chapter.)

-eoms followed by ...

Perfective:	V-*eoms*-**eos**...
Modality:	V-*eoms*-**ineu**...or V-*eoms*-**ik**...
Tense:	V-*eoms*-**eon**...or V-*eoms*-**in**...or V-*eoms*-**il**...
Sentence ender:	V-*eoms*-**jeo**

Similarly, *-eos* can be immediately followed by *-(eu)neu* or *-euk*, by a tense marker, or by just a sentence ender.

-eos followed by...

Modality:	V-*eos*-**ineu**...or V-*eos*-**ik**...
Tense:	V-*eos*-**eon**...or V-*eos*-**in**...or V-*eos*-**il**...
Sentence ender:	V-*eos*-**jeo**

And the modal suffix *-euk* can be immediately followed by a tense marker, or by a sentence ender.

-euk followed by . . .

Tense:	V-*euk*-**eon** . . . or V-*euk*-**eun** . . . or V-*euk*-**eul** . . .
Sentence ender:	V-*euk*-**yeo**

The only (partially) exceptional suffix is the indicative marker *-(eu) neu*, which must always be accompanied by the nonpast suffix *-eun*; see section 2.3.)

-*(eu)neu* followed by . . .

Tense:	V-*(eu)neu*-**n**
Sentence ender:	V-*(eu)neu*-n-**ga**

Two cases fall outside the purview of the template. One such case, involving the appearance of *-eon* in an unexpected position, is discussed in the next section of this chapter. Another problematic case, permitted by at least some speakers, is exemplified in patterns such as the following. Here, the perfective suffix *-eos* occurs far to the right of its normal position, sometimes even in patterns that also contain an instance of *-eos* in the expected position next to the verb.

*Mansu-man nalog mawn singgeu-k-eul-**as**-ib-de-da.*

Mansu-only rice all   plant-PROSP-FUT-PFV-AH-EVI-SE

(만수만 나록 몬 싱그클앗입데다)

'(I noticed) Mansu could have planted all the rice (plants).'

*Mansu pudeoji-k-eul-**as**-jeo.* (만수 푸더지클앗저)

Mansu   fall.down-PROSP-FUT-PFV-SE

'Mansu could have fallen down (but he didn't).'

*Mansu gwegi meog-**eos**-ik-eul-**as**-jeo.* (만수 궤기 먹엇이클앗저)

Mansu   meat   eat-PFV-PROSP-FUT-PFV-SE

'It was possible Mansu had eaten the meat (but he didn't).'

*Mikkang   mag dawl-**as**-ik-eul-**as**-jeo.* (미깡 막 둘앗이클앗저)

Tangerine very sweet-PFV-PROSP-FUT-PFV-SE

'The tangerines could have been very sweet (but they weren't).'

All these patterns involve the fixed sequence *euk-eul-as*, which we take to be a frozen pattern; see section 4.8.

3. A Note on Evidentiality

The fifth inflectional slot, which is positioned right after tense, is normally reserved for connectives (in the case of dependent clauses) and sentence enders (in all other cases)—the focus of chapters 7 and 8. Certain of these items have an evidential function, making explicit how the speaker came to have the information that s/he is expressing—through direct observation, reports from others, or inferences based on other observed clues. Because evidentiality interacts in intricate ways with tense- and aspect-related contrasts, it is worth examining in a preliminary way here, which we will do with the help of the three sentence enders discussed below: *-eola, -eogo,* and *-ge.* Other evidential markers, including *-eume, -de, -ya, -ye, -eub-de/ di-da, -eub-ne-da,* and *eub-de/di-ga(ng),* will be discussed in the next chapter. A further set of evidentiality-related suffixes, associated with reported speech and thought, is dealt with in chapter 8, section 3.

-eola (어라)

The sentence ender *-eola* (어라) can be used to express previous direct observations by the speaker, thereby implying that the observed event has already taken place. (*-ala* and *-la* are allomorphs of *-eola;* see chapter 7.)

With a bare stem (direct observation of an event or capacity):

*Haleubang   jiseul   eonju-**ala**.* (하르방 지슬 언주아라)
grandfather potato gather-SE
'(I saw) grandfather gather potatoes.'

*Gaui-n   gingi jal   sim-**eola**.* (가읜 깅이 잘 심어라)
3SG-TOP crab   well catch-SE
'(I saw) him/her catch a lot of crabs.'/'I saw that s/he could catch a lot of crabs.' (based on H.-K. Choi 1989, 30)

With the continuative marker (direct observation of an event as it occurred):

*Haleubang   mikkang   eonju-ams-**eola**.* (하르방 미깡 언주앎어라)
grandfather tangerine gather-CONT-SE
'(I saw) grandfather gathering tangerines.'

Where the sentence contains a perfective marker, *-eola* has a slightly different effect, implying that the speaker inferred that grandfather had picked the tangerines (perhaps because there were some in a bowl), although s/he did not directly witness the event.

With the perfective marker (inference that a previous event occurred):

*Haleubang   mikkang   eonju-as-**eola**.* (하르방 미깡 언주앗어라)
Grandfather tangerine gather-PFV-SE
'(I noticed that) grandfather had gathered tangerines.'

*Geu yecheong-i   ban   mawn tew-as-**eola**.*
that married.woman-NOM share all   distribute-PFV-SE
(그 예청이 반 믄 테왓어라)
'(I noticed that) the woman distributed a share to everyone.'

-eogo (어고)

The sentence ender *-eogo* (어고) shows similar effects. (*-ago* and *-yeogo* are allomorphs of *-eogo*; see chapter 7.)

With a bare stem (direct observation of an event or habit):

*Eomeong-i   neu chawj-**ago**.* (어멍이 느 춫아고)
mother-NOM 2SG look.for-SE
'(I saw) mother look for you.'

*Mansu-n   eodeule   menal   dawl-**ago**.* (만순 어드레 메날 돌아고)
Mansu-TOP somewhere every.day run-SE
'(I noticed) Mansu run somewhere every day.'

*Neu-ne abang eonchinyag mag   we-**yeogo**.*
2-PL   father last.night   very.much shout-SE
(느네아방 언치냑 막 웨여고)
'(I heard) your father shout last night.'

With the continuative marker (direct observation of an event as it occurred):

Neu-ne seong   *tal*   *ta-ms-**eogo**.* (느네 성 탈 닯어고)
2-PL   older.sibling wild.berry pick-CONT-SE
'(I saw) your older sibling picking wild berries.'

In the above examples, with a root that is either bare or inflected by the continuative marker, we get the interpretation in which the speaker directly observed the action expressed by the verb. In contrast, when there is a perfective marker, it is understood that the speaker observed that someone had picked the berries but did not witness the event itself.

With the perfective marker (inference that a previous event occurred):

Neu-ne seong   *tal*   *ta-s-**eogo**.* (느네 성 탈 탔어고)
2-PL   older.sibling wild.berry pick-PFV-SE
'(I noticed that) your older sibling picked wild berries.'

-ge (게)

The evidential marker *-ge* works somewhat differently. It is directly preceded by a tense marker (*-eun* or *-eon*) that indicates the time of the speaker's observation or inference, which need not match the time of the event denoted by the verb. For example, both sentences below describe an event (a marriage) that has already occurred, as indicated by the perfective suffix *-eos*. Use of the past tense marker *-eon* in conjunction with the evidential marker *-ge* indicates that the speaker learned of the event in the past, whereas the nonpast suffix *-eun* signals that s/he just now realizes it.

-eon-ge: the speaker learned of the event in the past:
Seonsuing gelhon   *haw-yeos-**eon-ge**.* (선싱 겔혼ᄒ엿언게)
teacher   marriage do-PFV-PST-SE
'(I learned that) the teacher got married.'

-eun-ge: the speaker just now becomes aware of a previous event:
Seonsuing gelhon   *haw-yeos-**in-ge**.* (선싱 겔혼ᄒ엿인게)
teacher   marriage do-PFV-NPST-SE
'(I see that) the teacher got married.'

A similar contrast is found in the following two pairs of sentences.

*Banong-keul   pan-na-bul-eos-**eon-ge**.* (바농클 판나불엇언게)
needle-machine breakdown-come.out-COMPL-PFV-PST-SE
'(I learned that) the sewing machine was completely broken.'

*Banong-keul   pan-na-bul-eos-**in-ge**.* (바농클 판나불엇인게)
needle-machine breakdown-come.out-COMPL-PFV-NPST-SE
'(I see that) the sewing machine is completely broken.'

A very striking indication of the role of the tense marker in the expression of evidentiality comes from the following example.

Mansu duli-n   ttae jile-ga   mag
Mansu young-NPST.CON time height-NOM very
*keu-k-eul-**an-ge**   hawneosi   an k-eos-eola.*
tall-PROSP-FUT-PST-CON so.much   not grow-PFV-SE
(만수 두린 때 지레가 막 크클안게 흔엇이 안 컷어라)
'(I noticed that) when Mansu was a child, it seemed that he
    would grow tall, but then (I saw that) he did not grow
    much.'

Here the event denoted by the main verb (growing tall) is presented
as a possible outcome for a future time—hence the presence of the
prospective marker *-(eu)k* and the future tense marker *-eul* on *keu-*
'tall.' However, because the prediction is based on a past observation
made when Mansu was a child, the evidential marker *-ge* is accompanied by the past-tense suffix *-eon*. Normally, *-eul* and *-eon* cannot co-
occur, both because they denote mutually incompatible periods in
time and because they compete for a place in the same inflectional
slot (see section 2.6). However, in the situation illustrated here, *-eon*
applies not to the growing event denoted by the verb, but rather to
the observation referenced by the evidential marker. We discuss the
use of *-ge* at greater length in chapter 7, section 3.2.

4. Phrasal Expressions of Modality

Thus far we have focused on the use of suffixes to express various
contrasts related to temporality, evidentiality, and modality. In some
cases, especially those involving modality, the relevant contrasts are
expressed in other ways. One strategy involves the use of "auxiliary"

verbs, especially *ji-da* 'be able,' *na-da* 'used to,' and *sa-da* 'must,' as discussed in chapter 5, section 2.3. Another strategy makes use of patterns of words and morphemes to express modal notions. Many of these patterns have quite similar Korean counterparts.

4.1 Desiderative

V-gujeong hawda (V-구정 ᄒ다)

> *Dolegi dunggeuli-**gujeong haw-da**.* (도레기 둥그리구정 ᄒ다)
> top   roll-desire   do-SE
> '(I) want to roll the top.'

> *Al-nyeog-chib-deole   dawd-**gujeong haw-da**.* (알녁칩더레 돋구정 ᄒ다)
> below-side-house-DIR run-desire   do-SE
> '(I) want to run to the house in the lower area.'

4.2 Permission/Request

(V . . . eodo) dwe-kuga/gwa (V . . . 어도 뒈쿠가/과)

> *I-geo   hawssawl ib-eo-bw-**ado**   dwe-**k-u-ga/gwa**?*
> this-thing a.little   wear-LV-try-CON become-PROSP-AH-SE
> (이거 ᄒ쏠 입어봐도 뒈쿠가/과?)
> 'Can I try this on?' (lit. 'Is it okay if I try this on?')

> *I-geo   hawssawl nawly-eo-ju-**k-u-gwa**?* (이거 ᄒ쏠 ᄂ려주쿠과?)
> this-thing a.little   drop-LV-give-PROSP-AH-SE
> 'Can you lower the price a little?'

4.3 Prohibition

V-eumin ani dweda (V-으민 아니뒈다)

> *I-dui-seo-n   haw-**min** ani dwe-b-ne-da.* (이듸선 ᄒ민 아니뒙네다)
> this-place-LOC-TOP do-CON   not become-AH-EVI-SE
> 'It is prohibited to do that here.'

> *Manung-eun dekki-**min**   ani dwe-b-ne-da.* (마눙은 데끼민 아니뒙네다)
> garlic-TOP   throw-CON not become-AH-EVI-SE
> 'It is prohibited to throw away garlic.'

4.4 Obligation/Necessity

V-eong ani dweda (V-엉 아니뒈다)

Geu-le-n   dam daw-ang   ani dwe-masseum.
that-LOC-TOP wall build-CON not become-AH.SE
(그렌 담 다왕 아니 뒈마씀)
'You shouldn't build a wall there.'

V-eo-sa haw-da (V-어사 ᄒ다)

Sawdab haw-yeo-sa haw-n-da. (ᄉ답ᄒ여사 ᄒ다)
laundry do-LV-OBLG do-NPST-SE
'(I) have to do the laundry.'

Sawngki-do jal   meog-eo-sa haw-ju. (ᄉ키도 잘 먹어사 ᄒ주)
vegetable-too well eat-LV-OBLG do-SE
'(You) have to eat vegetables a lot too.'

4.5 Knowledge

V-eul jung/chung alajida (V-을 중/충 알아지다)

Jimchi   dawmgeu-l   jung al-a-jy-eo? (짐치 ᄃ글 중 알아져?).
kimchi make-FUT.CON way know-LV-ABIL-SE
[verb root = *dawmgeu-*]
'Do you know how to make kimchi?'

Mulkkuleog sim-ul   chung al-a-ji-n-da. (물꾸럭 심울 충 알아진다)
octopus   catch-FUT.CON way   know-LV-ABIL-NPST-SE
'(I) know how to catch octopus.'

V-eul-di/ V-eul-ti molleukyeo (V-을디/을티 몰르켜) 'not sure whether . . . or . . . not'

ALLOMORPHY:

• *-ildi* after a stem ends in *s, j, or ch*
• *-uldi* after a stem that ends in a labial consonant
• *-ldi* when the stem ends in a vowel or *l* (which is then deleted)

USAGE: Used for the expression of doubt or uncertainty.

*Mansu nang ssa-ms-**il-di***   ***molleu-k-yeo.***

Mansu tree   cut.down-CONT-FUT-NMLZ not.know-PROSP-SE

(만수 낭 쌌일디 몰르켜)

'I am not sure whether Mansu is cutting down the tree.'

Seong-i   *mul jil-eo-nw-as-**il-di***

older.sibling-NOM water draw-LV-come.out-PFV-FUT-NMLZ

molleu-k-yeo. (성이 물 질어낫일디 몰르켜)

not.know-PROSP-SE

'I am not sure whether the older sibling has drawn water.'

4.6 Possibility

V-eunji(di)do molleuda (V-은지(디)도 몰르다)

Geu heoju-ga   *maj-**in-ji-do***   ***molleu-k-yeo***.

that rumor-NOM correct-NPST-NMLZ-even not.know-PROSP-SE

(그 허주가 맞인지도 몰르켜)

'That rumor may be right.'

Eodui   *gwuigyeong-ga-s-**in-ji-do***   ***molleu-k-yeo***.

somewhere sightseeing-go-PFV-NPST-NMLZ-even not.know-PROSP-SE

(어듸 귀경갓인지도 몰르켜)

'(S/he) may have gone on a trip to somewhere.'

V-(eu)neun suga isda/eusda (V-(으)는 수가 잇다/읏다)

Neu gyeong   *nawbde-dang*   *nuge-sindi*

2SG like.that act.superior-CON someone-DAT

*maj-**ineu-n***   ***su-ga***   *is-eo-i*.

be.beaten-INDC-NPST.CON possibility-NOM be-SE-EMPH

(느 경 눕데당 누게신디 맞이는 수가 잇어이)

'You may get beaten up by someone if you keep acting
    superior.'

V-eosilliga eusda (V-엇일리가 읏다)

*Geu bibali-ga gob-**as-il-li-ga***   ***eus**-jeo*.

that girl-NOM hide-PFV-FUT-NMLZ-NOM not.be-SE

(그 비바리가 곱앗일리가 읏저)

'There is no possibility that the girl would hide.'

4.7 Regret, Desire, and Doubt

V-eoseosa hawyeosindi/hesindi (V-엇어사 ᄒ엿인디/헷인디)

Mileuse bengweon-deole ga-s-eo-sa   *haw-yeos-in-di.*

early   hospital-DIR   go-PFV-LV-OBLG   do-PFV-NPST-SE

(미르세 벵원더레 갓어사 ᄒ엿인디)

'I should have gone to hospital earlier.'

V-eulgeol (V-을걸)

Eomeong-sindi hawssawl deo   *jal*   *haw-lgeo-l* (*mos he-s-jeo*).

mother-DAT   little   more well do-FUT-ACC (cannot do-PFV-SE)

(어멍신디 ᄒ쓸 더 잘 홀걸 (못 헷저))

'I should have treated my mother a little better (but couldn't).'

V-jumaneun (V-주만은)

Don   *hayeong ju-juman-eun* (*ani ju-eos-guna*).

money a.lot   give-CON-TOP   (not give-PFV-SE)

(돈 하영 주주만은 (아니 주엇구나))

'(You) should have given me a lot of money (but you haven't).'

V-(eu)neun geondi (V-으는 건디)

Jil-do   *mul-eo-bo-gog haw-yeong ga-neu-n*

street-too ask-LV-try-CON do-CON   go-INDC-NPST.CON

geo-n-di (*ani haw-yeon*). (질도 물어보곡 ᄒ영 가는 건디 (아니 ᄒ연))

thing-NPST-SE (not do-PST)

'I should have asked for directions.'

V-eosimin johda (V-엇이민 좋다)

Pengseng Hawaii-seo sal-a-jy-eos-imin   *joh-(eu)k-yeo.*

for.good   Hawaii-LOC live-LV-ABIL-PFV-CON good-PROSP-SE

(펭셍 하와이서 살아졋이민 좋(으)켜)

'It would be nice if I could live in Hawaii for good.'

V-eosillogo (**V-엇일로고**)

> *Dandan jigeum-kkawjeong ani meog-**eos-il-logo**?*
>
> no.way   now-until   not eat-PFV-FUT-SE
>
> (단단 지금꺼정 아니 먹엇일로고?)
>
> '(Do you think s/he) hasn't eaten until now? (I don't think so.)'

4.8 Appearance/Speculation

V-(eu)neun/eun geo dalmda/dalmabeda (**V-(으)는/은 거 닮다/닮아베다**)

> *Eomeong seodab   haw-**neu-n**   geo*
>
> mother   laundry do-INDC-NPST.CON NMLZ
>
> ***dalm-da/dalm-a-be-da***. (어멍 서답 하는 거 닮다/닮아베다)
>
> appear-SE/appear-LV-see.PASS-SE
>
> 'It looks like mother is washing the laundry.'

> *Mogpil ill-eo-bu-**n**   geo   **dalm-da**.* (목필 일러분 거 닮다)
>
> pencil   lose-LV-COMPL-PST.CON NMLZ appear-SE
>
> 'It looks like I've lost my pencil.'

V-eumjig/jeoghawda (**V-음직/적하다**)

> *Hawssol neuj-eo-do   dwe-**m-jig-haw-da**.* (하쏠 늦어도 뒘직하다)
>
> little   late-LV-CON become-NMLZ-probability-do-SE
>
> 'It seems okay to be a little late.'

> *Bingtteog meog-**eum-jeog-haw-da**.* (빙떡 먹음적하다)
>
> bingtteog eat-NMLZ-appearance-do-SE
>
> 'The bingtteog looks delicious.' (*Bingtteog* is a buckwheat roll filled with cooked radish.)

> *Gudeul-i   daws-**im-jig-haw-da**.* (구들이 돗임직하다)
>
> room-NOM   warm-NMLZ-appearance-do-SE
>
> 'The room appears warm.'

V-eun sengida (**V-은 셍이다**)

> *Mag dwe-**n**   **seng-i-yeo**.* (막 뒌 셍이여)
>
> very tired-PST.CON appearance-be-SE
>
> 'S/he looks very tired.'

V-eobeda (V-어베다)

*Seongjeong-i   guj-**eo-be-da**.* (성정이 궂어베다)

personality-NOM bad-LV-see.PASS-SE

'(His) personality looks bad.'

N-do V-eosilgeondi (N-도 V-엇일건디)

*Jil-e   cha-deol-**do** ha-**s-ilgeo-n-di**   joyeongge ta-ng*

road-LOC car-PL-even a.lot-PFV-FUT-NPST-CON bicycle   ride-CON

ga-b-seo. (질에 차덜도 핫일건디 조영게 탕 갑서)

go-AH-SE

'Take a bus, as there must be a lot of cars on the road.'

N-ilabunan V-eosilgeoda (N-이라부난 V-엇일거다)

*Jeoseul-i-la-bu-nan   jideulkeo demy-eo-nw-**as-ilgeo**-u-da.*

winter-be-SE-COMPL-CON firewood pile.up-LV-put-PFV-FUT-AH-SE

(저슬이라부난 지들커 데며낫일거우다)

'Because it is winter, firewood must have been piled up.'

V-eobunan V-eosilgeoda (V-어부난 V-엇일거다)

*Abang jug-**eo-bu-nan**   simdeul-**eos-ilgeo**-u-da.*

father die-LV-COMPL-CON hard-PFV-FUT-AH-SE

(아방 죽어부난 심들엇일거우다)

'It must have been difficult because father died.'

V-eukeulasjeo (V-으클앗저)

*Gingi meog-**euk-eul-as-jeo**.* (깅이 먹으클앗저)

crab   eat-PROSP-FUT-PFV-SE

'S/he would have eaten crab (but didn't).'

V-eukeulanasjeo (V-으클아낫저)

*Gingi meog-**euk-eul-a-na-s-jeo**.* (깅이 먹으클아낫저)

crab   eat-PROSP-FUT-LV-come.out-PFV-SE

'S/he would have eaten crab (but didn't).'

V-eosikeulasjeo (V-엇이클앗저)

Gingi meog-eos-ik-eul-as-jeo. (깅이 먹엇이클앗저)

crab   eat-PFV-PROSP-FUT-PFV-SE

'S/he would have eaten crab (but didn't).'

V-eosikeulanasjeo (V-엇이클아낫저)

Gingi meog-eos-ik-eul-a-na-s-jeo. (깅이 먹엇이클아낫저)

crab   eat-PFV-PROSP-FUT-LV-come.out-PFV-SE

'S/he would have eaten crab (but didn't).'

Sentence Enders

1. Introduction

A large set of clause-final suffixes, which we will call "sentence enders," provides information about a variety of factors, including evidentiality, sentence type, the formality of the speech act, and the degree of deference shown by the speaker to his or her addressee(s).

Almost all utterances in Jejueo include a sentence ender. Among the few exceptions are sentences that end in the past-tense suffix *-eon* (see chapter 6, section 2.4.2), nominalized sentences (see chapter 5, section 2.5), and sentences such as the final three below, in which there is an implicit copula verb with a nonpast interpretation.

Past-tense *-eon*:

*Gingi sim-**eon**.* (깅이 심언)

crab   catch-PST

'S/he caught a crab.'

Nominalized sentences:

*Neu musigeo haw-**m**?* (느 무시거 홈?)

2SG   what   do-NMLZ

'What are you doing?'

Implicit copula:

I-geo   dosegi. (이거 도세기)
this-thing pig
'This is a pig.' / 'Is this a pig?'

I-geo   musigeo? (이거 무시거?)
this-thing what
'What is this?'

I-dui-ga   sangbang? (이듸가 상방?)
this-place-NOM living.room
'Is this the living room?'

An important factor in the use of sentence enders lies in their inter-action with other suffixes on the verb, as mentioned in the preced-ing chapter.

2. Interaction with Tense and Aspect

Two major types of sentence enders can be identified in relation to tense and aspect (table 7.1).

2.1 Type 1

The first and largest group of sentence enders, which we will refer to as Type 1, is most easily identified by the fact that they can occur with an uninflected verb stem, or with a stem ending in the continua-tive suffix *-eoms* or the perfective suffix *-eos* (and sometimes *-euk*). The sentence ender *-ju* (주) works this way.

Bare stem (uninflected):

Sonang   singgeu-ju. (소낭 싱그주)
pine.tree plant-SE
'(S/he) plants pine trees.'

Continuative suffix *-eoms*:

*Nawmppi sichy-**eoms-ju**.* (눔삐 시쳤주)
radish   wash-CONT-SE
'(S/he) is washing the radishes.'

Perfective suffix *-eos*:

*Dawlbengi dekky-**eos-ju**.* (돌벵이 데꼇주)

snail   throw-PFV-SE

'(S/he) threw away the snails.'

2.2 Type 2

A second, much smaller group of sentence enders (Type 2) can occur only with a verb stem whose final suffix is *-eun, -eon, -eul,* or *-eom* (a version of *-eoms*, as explained below),[1] none of which can co-occur with Type 1 sentence enders. There appear to be very few sentence enders of this type, three of which are discussed in this book: *-di, -dia,* and *-ga*. The examples below involve *-ga* (recall that *-in* and *-n* are allomorphs of *-eun*).

*Jiseul singgeu-neu-**n-ga**?* (지슬 싱그는가?)

potato plant-INDC-NPST-SE

'Does (s/he) plant potatoes?'

*Daejugbulegi singg-**eon-ga**?* (대죽부레기 싱건가?)

corn   plant-PST-SE

'Did (s/he) plant corn?'

*Dawlbengi dekky-eos-**in-ga**?* (돌벵이 데꼇인가?)

snail   throw-PFV-NPST-SE

'(I wonder whether s/he) has thrown out the snails.'

*Halmang   gamjeo   mawn jus-eos-ilgeo-**n-ga**?*

grandmother sweet.potato all   gather-PFV-FUT-NPST-SE

(할망 감저 믄 줏엇일건가?)

'Would grandmother have gathered all the sweet potatoes?' /
   '(I wonder whether) grandmother has gathered all the sweet
   potatoes.'

---

1. Suffixes ending in *-n, -m,* and *-l* had a nominalizing function in Middle Korean and, apparently, in earlier versions of Jejueo as well (K.-M. Lee 1993, 150; J.-r. Hong 1993, 11).

Table 7.1   Two major classes of sentence enders, depending on stem type

STEM TYPE 1	STEM TYPE 2
Can occur with a bare stem, or a stem ending in *-eos* or *-eoms* (and sometimes *-euk*)	Requires a stem ending in *-eun, -eon, -eul,* or *-eom*

When the continuative suffix occurs with a Type 2 sentence ender, there is an interesting phonological consequence: the initial consonant of the sentence ender is not tensed, contrary to what we would expect if the aspectual suffix ended in *s*.

*Neu musigeo sichy-**eom-ga**?* (느 무시거 시쳠가?)

2SG what   wash-CONT-SE

[pronounced *sichyeom-**ga***, not *sichyeom-**kka***]

'What are you washing?'

As noted in chapter 6, section 2.1, we will represent the continuative suffix in such cases as *-eom* (엄), minus the *s* that would normally trigger tensing, with the understanding that it is an allomorphic variant of the more common *-eoms* (었).

A small number of sentence enders, including *-da, -i, -go, -ya,* and *-ye*, appear to have mixed properties in that they can occur with *-eoms* and *-eos* (a Type 1 property) or with *-eun* (a Type 2 property). We will refer to the stem type in this case as "mixed."

*Na jiseul   sichy-**eoms-da**.* (나 지슬 시쳤다)

1SG potato wash-CONT-SE

[*da* is pronounced *tta*, with tensing]

'I am washing the potatoes.'

*Gaui sabal-nawmawl singg-**eun-da**.* (가의 사발ㄴ 몰 싱근다)

3SG   bowl-vegetable plant-NPST-SE

'S/he plants cabbage.'

*Gasi-eomong jiseul   sichy-**eoms-in-da**.* (가시어멍 지슬 시쳤인다)

wife-mother potato wash-CONT-NPST-SE

'Mother-in-law must be washing the potatoes.'

When the continuative marker occurs with a mixed-type sentence ender, it can have either the form *-eoms* or *-eom*. In the first case, the *s* is pronounced if the sentence ender begins with a vowel or glide, and it causes tensing if the sentence ender begins with a consonant.

-eoms with the sentence ender *-ya*:

*Malchug   chawj-**ams**-ya?* (말축 촞았야?) [*s* is pronounced]

grasshopper look.for-CONT-SE

'Is s/he looking for grasshoppers?'

-eoms with the sentence ender *-go*:

*Mansu-n   badang-deole dawl-**ams**-go?* (만순 바당더레 돌았고?)

Mansu-TOP sea-DIR   run-CONT-SE

[*s* triggers tensing of the consonant in *-go*]

'Is Mansu heading to the sea?'

On the other hand, if the continuative marker has the form *-eom*, no *s* is pronounced and there is no tensing of a following consonant. (For a discussion of the *n* that appears in the first example below, see chapter 6, section 2.1.)

-eom with the sentence ender *-ya*:

*Malchug   chawj-am-n-**ya**?* (말축 촞암냐?) [no *s*]

grasshopper look.for-CONT-EXC-SE

'Is s/he looking for grasshoppers?'

-eom with the sentence ender *-go*:

*Mansu eodeule dawl-**am**-go?* (만수 어드레 돌암고?)

Mansu where run-CONT-SE

[no *s*; no tensing of the consonant in *-go*]

'Where is Mansu going?'

The next sections survey the more common sentence enders in Jejueo, beginning with those that are used in informal situations.

3. Informal Sentence Enders

Jejueo has a large set of sentence enders that are used in informal situations—with family members, friends, and acquaintances of various sorts. They are usually not appropriate for speech to an elder or someone of higher social rank. In the absence of a comprehensive study, we can offer only a preliminary description of their usage.

3.1 Informal Sentence Enders Compatible with Both Statements and Questions

The following sentence enders can be used for both statements and questions.

-di (디)

ALLOMORPHY: *-ti* after the suffix *-eul*.

STEM TYPE: Type 2 (ending in *-eun* in a statement, and in *-eun*, *-eon*, *-eul*, or *-eom* in a question).

USAGE: For statements and *wh* questions; see also section 3.3.2.

Na gingi da meog-eos-in-di. (나 깅이 다 먹엇인디)
1SG crab all eat-PFV-NPST-SE
'I already ate the crab.'

Neu-n   musigeo sim-ul-ti? (는 무시거 심울티?)
2SG-TOP what   catch-FUT-SE
'What do you want to catch?'/'What will you catch?'

Na halmang   chib-deole menal   dawl-euneu-n-di.
1SG grandmother house-DIR everyday run-INDC-NPST-SE
(나 할망칩더레 메날 둘으는디)
'I go to grandmother's house every day.'

Gaui ije jib-ui   ga-ms-ilgeo-n-di. (가의 이제 집의값일건디)
3SG   now house-DIR go-CONT-FUT-NPST-SE
'(I assume that) s/he must be going home now.'

Abang-i   eomeong dugji   nuleutt-eoms-in-di.
father-NOM mother   shoulder press-CONT-NPST-SE
(아방이 어멍 둑지 누르떲인디)
'Father is massaging mother's shoulder.'

For further discussion of the use of *-di* in question patterns, see section 3.3.2.

-eo (어)

ALLOMORPHY:

- *-a* (vowel harmony; see chapter 2, section 4.2.4)
- either Ø or *-yeo* after a stem ending in *e* or *ae*: *me* (메) or *me-yeo* (메여) 'pull'
- Ø after a stem ending in *a*: *ka* (카) 'burn'
- *-yeo* after a stem ending *i* or *aw*: *haw-yeo* (ㅎ여) 'do'

STEM TYPE: Type 1 (bare, or ending in *-eos* or *-eoms*).

USAGE: Statements or questions (both *yes–no* and *wh* questions). In statements, *-eo* creates a somewhat softer impression than *-ju* (see below).

*Neu chawlle   jal   menggeul-**a**?* (느 출레 잘 멩글아?)
2SG side.dishes well make-SE
'Do you make side dishes well?'

*Na chawlle   jal   menggeul-**a**.* (나 출레 잘 멩글아)
1SG side.dishes well make-SE.
'I can make side dishes well.'

*Mansu menal   ganse-haw-**yeo**.* (만수 메날 간세ㅎ여)
Mansu everyday laziness-do-SE
'Mansu slacks off every day.'

*Sunja geomjil jal   me-**yeo**.* (순자 검질 잘 메여)
Sunja weed   well pull-SE
'Sunja can pull weeds well.'

I   jideulkeo chujy-eos-in-di   ka? (이 지들커 추졋인디 카?)
this firewood damp-PFV-NPST-CON burn
'Would this firewood burn when it is damp?'

*Gaui musigeo bongg-ams-**eo**?* (가의 무시거 봉갊어?)
3SG what   gather-CONT-SE
'What is s/he is gathering?'

Gaui jiseul   sichy-eoms-eo. (가의 지슬 시쳤어)

3SG   potato wash-CONT-SE

'S/he is washing a potato.'

Na   yeobcho   chawj-as-eo. (나 엽초 춫앗어)

1SG cigarette find-PFV-SE

'I found a hand-rolled cigarette.'

-eogo (어고)

ALLOMORPHY:

- *-ago* (vowel harmony; see chapter 2, section 4.2.4)
- either *-go* or *-yeogo* after a stem ending in *e* or *ae*: *gwe-go* (궤고) or *gwe-yeogo* (궤여고) 'boiled'
- Ø after a stem ending in *a*: *ka-go* (카고) 'burned'
- *-yeogo* after a stem ending in *aw*: *haw-yeogo* (ᄒ여고) 'did'

STEM TYPE: Type 1 (bare, or ending in *-eos, -eoms,* or *-euk*).
USAGE: Evidential marker; used for statements and questions that rely on direct observation or inference.

With a bare stem (direct observation of an event, habit or fact):

Eomeong-i   neu sungteol-eogo. (어멍이 느 숭털어고)

mother-NOM 2SG imitate-SE

'(I saw your) mother imitate you.'

Mansu-n   eodeule menal   dawl-ago. (만순 어드레 메날 돌아고)

Mansu-TOP where   everyday run-SE

'(I noticed that) Mansu went somewhere every day.'

Geu badang-do mag jip-eogo. (그 바당도 막 짚어고)

that sea-too   very deep-SE

'(I found out that) that sea is also very deep.'

With the continuative marker (direct observation of an event as it occurred):

Abang sawngki   tawd-ams-eogo. (아방 숭키 톤앖어고)

father vegetable pluck-CONT-SE

'(I saw) father picking vegetables.'

With the perfective marker (inference based on evidence of a previous event):

*Eomeong seodab   mawn haw-yeos-**eogo**.* (어멍 서답 몬 ㅎ엿어고)
mother   laundry all   do-PFV-SE
'(I noticed that) mother had already done the laundry.'

This sentence ender can also be used with *wh* questions on the assumption that the addressee can answer the question based on direct observation of a prior event. (This usage is apparently reserved for speech by an older person to a younger person.)

*I-dui   heobeog   nuge-ga   beoll-**eogo**?* (이듸 허벅 누게가 벌러고?)
this-place water.pot who-NOM break-SE
'(Did you see) who broke the water pot here?'

*Gai-ne beos-deol-eun   geu-dui-seo   musigeo jus-**eogo**?*
3SG-PL friend-PL-TOP   that-place-LOC what   gather-SE
(가이네 벗덜은 그듸서 무시거 줏어고?)
'(Did you see) what their friends were gathering up there?'

-eola (어라)

ALLOMORPHY:

- *-ala* (vowel harmony; see chapter 2, section 4.2.4)
- either *-la* or *-yeola* after a stem ending in *e* or *ae*: *gwe-la* (궤라) or *gwe-yeola* (궤여라) 'boiled'
- *-la* after a stem ending in *a* or *eo*: *ka-la* (카라) 'burned'
- *-yeola* after a stem ending in *i* or *aw*: *haw-yeola* (ㅎ여라) 'did'

STEM TYPE: Type 1 (bare, or ending in *-eos*, *-eoms*, or *-euk*).

USAGE: Statements, *yes–no* or *wh* questions; appropriate for use by an elder person to a younger one, as well as between friends and people who know each other well.

When used in statements about past situations, *-eola* has an evidential function, indicating that the speaker's statement is based on either direct observation or an inference based on observation.

With a bare stem (direct observation of an event or capacity):

Mansu-do mulkkuleog sim-eola. (만수도 물꾸럭 심어라)
Mansu-too octopus   catch-SE
'(I saw) Mansu too catch octopus.' (based on H.-K. Choi 1989: 30)

Gaui-n mul jal jil-eola. (가읜 물 잘 질어라)
3SG-TOP water well draw-SE
'(I saw) him/her draw water skillfully.'

With the continuative marker (direct observation of an event as it occurred):

Haleubang mikkang ta-ms-eola. (하르방 미깡 탒어라)
grandfather tangerine pick-CONT-SE
'(I saw) grandfather picking tangerines.'

With the perfective marker (inference based on evidence of a previous event):

Ga-ne-deol jiseul mawn dekky-eos-eola. (가네덜 지슬 몬 데꼇어라)
3-PL-PL   potato all   throw-PFV-SE
'(I noticed that) they had thrown away all the potatoes.'

When combined with the future marker *-eulgeo*, *-eola* can be associated with the expression of a conjecture based on the speaker's feeling or opinion.

Yaui-n Yeongsu-ne sawnji-lgeo-la. (야읜 영수네 손질거라)
3SG-TOP Yeongsu-PL grandchild-FUT-SE
'This child may be Yeongsu's grandchild.'

I-dui-ga   ja-ne bas-i-lgeo-la. (이듸가 자네 밧일거라)
this-place-NOM 3-PL field-be-FUT-SE
'This place may be their field.'

Sunja ije jib-deole dawl-eulgeo-la? (순자 이제 집더레 돌을거라?)
Sunja now house-DIR run-FUT-SE
'Is Sunja going to rush back home now?'

*Nuge-ga   ssawl kkab chuli-**lgeo-la**?* (누게가 쏠깝 추릴거라?)

who-NOM rice   price pay-FUT-SE

'Who will pay for the rice?'

The conjectural interpretation becomes obligatory when *-eulgeo-la* is added to an inflected verb stem.

*Gai-ne beos   ije   jib-deole   dawl-ams-**ilgeo-la**.*

3-PL   friend now house-DIR run-CONT-FUT-SE

(가이네 벗 이제 집더레 돌앖일거라)

'His friend might be running home now.'

*Mansu ije   mal   da gawl-as-**ilgeo-la**.* (만수 이제 말 다 굴앗일거라)

Mansu now speech all talk-PFV-FUT-SE

'Mansu might have finished talking by now.'

-eumen (으멘)[2]

ALLOMORPHY:

- *-imen* after a stem that ends in *s, j,* or *ch*
- *-umen* after a stem that ends in a labial consonant
- *-men* after a stem that ends in a vowel or *l*

STEM TYPE: Type 1 (bare, or ending in *-eos* or *-eoms*).

USAGE: Statements and *yes–no* or *wh* questions addressed to close friends and family members; creates an impression of friendliness and intimacy.

When attached to a noninflected verb stem, *-eumen* is used to report or ask about an ongoing current event.

*Na-ga   ssawl gwe-u-**men**.* (나가 쏠 궤우멘)

1SG-NOM rice   boil-CAUS-SE

'I am boiling the rice.'

*Halmang   mulkkuleog meog-**eumen**.* (할망 물꾸럭 먹으멘)

grandmother octopus   eat-SE

'(I know) grandmother is eating octopus.'

---

2. This sentence ender seems to have originated in the combination of the nominalizer *-eum* and the reportive marker *-en*. An apparent semantic reflex of this etymology is the continuative meaning exemplified in the first set of examples below. (As noted in chapter 6, section 2.1, the continuative marker originated as a nominalizer.)

Eomeong chawj-imen? (어멍 춫이멘?)

mother   look.for-SE

'(Is s/he) looking for mother?'

Neu musigeo sichi-men? (느 무시거 시치멘?)

2SG what   wash-SE

'What are you washing?

When attached to an inflected verb, *-eumen* has an evidential function in that it is used to report or ask about a past event that was directly observed or whose occurrence was inferred from an observation.

Ga-ng bo-nan, eomeong jiseul   mawn sichy-eos-imen.

go-CON see-CON mother potato all   wash-PFV-SE

(강 보난, 어멍 지슬 문 시첫이멘)

'When (I) went (there), (I noticed that) Mom had washed all
    the potatoes.'

Ga-ng bo-nan   eomeong abang mal   gawl-ams-imen.

go-CON see-CON mother   father speech talk-CONT-SE

(강 보난 어멍 아방 말 굴앖이멘)

'When I went (there), I saw mother and father talking.'

Uli   ses-ttawl   chawlle   menggeul-ams-imen?

1PL second.daughter side.dishes make-CONT-SE

(우리 셋뚤 출레 멩글앖이멘?)

'(Did you see) my second-oldest daughter making side dishes?'

Mina mom gawm-as-imen? (미나 몸 곱앗이멘?)

Mina body wash-PFV-SE

'(Did you notice that) Mina had bathed?'

-ji (지)

ALLOMORPHY: None.

STEM TYPE: Type 1 (bare, or ending in *-eos* or *-eoms*).

USAGE: Statements and confirmatory *yes–no* questions. When used for statements, *-ji* implies certainty on the part of the speaker.

Na-ga   menal   halmang   chib-deole dawd-ji.
1SG-NOM everyday grandmother house-DIR run-SE
(나가 메날 할망칩더레 돋지)
'(I assure you that) I go to grandmother's house every day.'

Uli asi-ga   banong chawj-as-ji. (우리 아시가 바농 촞앗지)
1PL younger.sibling-NOM needle find-PFV-SE
'(I assure you that) my younger sibling found the needle.'

Mina ije   jingsim chawlly-eoms-ji. (미나 이제 징심 출렸지)
Mina now lunch   prepare-CONT-SE
'(I assure you that) Mina is preparing for lunch now.'

When used for questions, *-ji* implies that the speaker is seeking agreement with an assumption or judgment.

Neu menal badang-deole dawl-eulgeo-ji? (느 메날 바당더레 둘을거지?)
2SG daily   sea-DIR   run-FUT-SE
'(I believe that) you will go to the sea every day, right?

Neu mawncheo gwendang chib-deole dawl-ams-ilgeo-ji?
2SG first   relative   house-DIR run-CONT-FUT-SE
(느 믄처 궨당칩더레 둘았일거지?)
'(I believe that) you are going to go to your relative's house
   first, right?'

Yaui neomui   hayeong bongg-ams-ji-i? (야의 너믜 하영 봉갊지이?)
3SG too.much a.lot   gather-CONT-SE-EMPH
'S/he is gathering up too much, right?'

Na-sindi jeonhwa ani w-as-ji? (나신디 전화 아니 왓지?)
1SG-DAT phone   not come-PFV-SE
'(I believe that) nobody called me, right?'

Neu menal   mom gawm-ji? (느 메날 몸 곰지?)
2SG everyday body wash-SE
'(I believe that) you have a bath every day, right?'

-na (나)

ALLOMORPHY: None.
STEM TYPE: Type 1 (bare, or ending in *-eos* or *-eoms*).
USAGE: Statements of fact, and *yes–no* or *wh* questions about factual matters.

*I   aegi-n   mal   jal   gawd-**na**.* (이 애긴 말 잘 곧나)
this child-TOP speech well speak-SE
'This baby can speak well.'

*Neu mulkkuleog sim-eo-ji-**na**?* (느 물꾸럭 심어지나?)
2SG octopus   catch-LV-ABIL-SE
'Can you catch octopus?'

*Neu menal eodeule dawd-**na**?* (느 메날 어드레 돋나?)
2SG daily   where   run-SE
'Where do you run to every day?'

*Neu musigeo sichy-eoms-**na**?* (느 무시거 시쳤나?)
2SG what   wash-CONT-SE
'What are you washing?'

A question marked by *-na* sounds quite direct, giving it a somewhat authoritative tone.

3.2 Informal Sentence Enders for Statements Only

The following sentence enders are used only for statements.

-de (데)

ALLOMORPHY: None.
STEM TYPE: Type 1 (bare, or ending in *-eos* or *-eoms*).
USAGE: Evidential marker; used for statements about past events directly observed by the speaker; implies surprise. For more discussion, see Y.-J. Jung (1983, 315).

*Gaui giyeong haw-n   il   haw-**de**.* (가의 기영흔 일 ㅎ데)
3SG   like.that do-NPST.CON work do-SE
'(I saw) him/her doing that kind of work (surprisingly).'

Gaui buleumssi haw-de. (가의 부름씨 ᄒ데)

3SG   errand   do-SE

'(I saw) him/her doing an errand (surprisingly).'

Gaui banong gob-jy-eo-bul-eos-de. (가의 바농 곱져불엇데)

3SG   needle   hide-CAUS-LV-COMPL-PFV-SE

'(I noticed that) s/he had hidden the needle (surprisingly).'

Mansu nang singg-eoms-de. (만수 낭 싱겄데)

Mansu tree   plant-CONT-SE

'(I saw that) Mansu was (in the middle of) planting a tree (surprisingly).'

As noted in section 4.1, *-de* is not a past-tense marker per se. The past interpretation associated with it comes from the fact that, as an evidential, it reports previously observed events.

-*(eu)da* ((으)다)

ALLOMORPHY: See below.

STEM TYPE: Mixed (bare, or ending in *-eos*, *-eoms*, or *-eun*).

USAGE: Statements; more likely to be used by older speakers.

The sentence ender has a quite intricate allomorphy which we will consider in steps. First, with action verbs and descriptive verbs that carry inflection for tense or aspect, only the form *-da* is permitted.

Inflected action verbs:

Bojegi   dos-gwegi hayeong meog-eun-da. (보제기 돗궤기 하영 먹은다)

fisherman pig-meat a.lot   eat-NPST-SE

'The fisherman eats pork a lot.'

Sunja buleumssi haw-yeos-in-da. (순자 부름씨 ᄒ엿인다)

Sunja errand   do-PFV-NPST-SE

'Sunja must have done an errand.'

Na bettwillag he-ms-da. (나 베뛸락 헸다)

1SG jump.rope do-CONT-SE

'I am jumping rope.'

*Ga-ng bo-min haleubang joban   mawn meog-eos-in-**da**.*
go-CON see-CON grandfather breakfast all   eat-PFV-NPST-SE
(강 보민 하르방 조반 믄 먹엇인다)
'Grandpa has (usually) eaten breakfast when I go and check.'

*Ga-ng bo-min   halmang   jawnyag menggeul-ams-in-**da**.*
go-CON look-CON grandmother dinner   make-CONT-NPST-SE
(강 보민 할망 ᄌ냑 멩글았인다)
'Grandmother is (usually) in the middle of making dinner
    when I go and check.'

*Na-ga   sawdab haw-lgeo-**da**.* (나가 ᄉ답홀거다)
1SG-NOM laundry do-FUT-SE
'I (not others) will do the laundry.'

*Gai seonsuing-i-la-s-**da**.* (가이 선싱이랏다)
3SG teacher-be-HAB-PFV-SE
'S/he used to be a teacher.'

Inflected descriptive verbs:

*Eodug-eos-**da**.* (어둑엇다)   *Eodug-eoms-**da**.* (어둑없다)
dark-PFV-SE   dark-CONT-SE
'It is dark.'   'It is getting dark.'

*Eol-eos-**da**.* (얼엇다)   *Eol-eoms-**da**.* (얼없다)
cold-PFV-SE   cold-CONT-SE
'It is cold.'   'It is getting cold.'

*Geu gudeul-eun mag daws-in-**da**.* (그 구들은 막 돗인다)
that room-TOP   very warm-NPST-SE
'That room is very warm.'

In contrast, the following pattern of allomorphy is observed with descriptive verbs that are not inflected for tense or aspect.

- *-(i)da* after a stem ending in *s* or *j* (no stems end in *ch*)
- *-(u)da* after a stem ending in a labial consonant
- *-da* after a stem ending in a vowel or *l*

Uninflected descriptive verbs:

Jog-(eu)da. (족(으)다) *Yawm-(u)da.* (욤(우)다) *Daws-(i)da.* (돗(이)다)
small-SE   ripe-SE   hot-SE
'It is small.'   'It is ripe.'   'It is hot.'

Ha-da. (하다)   *Gob-da.* (곱다)
a.lot-SE   pretty-SE
'It is a lot.'   'She is pretty.'

-*(eu)jeo* ((으)저)

ALLOMORPHY:

- -*(i)jeo* after a stem that ends in *s, j,* or *ch*
- -*(u)jeo* after a stem that ends in a labial consonant
- -*jeo* after a stem that ends in a vowel or *l*

STEM TYPE: Type 1 (bare, or ending in -*eos* or -*eoms*).
USAGE: Can only be used with action verbs.
When it has a first-person subject, -*jeo* is associated with the expression of the speaker's intention or will.

Na-lang i-geo   dekki-jeo. (나랑 이거 데끼저)
1SG-TOP this-thing throw-SE
'I will throw away this (not you).'

Uli-ga   sawdab haw-jeo. (우리가 ㅅ답ㅎ저)
1PL-NOM laundry do-SE
'We will do the laundry.'

I-le   do-la.   Nae sichi-jeo. (이레 도라. 내 시치저.)
this-DIR give-SE 1SG wash-SE
'Give (it) (to me) here. I will wash it.' (P.-h. Hyun 1977b, 242)

Gawman is-ila. Na-ga   gawd-jeo/gawl-eujeo.
still   be-SE 1SG-NOM talk-SE
(ㄱ만 잇이라. 나가 곧저/굴으저)
'Keep quiet. I will talk.' (based on P.-h. Hyun 1977b, 242)

Neu-lang aj-a-si-la.   Nae haw-jeo. (느랑 앚아시라. 내 ᄒ저)
2SG-TOP   sit-LV-be-SE 1SG do-SE
'You sit down (and wait). I will do (it).' (P.-h. Hyun 1977b, 242)

Na-ga   sim-(u)jeo. (나가 심 (우) 저)
1SG-NOM   catch-SE
'I will catch (it).'

Na-ga   jus-(i)jeo. (나가 줏 (이) 저)
1SG-NOM   gather-SE
'I will gather (them).'

Na-ga   gwe-u-jeo. (나가 궤우저)
1SG-NOM   boil-CAUS-SE
'I will boil (it).'

Where *-jeo* is attached to a bare stem, as in the preceding examples, the subject must be the speaker. There is no such restriction when the verb is inflected.[3]

I-geo   mag jal menggeul-a-jy-eos-jeo. (이거 막 잘 멩글아졋저)
this-thing really well make-LV-become-PFV-SE
'Wow, this is well made!'

Neu nang jal   singg-eoms-jeo. (느 낭 잘 싱겂저)
2SG tree   well plant-CONT-SE
'You are planting trees well.'

---

3. J.-h. Kim (2014b, 121) reports a further use of *-jeo* as a sentence-internal connective.

*Geu mos-e   mul-i   **eol-jeo**   **nog-jeo**   haw-neu-n-di...*
that pond-in water-NOM frozen-CON melt-CON do-INDC-NPST-SE
(그 못에 물이 얼저 녹저 ᄒ는디 ...)
'The water in the pond freezes and melts, back and forth.'

*Gaui mal   **deud-jeo mal-jeo**   haw-l-geos-do   eus-da.*
3SG speech hear-SE   do.not-CON do-FUT-thing-even not.be-SE
(가의 말 듣저 말저 ᄒ 것도 웃다)
'There is nothing to take seriously in what s/he says.'

Na jeongji-e gob-ams-jeo. (나 정지에 곱았저)
1SG kitchen-LOC hide-CONT-SE
'I am hiding in the kitchen.'

Haleubang mom gawm-as-jeo. (하르방 몸 굼앗저)
grandfather body wash-PFV-SE
'Grandfather took a bath.'

A curious feature of *-jeo* in patterns with a first-person subject is that the presence of epenthetic *-i* after continuative *-eoms* or perfective *-eos* creates a future interpretation. Examples of this can be seen in the following set of sentences.

No epenthetic vowel (present-time interpretation):

Na nang-gaji bongg-ams-jeo. (나 낭가지 봉값저)
1SG tree-branch gather-CONT-SE
'I am gathering sticks.'

Uli mawncheo joban meog-eoms-jeo. (우리 몬처 조반 먹없저)
1PL first breakfast eat-CONT-SE
'We are eating breakfast first (without you).'

Na mawnyeo gingi meog-eos-jeo. (나 몬여 깅이 먹엇저)
1SG first crab eat-PFV-SE
'I ate the crabs first.'

Epenthetic vowel (future-time interpretation):

Na mawnyeo joban meog-eos-ijeo. (나 몬여 조반 먹엇이저)
1SG first breakfast eat-PFV-SE
'I will have eaten breakfast first.'

Uli mawncheo gingi meog-eoms-ijeo. (우리 몬처 깅이 먹없이저)
1PL first crab eat-CONT-SE
'We will be eating the crabs first (without you).'

Na-ga gangsengi chawj-ams-ijeo. (나가 강셍이 촞았이저)
1SG-NOM puppy search-CONT-SE
'I will be searching for the puppy (without you).'

-(eu)ju ((으)주)

ALLOMORPHY:

- *-(i)ju* after a stem that ends in *s*, *j*, or *ch*
- *-(u)ju* after a stem that ends in a labial consonant
- *-ju* after a stem that ends in a vowel or *l*

STEM TYPE: Type 1 (bare, or ending in *-eos* or *-eoms*).
USAGE: Has a variety of semantic effects, as discussed below.
When used with a bare stem and a first-person subject, *-ju* indicates an intention or strong assertion.

Na-ga   meog-(eu)ju.   *Na-ga   ig-(eu)ju.* (나가 익(으)주)
1SG-NOM eat-SE   1SG-NOM read-SE
(나가 먹(으)주)⁴   'I will read (it).'
'I will eat (it).'

Na-ga   gawl-(eu)ju.   *Na-ga   gawd-ju.* (나가 굳주)
1SG-NOM tell-SE   1SG-NOM tell-SE
(나가 굴(으)주)   'I will talk.'
'I will talk.

Na-ga   dawd-ju. (나가 돋주)   *Na-ga   chawj-(i)ju.* (나가 촞(이)주)
1SG-NOM run-SE   1SG-NOM find-SE
'I will run.'   'I will find (it).'

Na-ga   sim-(u)ju. (나가 심(우)주)
1SG-NOM hold-SE
'I will catch (it).'

With a third-person subject and a bare stem, *-ju* expresses the speaker's judgment or assumption.

Geu-dui-n   mag neolleu-ju. (그뒨 막 널르주)
that-place-TOP very spacious-SE
'That place is very spacious.'

---

4. Some speakers report that the epenthentic vowel sounds less than fully natural
    with this verb.

Mansu mal   jal   gawd-ju. (만수 말 잘 걷주)
Mansu speech well speak-SE
'Mansu talks well.'

Mina-ga   gob-ju. (미나가 곱주)
Mina-NOM pretty-SE
'Mina (is the one who) is pretty.'

I-dui-ga   Mansu-ne bas-i-ju. (이듸가 만수네 밧이주)
this-place-NOM Mansu-PL field-be-SE
'This is (is the location of) Mansu's family field.'

Uli seong   ije   jiseul   jus-eoms-ju. (우리 성 이제 지슬 줏없주)
1PL older.sibling now potato gather-CONT-SE
'My older sibling is gathering potatoes now (quite or very
   certainly).'

Geu bibali-ga mul   jil-eos-ju. (그 비바리가 물 질엇주)
that girl-NOM water draw-PFV-SE
'The girl has drawn the water (quite or very certainly).'

Uli asi   badang-deole dawl-eulgeo-ju.
1PL younger.sibling sea-DIR   run-FUT-SE
(우리 아시 바당더레 돌을거주)
'My younger sibling is going to the sea (quite or very
   certainly).'

-ju can also be used to express regret or give advice.

Neu-ga   buleumssi haw-ju. (느가 부름씨 ᄒ주)
2SG-NOM errand   do-SE
'You should have done the errand.'/'You (not others) should
   do the errand.'

Neu-ga   sim-ju. (느가 심주)
2SG-NOM catch-SE
'You (not others) should have caught it.'/'You'd better catch (it).'

Neu-ga   chawj-(i)ju. (느가 촞(이)주)

2SG-NOM search-SE

'You (not others) should have searched.'/'You'd better search.'

Sawgnki   neu-ga   sichi-ju-ge. (슝키 느가 시치주게)

vegetable 2SG-NOM wash-SE-EMPH

'You should have washed the vegetables.'/'You should wash the vegetables.'

Geul   ig-(eu)ju-ge. (글 익(으)주게)

letter read-SE-EMPH

'(You) should have studied.'/'(You) should study.'

Finally, *-(eu)ju* can be used to express a proposal.

Mulkkuleog sim-ju. (물꾸럭 심주)

octopus   catch-SE

'Let's catch the octopus.'

Jiseul   jus-ju. (지슬 줏주)

potato gather-SE

'Let's gather the potatoes.'

A striking feature of this use is that it is compatible with the continuative and perfective suffixes, yielding the interpretations illustrated below.

Uli-man sawdab haw-yeos-(i)ju. (우리만 ᄉ답ᄒ엿(이)주)

1PL-only laundry do-PFV-SE

'Let's get the laundry done.'/'We'd better get the laundry done.'

Ga-ms-(i)ju. (갌(이)주)

go-CONT-SE

'Let's get going first.'/'We'd better (start) going.'

-euma (으마)

ALLOMORPHY:

- *-ima* after a stem ending in *s, j,* or *ch* (for some speakers)
- *-uma* after a stem ending in a labial consonant (for some speakers)
- *-ma* after a stem that ends in a vowel or *l*

STEM TYPE: Type 1 (bare, or ending in *-eos* or *-eoms*).
USAGE: Expresses the speaker's intention (or willingness) to do something in the future. It requires a first-person subject, and cannot be used when speaking to an elder.

> *Na-ga   geyeog   ka-s-ima.* (나가 게역 캇이마)
> 1SG-NOM roasted.barley.flour mix-PFV-SE
> 'I will have first mixed roasted barley flour (with water).'

> *Na-ga   bulu   tawd-ams-ima.* (나가 부루 톤앖이마)
> 1SG-NOM lettuce pick-CONT-SE
> 'I will be picking lettuce (first).'

> *Na-ga   banong chawj-ima.* (나가 바농 춫이마)
> 1SG-NOM needle find-SE
> 'I will find the needle.'

> *Na-ga   kong gwe-u-ma.* (나가 콩 궤우마)
> 1SG-NOM bean boil-CAUS-SE
> 'I will boil the beans.'

-eume (으메)[5]

ALLOMORPHY:

- *-ime* after a stem ending in *s, j,* or *ch*
- *-ume* after a stem that ends in a labial consonant
- *-me* after a stem ending in a vowel or *l*

STEM TYPE: Type 1 (bare, or ending in *-eos* or *-eoms*).
USAGE: Evidential marker; used for statements based on current

---

5. It has been suggested that this sentence ender originated from the nominalizing suffix *-eum* and the postposition *-e*; see chapter 6, section 2.1, as well as J.-h. Kang (1987, 525) and N.-S. Sung (1982, 5).

or past personal experience or judgment, but with less conviction than is associated with *-na* or *-da*.

When used with a bare stem, *-eume* implies that the statement represents the speaker's assumption or a guess that has not yet been confirmed by others.

> *Dawg-gwegi   menal meog-eume*. (독궤기 메날 먹으메)
>
> chicken-meat daily   eat-SE
>
> '(S/he) eats chicken every day.' / '(S/he) will probably eat chicken every day.'

> *Menal gaekkaws-deole dawl-eume*. (메날 개껏더레 돌으메)
>
> daily   seashore-DIR   run-SE
>
> '(S/he) goes to the seashore daily.' / '(S/he) will probably go to the seashore daily.'

> *Geu gudeul mag daws-ime*. (그 구들 막 돗이메)
>
> that room   very warm-SE
>
> 'That room is (usually) very warm.'

> *Halmang-i   sawdab bawlleu-me*. (할망이 ᄉ답 볼르메)
>
> grandmother-NOM laundry step.on-SE
>
> 'Grandmother steps on the laundry (to press it flat).' / 'Grandmother will probably step on the laundry.'

> *Uli asi   kong jal sawlm-ume*. (우리 아시 콩 잘 숢우메)
>
> 1PL younger.sibling bean well boil-SE
>
> 'My younger sibling boils beans well.' / 'My younger sibling will probably boil beans well.'

> *Gaui ga-bul-me*. (가의 가불메)
>
> 3SG   go-COMPL-SE
>
> 'S/he goes away.' / 'S/he may go away.' (Y.-J. Jung 1983, 319)

Use of *-eume* with an inflected verb often makes the sentence less assertive and frequently expresses conjecture on the part of the speaker, based on his or her personal knowledge of the situation.

> *Gaekkaws-deole dawl-as-ime*. (개껏더레 돌앗이메)
>
> seashore-DIR   run-PFV-SE
>
> 'S/he may have run to the seashore.'

*Mikkang   jus-eoms-**ime**.* (미깡 줏없이메)

tangerine gather-CONT-SE

'S/he may be gathering tangerines.'

*Nuil   Mansu gwendang chib-ui   ga-lgeo-**me**.*

tomorrow Mansu relative   house-DIR go-FUT-SE

(닐 만수 궨당칩의 갈거메)

'Mansu may be going to his relative's house tomorrow.'

*Ije   Mansu gwendang chib-ui   ga-s-ilgeo-**me**.*

now Mansu relative   house-DIR go-PFV-FUT-SE

(이제 만수 궨당칩의 갓일거메)

'Mansu may have left for his relative's house by now.'

*Ije   Mansu buleumssi he-ms-ilgeo-**me**.* (이제 만수 부름씨 헴일거메)

now Mansu errand   do-CONT-FUT-SE

'Mansu may be doing an errand now.'

-(eu)ne ((으)네) (S.-T. Kim 1972, 70; S.-N. Lee 1957, 183;
S.-J. Song 2007, 100)

ALLOMORPHY:

- *-(i)ne* after a stem ending in *s, j,* or *ch*
- *-(u)ne* after a stem that ends in a labial consonant
- *-ne* after a stem ending in a vowel or *l* (which is then deleted),
  as well as after the continuative marker *-eoms* and the perfective
  marker *-eos*

STEM TYPE: Type 1 (bare, or ending in *-eos* or *-eoms*).

USAGE: Permits various interpretations, including emphasis, surprise, and the implication that the addressee either already knows
or should know something; can be used to scold a listener for not
remembering something, and is therefore not appropriate when
speaking to an elder or a stranger.

*Mansu jal   meog-(**eu**)ne!* (만수 잘 먹(으)네!)

Mansu well eat-SE

'(I see that) Mansu eats well!'/'(Don't you know that) Mansu
   eats well?'/'Mansu eats well (so give him more)!'

Mansu menal   eomeong chawj-(i)ne! (만수 메날 어멍 츷(이)네!)

Mansu everyday mother look.for-SE

'(Don't you know that) Mansu always looks for mother?' /
  'Mansu always looks for mother (so don't go away too long)!'

Mansu gwegi nakk-eune! (만수 궤기 낚으네!)

Mansu fish   fish-SE

'(I see that) Mansu catches fish.' / '(Don't you know that) Mansu
  catches fish?' / 'Mansu catches fish (so take him with you)!'

Eomeong-i   kong gaw-ne! (어멍이 콩 ㄱ네!) [root = *gawl-*]

mother-NOM bean grind-SE

'(I see that) mother grinds beans.' / '(Don't you know that)
  mother grinds beans!' / 'Mother is grinding beans (so
  help her).'

Na badang-deule dawl-ams-ne! (나 바당드레 돌앖네!)

1SG sea-DIR   run-CONT-SE

'(Don't you know that) I'm going to the sea?' / 'I am going to
  the sea!'

Haleubang nuilmoli   gawchi ta-lgeo-ne!

grandfather day.after.tomorrow chili   pick-FUT-SE

(하르방 늴모리 ㄱ치 탈거네!)

'(I notice that) grandfather is going to pick chilis the day after
  tomorrow.' / 'Grandfather is going to pick chilis the day after
  tomorrow, don't you know that?' / 'Grandfather is going to
  pick chilis the day after tomorrow!'

Eonchinag eomeong-i   chawlle   menggeul-as-ne!

last.night mother-NOM side.dish make-PFV-SE

(언치낙 어멍이 출레 멩글앗네!)

'(I notice that) mother made side dishes last night.' / '(Don't
  you know that) mother made side dishes last night?' /
  'Mother made side dishes last night (so you should cook this
  morning).'

Geu-geo   Yeongsu-ga   bongg-as-ne! (그거 영수가 봉갓네!)

that-thing Yeongsu-NOM find-PFV-SE

'(I notice that) Yeongsu came upon the thing'/'As you should know, Yeongsu came upon the thing.'/'Yeongsu came upon the thing (so let him have it).'

-ge (게)

ALLOMORPHY: None.

STEM TYPE: Type 2 (ending in *-eun* or *-eon*).

USAGE: Evidential marker for statements in which the speaker reports an event of which s/he has knowledge, either through observation or inference.

As noted in chapter 6, section 3, a distinctive feature of *-ge* is its interaction with the tense markers *-eon* and *-eun*, which indicate the time of the speaker's observation or inference. In the examples that follow, use of *-eun-ge* or *-neu-n-ge* signals direct observation of a current habitual act, a state, or an ongoing event.

Habitual act:

Geu chogi   saleum-deol ta-neu-n-ge. (그 초기 사름덜 타는게)

that mushroom person-PL   pick-INDC-NPST-SE

'(I know from experience that) people pick that mushroom.' (based on J.-h. Kim 2014b:194)

State:

I   mulwe-deol-eun   mag guj-in-ge. (이 물웨덜은 막 궂인게)

this cucumber-PL-TOP very bad-NPST-SE

'(I see that) these cucumbers are very bad (in quality).'

Ongoing event (*-eoms* required):

Abang mikkang-nang singg-eoms-in-ge. (아방 미깡낭 싱겂인게)

father tangerine-tree plant-CONT-NPST-SE

'(I see) father planting tangerine trees.'

Halmang-i   haleubang-sindi bue-nae-ms-in-ge.

grandmother-NOM grandfather-DAT anger-show-CONT-NPST-SE

(할망이 하르방신디 부에냈인게)

'(I see) grandmother getting angry at grandfather.'

*Jaui Yeongsu eomeong sungteol-**eoms-in-ge**.* (자의 영수어멍 숭털없인게)

3SG Yeongsu mother imitate-CONT-NPST-SE

'(I see) him/her imitating Yeongsu's mother.'

*Haleubang hwagwag chawj-**ams-in-ge**.* (하르방 화곽 춪앖인게)

grandfather match   look.for-CONT-NPST-SE

'(I see) grandfather looking for the matches.'

*Eomeong sawngki   tawd-**ams-in-ge**.* (어멍 숭키 톤앖인게)

mother   vegetable pluck-CONT-NPST-SE

'(I see) mother picking vegetables.'

When *-eun-ge* is used in conjunction with the prospective marker *-euk*, the result is a conjecture that is based on a current observation.

*Dos-gwegi galleu-dang bo-nan na jeogsi-n jog-**euk-eun-ge**.*

pig-meat split-CON   see-CON 1SG share-TOP small-PROSP-NPST-SE

(돗궤기 갈르당 보난 나 적신 족으큰게)

'Upon dividing the pork, (I can see that) my share will be
    small.'

*Ttawl-i   chawj-**ik-eun-ge**.* (똘이 춪이큰게)

daughter-NOM search-PROSP-NPST-SE

'(I can see that) your daughter may/will look for you.'

In contrast, the form *-eon-ge* is used to indicate a previous observation.

*Neu-ne sawnji   pachi   jal jus-**eon-ge**.*

2-PL   grandchild fallen.tangerines well pick-PST-SE

(느네 손지 파치 잘 줏언게)

'(I saw) your grandchild pick fallen tangerines well.'

*Neu-ne dosegi hwaleuleug-haw-ge jal-do   jal dawl-a-na-**n-ge**.*

2-PL   pig   quick-do-ADV   well-even well run.away-LV-out-PST-SE

(느네 도세기 화르륵ᄒ게 잘도 잘 돌아난게)

'(I saw) your pig run away really quickly.'

*Halmang-i   haleubang-sindi   bue-nae-ms-**eon-ge**.*
grandmother-NOM grandfather-DAT anger-show-CONT-PST-SE
(할망이 하르방신디 부에냈언게)
'(I saw) grandmother getting angry at grandfather.'

*Haleubang   gawse   gob-jy-eoms-**eon-ge**.* (하르방 ᄀ세 곱졌언게)
grandfather scissors hide-CAUS-CONT-PST-SE
'(I saw) grandfather hiding the scissors.'

A different set of effects arise when the verb carries the perfective marker *-eos*. In this case, use of the nonpast *-eun* implies a current inference about a previous event that the speaker did not actually witness but nonetheless believes to have occurred based on evidence of some sort.

*Eomeong-i   so-nang   geuchy-a-bul-**eos-in-ge**.* (어멍이 소낭 그챠불엇인게)
mother-NOM pine-tree cut-LV-COMPL-PFV-NPST-SE
'(I see that) mother cut the pine tree completely down.'

*Abang gawse   chawj-**as-in-ge**.* (아방 ᄀ세 촞앗인게)
father scissors search-PFV-NPST-SE
'(I see that) father found the scissors.'

*Banong-keul   pan-na-bul-**eos-in-ge**.* (바눙클 판나불엇인게)
needle-machine breakdown-come.out-COMPL-PFV-NPST-SE
'(I see that) the sewing machine is completely broken.'

In contrast, use of the past-tense suffix *-eon* indicates a past inference (rather than a direct observation) about a previously occurring event.

*Eomeong-i so-nang   geuchy-a-bul-**eos-eon-ge**.* (어멍이 소낭 그챠불엇언게)
mother   pine-tree cut-LV-COMPL-PFV-PST-SE
'(I figured) that mother had cut the pine tree completely
    down.'

*Abang hwagwag chawj-**as-eon-ge**.* (아방 화꽉 촞앗언게)
father match   find-PFV-PST-SE
'(I figured) that father had found the matches.'

Table 7.2 summarizes the various evidential interpretations associated with the use of *-ge*.

Table 7.2   Summary of interpretations associated with *-ge*

-eon-ge	*-eun-ge*
V-*eon-ge*=I saw *x* V(-ing)	V-*neu-n-ge*=I know that *x* Vs
V-*eoms-eon-ge*=I saw *x* V-ing	V-*eoms-in-ge*=I see *x* V-ing
V-*eos-eon-ge*=I noticed that *x* V'ed	V-*eos-in-ge*=I see that *x* V'ed
	V-*euk-eun-ge*=I see that *x* will V

-guna (구나)

ALLOMORPHY: *-loguna* after the copula verb *i-da*.

STEM TYPE: Type 1 (ending in *-eos* or *-eoms*; a bare stem is possible for descriptive and copula verbs).

USAGE: To express surprise or excitement.

*I-dui   mag neolleu-**guna**!* (이듸 막 널르구나!)
this-place very wide-SE
'What a spacious place!'

*Jawg-haw-n   geo   mawn sod-a-bul-eos-**guna**-ge!*
precious-do-NPST.CON thing all   spill-LV-COMPL-PFV-SE-EMPH
(죽흔 거 믄 솓아불엇구나게!)
'Oh, you've spilled the precious thing completely!'

*Mikkang jus-eoms-**guna**!* (미깡 줏없구나!)
tangerine gather-CONT-SE
'(I see) you're gathering tangerines!'

*Jjokkeulag-haw-n   mawl-i-(**lo**)**guna**!* (쪼끌락흔 몰이(로)구나!)
small-do-NPST.CON horse-be-SE
'What a small horse it is!'

-ye (예)[6]

ALLOMORPHY: None.

STEM TYPE: Mixed (ending in *-eos, -eoms, -eun,* or *-eon*).

---

6. J.-h. Kim (2014b, 212) suggests that *-ye* may have originated as a combination of the copula root *i-* and the suffix *-e*.

USAGE: Use of -*ye* implies that the speaker is aware of a fact or situation, through observation or inference, and is either calling the addressee's attention to it or seeking agreement on it.

With -*eos* and -*eoms*:

*Na   naws sichy-**eos**-ye.* (나 놋 시쳣예)
1SG face   wash-PFV-SE
'(You know that) I washed my face (right?).'

*Na chawlle   menggeul-**ams**-ye.* (나 출레 멩글았예)
1SG side.dish make-CONT-SE
'(You know that) I'm making the side dish (right?).'

With *neu-n* (knowledge of a recurring event):

*Bojegi   badang-deole dawl-**euneu-n**-ye.* (보제기 바당더레 돌으는예)
fisherman sea-DIR   run-INDC-NPST-SE
'(We know that) the fisherman goes to the sea (right)?'

With -*eon* (direct observation of a previous event):

*Cheolsu gingi dekky-**eon**-ye.* (철수 깅이 데껸예)
Cheolsu crab   throw-PST-SE
'(We saw) Cheolsu throw away the crab, right?'

*Na joban   meog-**eon**-ye.* (나 조반 먹언예)
1SG breakfast eat-PST-SE
'(You saw) me eat breakfast, right?'

With -*eoms-in* (direct observation of a current event):

*Sunja sawdab haw-**yeoms-in**-ye.* (순자 스답ㅎ엾인예)
Sunja laundry do-CONT-NPST-SE
'(Look, you can see that) Sunja is doing the laundry (right).'

*Jaui-ga   neu-ne seong   michy-eo-ga-bul-**eoms-in**-ye.*
3SG-NOM 2-PL   older.sibling catch.up-LV-go-COMPL-CONT-NPST-SE
(자의가 느네 성 미쳐가불엾인예)
'(Look, you can see that) s/he is catching up with your older
    sibling (right).'

*Neu-ne asi   mag jegi dawl-**ams-in-ye**.*

2-PL   younger.sibling very fast run-CONT-NPST-SE

(느네 아시 막 제기 돌았인예)

'(Look, you see that) your younger sibling is running really fast
  (right).'

With *-eoms-eon* (direct observation of a past event):

*Sunja sawdab haw-**yeoms-eon-ye**.* (순자 ᄉ답ᄒ였언예)

Sunja laundry do-CONT-PST-SE

'(We saw) Sunja was doing the laundry (right).'

With *-eos-in* (inference about a past event from currently available evidence):

*Sunja joban   meog-**eos-in-ye**.* (순자 조반 먹엇인예)

Sunja breakfast eat-PFV-NPST-SE

'(Look, you can see) Sunja has finished eating breakfast
  (right).'

*Eomeong eonchinag gawse   chawj-**as-in-ye**.* (어멍 언치낙 ᄀ세 ᄎ앗인예)

mother   last.night scissors find-PFV-NPST-SE

'(Look, you can see that) mother found the scissors last night
  (right).'

*Neu ap-**as-in-ye**.* (느 아팟인예)

2SG sick-PFV-NPST-SE

'(We know) you are sick (so don't work).'

With *-eos-eon* (past inference about a previous event):

*Mansu sawngki sichy-**eos-eon-ye**.* (만수 숭키 시쳣언예)

Mansu vegetable wash-PFV-PST-SE

'(You noticed that) Mansu washed the vegetables (right).'

3.3 Informal Sentence Enders for Questions

Yet another set of sentence enders appear only on questions. An
important issue in the study of these items has to do with whether
they systematically distinguish between *yes–no* questions and *wh*

questions—a feature of Middle Korean that has also been reported in one form or another for Jejueo by some scholars (e.g., Y.-G. Han 1984, 235; S.-J. Song 2007; H.-K. Choi 1989; J.-h. Kim 2014b; S.-Y. Chung 2017). One view is that *-dia*, *-ga* and *-(n)ya* are used only for *yes-no* questions, while *-di*, *-go* and *-(n)i* indicate *wh* questions. As we will see next, however, this view appears to be inaccurate: although certain sentence enders can occur only with *wh* questions, none can occur only with *yes–no* questions.

3.3.1 Sentence Enders for Both *Wh* Questions and *Yes–No* Questions

A number of sentence enders can be used to indicate interrogative sentences, regardless of whether they are *wh* questions or *yes–no* questions.

***-dia* (디아)**

ALLOMORPHY:

• *-tia* or *-ttia* is possible after the suffix *-eul*

STEM TYPE: Type 2 (ending in *-eun*, *-eon*, *-eul*, or *-eom*).
USAGE: *Yes–no* and *wh* questions directed toward a person with relevant personal experience (J.-h. Kim 2014b, 303).

*Neu sawngki sichy-eon-**dia**?* (느 승키 시쪈디아?)
2SG vegetable wash-PST-SE
'Have you washed the vegetables?'

*Nuil   halmang   chib-ui   ga-l-**tia**?* (늴 할망칩의 갈티아?)
tomorrow grandmother house-DIR go-FUT-SE
'Do (you) want to go to grandmother's house tomorrow?'

*Neu abang chawj-am-**dia**?* (느 아방 춫암디아?)
2SG father look.for-CONT-SE
'Are you looking for (your) father?'

*Neu-n   eodui gob-am-**dia**?* (는 어듸 곱암디아?)
2SG-TOP where hide-CONT-SE
'Where are you hiding?'

*Neu ajeog-do geu-dui   sal-am-**dia**?* (느 아적도 그듸 살암디아?)

2SG still-too that-place live-CONT-SE

'Are you still living in that place?'

*Neu musigeo jus-eom-**dia**?* (느 무시거 줏엄디아?)

2SG what   gather-CONT-SE

'What are you gathering?'

*Neu jaeyeol sim-eom-**dia**?* (느 재열 심엄디아?)

2SG cicada catch-CONT-SE

'Are you catching cicadas?'

*Neu-n   musa eol-eon-**dia**?* (는 무사 얼언디아?)

2SG-TOP why   cold-PST-SE

'Why are you cold?'

*Neu-n   eol-eon-**dia**?* (는 얼언디아?)

2SG-TOP cold-PST-SE

'Are you cold?'

*Neu-n   eoneuje-butteo seonsuing-i-la-n-**dia**?*

2SG-TOP when-from   teacher-be-HAB-PST-SE

(는 어느제부떠 선싱이란디아?)

'Since when have you been a teacher?'

*Neu-n   yeosnal-e   seonsuing-i-la-n-**dia**?* (는 엿날에 선싱이란디아?)

2SG-TOP old.days-in teacher-be-HAB-PST-SE

'Were you a teacher in the past?'

*Nuge-ga   seonsuing-i-yeon-**dia**?* (누게가 선싱이연디아?)

who-NOM teacher-be-PST-SE

'Who was a teacher?'

-ga (가)

ALLOMORPHY: None.

STEM TYPE: Type 2 (ending in *-eun*, *-eon*, or *-eom*); may appear with a bare copula.

USAGE: *Yes–no* questions and *wh* questions, regardless of verb type; can also be attached to a nominal in verbless sentences.

*I-geo   musigeos-**ga**?*
this-thing what-SE
(이거 무시것가?)
'What is this?'

*I-geo   neu-ne mawl(-i)-**ga**?*
this-thing 2-PL   horse (-be)-SE
(이거 느네 물(이)가?)
'Is this your horse?'

*Neu musigeo gob-ji-lgeo-**ga**?*
2SG what   hide-CAUS-FUT-SE
(느 무시거 곱질거가?)
'What will you hide?'

*Neu don   gob-ji-lgeo-**ga**?*
2SG money hide-CAUS-FUT-SE
(느 돈 곱질거가?)
'Will you hide (your) money?'

*Abang musigeo jus-eon-**ga**?*
father what   gather-PST-SE
(아방 무시거 줏언가?)
'What did father gather?'

*Abang jo-kogoli   jus-eon-**ga**?*
father millet-ear gather-PST-SE
(아방 조코고리 줏언가?)
'Did father gather ears of millet?'

*Geu-dui   daws-as-in-**ga**?*
that-place warm-PFV-NPST-SE
(그듸 둣안인가?)
'Is that place warm?'

*Geu-dui   musa daws-as-in-**ga**?*
that-place why   warm-PFV-NPST-SE
(그듸 무사 둣안인가?)
'Why is that place warm?'

Questions that are marked by *-ga* are often used to express curiosity or musing.

*Halmang-eun   chawlle-do   jal   menggeu-neu-n-**ga**?*
grandmother-TOP side.dishes-even well make-INDC-NPST-SE
(할망은 출레도 잘 멩그는가?)
'Does grandmother make even side dishes well, I wonder?'

*Abang-eun jawnyag mawn meog-eon-**ga**?* (아방은 ᄌ냑 몬 먹언가?)
father-TOP dinner   all   eat-PST-SE
'Has father eaten all his dinner, I wonder?'

*Geu saleum-eun ajeog-do geu-dui   sal-ams-in-**ga**?*
that person-TOP still-too that-place live-CONT-NPST-SE
(그 사름은 아젹도 그듸 살암신가?)
'Is the person still living there, I wonder?'

As previously noted (chapter 6, section 2.1), the continuative marker does not bring about tensing of the initial consonant of *-go* and is therefore represented as *-eom* rather than *-eoms*.

*Neu musigeo jus-eom-**ga**?*	*Neu jo-kogoli jus-eom-**ga**?*
2SG what gather-CONT-SE	2SG millet-ear gather-CONT-SE
(느 무시거 줏엄가?)	(느 조코고리 줏엄가?)
'What are you gathering?'	'Are you gathering ears of millet?'

-go (고)

ALLOMORPHY: None.
STEM TYPE: Mixed (bare, or ending in *-eos*, *-eoms*, or *-eun*).
USAGE: *Wh* questions and *yes–no* questions.

*Jai-n   musigeo sichi-m(-i)-**go**?* (자인 무시거 시침(이)고?)[7]
3SG-TOP what   wash-NMLZ(-be)-SE
'What is s/he washing?'

*I-geo   nuge mawl(-i)-**go**?* (이거 누게 몰(이)고?)
this-thing who   horse(-be)-SE
'Whose horse is this?'

*Nuge-**go**?* (누게고?)
who-SE
'Who is this?'

*Yai-n   neu-ne sawnji-**go**?* (야인 느네 손지고?)
3SG-TOP 2-PL   grandchild-SE
'Is s/he your grandchild?'

*Geu dui   daws-as-**go**?* (그듸 돗앗고?)
that place warm-PFV-SE
'Is that place warm?'

When used with the nonpast suffix *-eun*, *-go* helps create a conjectural 'I wonder...' interpretation.

---

7. According to S.-Y. Chung (2017, slides 20 and 28), use of the copula is common among younger speakers; however, elder speakers tend to drop it.

*Geu nongbani-n menal   musigeo meog-neu-**n-go**?*
that farmer-TOP every.day what   eat-INDC-NPST-SE
(그 농바닌 메날 무시거 먹는고?)
'I wonder what that farmer eats every day.'

*I-dui-n   musa yeong   daws-**in-go**?* (이딘 무사 영 돗인고?)
this-place-TOP why   like.this warm-NPST-SE
'I wonder why this place is warm like this.'

*Seonsuing musigeo tew-as-**in-go**?* (선싱 무시거 테왓인고?)
teacher   what   distribute-PFV-NPST-SE
'I wonder what the teacher distributed.'

*Mansu adeule dawl-ams-**in-go**?* (만수 어드레 돌았인고?)
Mansu where run-CONT-NPST-SE
'I wonder where Mansu is going.'

When used between friends and people who know each other well,
yes–no questions ending in *-go* can imply shared disbelief or surprise.

*Jai-n   musigeo   sichi-m(-**i**)-**go**?* (자인 무시거 시침(이)고?)
3SG-TOP something wash-NMLZ(-be)-SE
'Is she washing something? (I don't think so.)'

*Uli sawchun eodeule   dawl-ams-**go**?* (우리 ᄉ춘 어드레 돌았고?)
1PL cousin   somewhere run-CONT-SE
'(Do you think) our cousin is going somewhere? (I don't
  think so.)'

*Jigeum bekk-i-s-dui   bi   w-ams-**go**?* (지금 벡잇듸 비 왒고?)
now   outside-LOC-PGEN-place rain come-CONT-SE
'Is it raining outside? (I don't think so.)'

*Gasi-eomeong joban   meog-eos-**go**?* (가시어멍 조반 먹엇고?)
wife-mother   breakfast eat-PFV-SE
'(Do you think) mother-in-law ate breakfast? (I don't think so.)'

*Geo mawl-i-**go**?* (거 몰이고?)
that horse-be-SE
'Is that a horse? (I don't think so.)'

-ya (야)[8]

ALLOMORPHY: None.

STEM TYPE: Mixed (ending in *-eos, -eoms, -eun, -eon,* or *-eul*).

USAGE: *Wh* questions and *yes–no* questions; employed mostly by elderly speakers in informal contexts involving friends and people who know each other well.

Neu babjuli   sim-eos-ya? (느 밥주리 심엇야?)

2SG dragonfly catch-PFV-SE

'Did you catch a dragonfly?'

Yeongsu mom gawm-ams-ya? (영수 몸 곰았야?)

Yeongsu body wash-CONT-SE

'Is Yeongsu taking a bath?'

Gudeul daws-in-ya? (구들 돗인야?)

room   warm-NPST-SE

'Is the room warm?'

Eoneu gudeul-i   daws-in-ya? (어느 구들이 돗인야?)

which room-NOM warm-NPST-SE

'Which room is warm?'

Ga-ne abang-i-n-ya? (가네 아방인야?)

3-PL   father-be-NPST-SE

'Are you their father?'

Nuge-ne abang-i-n-ya? (누게네 아방인야?)

who-PL father-be-NPST-SE

'Whose father are you?'

With a third-person subject, *-ya* has an evidential function, implying that the addressee can answer the question on the basis of experience or inference.[9] As the next examples show, the effect of evidentiality is sensitive to the verb's aspect, modality, and tense.

8. J.-h. Kim (2014b, 213) suggests that *-ya* may originate as a combination of the copula root *i-* and the suffix *-a*.

9. C.-H. Woo (1995) reports the use of *-ya* with the evidential suffix *-deo*, which is normally associated with Korean; see the example that follows.

With *-neu-n* (direct observation of particular tendency):

*Mansu gawlgaebi sim-(u)neu-n-**ya**?* (만수 굴개비 심 (우) 는야?)
Mansu frog   catch-INDC-NPST-SE
'(In your experience,) does Mansu catch frogs?'

With *-eon* (direct observation of a previous event):

*Cheolsu badang-iseo   nol-an-**ya**?* (철수 바당이서 놀안야?)
Cheolsu seashore-LOC play-PST-SE
'(Did you see) Cheolsu hanging out at the sea?'

With *-eoms-in* (direct knowledge of a current event or tendency):

*Haleubang musigeo   sichy-eoms-in-**ya**?*
grandfather what/something wash-CONT-NPST-SE
(하르방 무시거 시쳤인야?)
'(Do you know whether) grandfather is washing
    something?'/'(Do you see) what grandfather is washing?'

*Nongbani jiseul   meog-eoms-in-**ya**?* (농바니 지슬 먹없인야?)
farmer   potato eat-CONT-NPST-SE
'(Do you see/know) a farmer is eating potatoes?'

With *-eul* or *-eulgeo* (conjecture, based on experience):

*Eotteong geu il-eul   haw-l-**ya**?* (어떵 그 일을 홀야?)
how   that work-ACC do-FUT-SE
'(Based on your experience with him/her,) how can s/he do
    that work?' (based on J.-h. Kim 2014b, 343)

*Cheolsu don   gob-ji-lgeo-n-**ya**?* (철수 돈 곱질건야?)
Cheolsu money hide-CAUS-FUT-NPST-SE
'(Do you know whether) Cheolsu will hide the money?'

---

*Mansu mul jil-**deo**-n-ya?* (만수 물 질던야?)
Mansu water draw-EVI-PST-SE
'Did (you see) Mansu drawing water?'

With *-eos-in* (current inference or observation about a previous event):

*Mansu mikkang   tew-**as-in**-ya?* (만수 미깡 테왓인야?)

Mansu tangerine distribute-PFV-NPST-SE

'(Based on your observation or inference), did Mansu distribute the tangerines?'

With *-eos-eon* (past inference related to a previous event):

*Olabang   manong me-**yeos-eon**-ya?* (오라방 마농 메엿언야?)

older.brother garlic   pull-PFV-PST-SE

'Did (you notice whether your) older brother had picked garlic?'

A Segmentation Controversy (*-ya* or *-nya*)

A different analysis of the patterns we have been considering holds that the sentence ender is *-nya* rather than *-ya*. This in turn forces reanalysis of the other suffixes, giving the result illustrated below (see, e.g., S.-Y. Chung 2017; P.-h. Hyun 1976, 124; S.-N. Lee 1957, 184).

*Neu gingi sim-eo-m-si-**nya**?* (느 깅이 심엄시냐?)

2SG crab catch-LV-NMLZ-be-SE

'Are you catching crabs?'

In contrast, we believe that the verbal complex contains the continuative marker *-eoms* followed by the nonpast marker *-in*, the expected allomorph of *-eun* in this context.

*Neu gingi sim-**eoms-in**-ya?* (느 깅이 심없인야?)

2SG crab catch-CONT-NPST-SE

'Are you catching crabs?'

As noted in O'Grady et al. (2018), two considerations support this conclusion. First, as we would predict, the basic form of the nonpast marker (*-eun*) shows up in patterns such as the following, where the preceding suffix ends in *k* rather than *s*.

*Gai gingi sim-**uk-eun-ya**?* (가이 깅이 심우큰야?)[10]

3SG crab catch-PROSP-NPST-SE?

'(Do you think that) s/he would catch crab?'

Second, as we also predict, the sentence ender has the form *ya* when the preceding suffix does not end in *n*.

*Neu babjuli   sim-eos-**ya**?* (느 밥주리 심엇야?)

2SG dragonfly catch-PFV-SE

'Did you catch a dragonfly?'

*Yeongsu mom gawm-ams-**ya**?* (영수 몸 곰았야?)

Yeongsu body wash-CONT-SE

'(Do you see) Yeongsu taking a bath?'

3.3.2 Sentence Enders for *Wh* Questions Only

In contrast to *-dia, -ga, -go,* and *-ya,* two sentence enders appear to occur only with *wh* questions: *-di* and *-i.*

-di (디)

ALLOMORPHY:

• *-ti* after the suffix *-eul*

STEM TYPE: Type 2 (ending in *-eun, -eon, -eul,* or *-eom*).

USAGE: *Wh* questions. As observed in section 3.1, *-di* can also be used in statements; however, it does not appear in *yes–no* questions.

*Neu-n   nuge adeol-i-n-**di**?* (는 누게 아덜인디?)

2SG-TOP who son-be-NPST-SE?

'Whose son are you?' (J.-r. Hong 1975,165)

*Neu-n   musigeo singgeu-l-**ti**?* (는 무시거 싱글티?)

2SG-TOP what   plant-FUT-SE

'What do you want to plant?'/'What will you plant?'

---

10. A similar pattern is also possible with the past tense suffix *-eon*: *sim-**uk-eon-ya*** (심우컨야).

When used with the continuative marker, there is no tensing.

> *Neu-n* **eodui** *gob-**am-di**?* (는 어듸 곱암디?)
>
> 2SG-TOP where hide-CONT-SE
>
> 'Where are you hiding?' (based on J.-r. Hong 1975, 165)

-i (이)

ALLOMORPHY: None.
STEM TYPE: Mixed (bare or ending in *-eos, -eoms, -eun,* or *-eon*).
USAGE: *Wh* questions that are addressed to friends or to younger listeners.

> *Gai* **eodui** *ga-s-**i**?* (가이 어듸 갓이?)
>
> 3SG where go-PFV-SE
>
> 'Where did s/he go?'

> *Gai* **musingeo**-len *gawl-ams-**i**?* (가이 무신거렌 굴앖이?)
>
> 3SG what-CON   say-CONT-SE
>
> 'What is s/he saying?'

> *Neu-n*   *seodab-haw-le*   **eodeule** *ga-neu-n-**i**?*
>
> 2SG-TOP laundry-do-CON where   go-INDC-NPST-SE
>
> (는 서답ᄒ레 어드레 가는이?)
>
> 'Where do you go to do your laundry?'

> *Eomeong-i*   **musingeo**-len *gawl-as-in-**i**?* (어멍이 무신거렌 굴앗인이?)
>
> mother-NOM what-CON   say-PFV-NPST-SE
>
> 'What has mom said?'

> *Haleubang* **musigeo** *gwe-w-ams-in-**i**?* (하르방 무시거 궤왎인이?)
>
> grandfather what   boil-CAUS-CONT-NPST-SE
>
> 'What is grandfather boiling?'

> **Nuge**-ga   *sawdab   haw-lgeo-n-**i**?* (누게가 ᄉ답훌건이?)
>
> who-NOM laundry do-FUT-NPST-SE
>
> 'Who is going to do the laundry?'

> *Neu* **musingeo** *ig-eoms-in-**i**?* (느 무신거 익엾인이?)
>
> 2SG what   read-CONT-NPST-SE
>
> 'What are you reading?'

Nuge-ne mikkang-i   daw-n-i? (누게네 미깡이 돈이?)

who-PL   tangerine-NOM sweet-NPST-SE

'Whose tangerines are sweet?'

Nuge-ne mawl-i-n-i? (누게네 몰인이?)

who-PL   horse-be-NPST-SE

'Whose horse is it?'

Another Segmentation Controversy (-*i* or -*ni*)

On the analysis put forward by P.-h. Hyun (1976), C. H. Woo (1995, 42) and others, the sentence ender in the preceding sentence is -*ni*, not -*i*, yielding an analysis very different from the one we propose.

Our analysis:

Eomeong musingeo jus-eoms-in-i? (어멍 무신거 줏없인이?)

mother   what   gather-CONT-NPST-SE

'What is mother gathering?'

The alternative analysis:

Eomeong musingeo jus-eo-m-si-ni? (어멍 무신거 줏엄시니?)

mother   what   gather-LV-NMLZ-be-SE

'What is mother gathering?'

O'Grady et al. (2018) argue that the alternative analysis cannot be right. As the past-tense version of the sentence immediately below reveals, *s* is clearly part of the continuative suffix and *n* must be part of the tense marker.

*Eomeong musingeo jus-**eoms-eon**-i?* (어멍 무신거 줏없언이?)

mother   what   gather-CONT-PST-SE

'What was mother gathering?'

This allows us to confirm our analysis of the nonpast version of the sentence as well: the sentence ender is -*i*. It is preceded by the nonpast suffix -*in*, which is the allomorph of the nonpast morpheme -*eun* that is expected after a stem ending in *s*.

Eomeong musingeo jus-eoms-in-i? (어멍 무신거 줏없인이?)

mother   what   gather-CONT-NPST-SE

'What is mother gathering?'

3.3.3 Summary

In sum, Jejueo appears to have a system of sentence enders that is sensitive to the distinction between *yes–no* questions and *wh* questions, but not along traditional lines. The key contrasts are reviewed in table 7.3.

Table 7.3   Sentence enders that distinguish between question types

SENTENCE ENDER	VERB TYPE	QUESTION TYPE
-dia	all	*wh* or *yes–no*
-ga	all	*wh* or *yes–no*
-go	all	*wh* or *yes–no*
-ya	all	*wh* or *yes–no*
*-di**	all	*wh* only
-i	all	*wh* only

* Can also occur in statements.

As this summary shows, *-di* and *-i* are used only with *wh* questions, but there are no clear examples of sentence enders that occur just with *yes-no* questions. The only possible candidates are *-ji*, which may be used for confirmatory questions (section 3.1), and *-eullogo*, which can sometimes call for a *yes* or *no* answer but also has a confirmatory connotation.

-eullogo (을로고)

ALLOMORPHY:

- *-illogo* after a stem ending in *s, j,* or *ch*
- *-ullogo* after a stem that ends in a labial consonant
- *-llogo* after a stem that ends in a vowel or *l* (in which case the stem-final *l* is deleted).

STEM TYPE: Type 1 (bare, or ending in *-eos, -eoms,* or *-euk*).
USAGE: Utterances that signal the speaker's doubt or skep-

ticism about an event, which is assumed to be shared by the addressee—thereby implying a request for confirmation.[11]

Halmang-i   galjungi menggeul-jen haw-l-logo?
grandmother-NOM galjungi make-CON   do-FUT-SE
(할망이 갈중이 멩글젠 흘로고?)
'I don't think grandmother will try to make *galjungi*, right?'
   (*Galjungi* are trousers made out of traditional cloth.)

Gai-ga   mikkang-nang singgeu-jen haw-l-logo?
3SG-NOM tangerine-tree plant-CON   do-FUT-SE
(가이가 미깡낭 싱그젠 흘로고?)
'I don't think he will plant tangerine trees, right?'

Mansu-ga   nang geuchi-l-logo? (만수가 낭 그칠로고?)
Mansu-NOM tree   cut-FUT-SE
'I don't think that Mansu is going to cut down the tree, right?'

Yeongsu mom gawm-ams-il-logo? (영수 몸 곱았일로고?)
Yeongsu body wash-CONT-FUT-SE
'I don't think Yeongsu is taking a bath, right?'

Geu gudeul daws-as-il-logo? (그 구들 돗앗일로고?)
that room   warm-PFV-FUT-SE
'I don't think the room has become warm, do you?'

3.4 Informal Sentence Enders for Imperatives and Propositives

A further set of sentence enders mark commands and proposals.

-(eu)ge ((으)게)

ALLOMORPHY:

• *-(i)ge* after a stem that ends in *s, j,* or *ch*
• *-(u)ge* after a stem that ends in a labial consonant
• *-ge* after a stem that ends in a vowel or *l* (the verb root *meog-* 'eat' is exceptional in allowing only *-ge*)

---

11. It is possible that this sentence ender, which clearly contains at least two (and perhaps three) component morphemes, may have a different interpretation. When used with falling intonation, it can apparently assert strong disbelief.

STEM TYPE: Type 1 (bare, or ending in *-eos* or *-eoms*).
USAGE: Propositives.

*Sawdab haw-**ge**!* (ㅅ답ㅎ게!)   *Mom gawm-(**u**)**ge**!* (몸 곰(우)게!)
laundry do-SE   body bathe-SE
'Let's do the laundry!'   'Let's take a bath!'

*Jus-(**i**)**ge**!* (줏(이)게!)   *Ig-(**eu**)**ge**!* (익(으)게!)
gather-SE   read-SE
'Let's gather (them)!'   'Let's read (it)!'

*Dawl-ams-(**i**)**ge**!* (돌앖(이)게!)   *Bongg-ams-(**i**)**ge**!* (봉값(이)게!)
run-CONT-SE   gather-CONT-SE
'Let's get running!'   'Let's start gathering (things)!'

*Meog-eos-(**i**)**ge**!* (먹엇(이)게!)
eat-PFV-SE
'Let's get finished eating!'

-eula (으라)

ALLOMORPHY:

• *-ila* after a stem ending in *s*, *j*, or *ch*
• *-ula* after a stem that ends in a labial consonant
• *-la* after a stem that ends in a vowel or *l*

STEM TYPE: Type 1 (bare, or ending in *-eos* or *-eoms*).
USAGE: Imperative, to demand an immediate action.

*Meog-**eula**!* (먹으라!)   *Aj-**ila**!* (앚이라!)
eat-SE   sit-SE
'Eat!'   'Sit down!'

*Sim-**ula**!* (심우라!)   *Seolleu-**la**!* (설르라!)
catch-SE   clean-SE
'Catch (it)!'   'Clean up!' (also 'Quit!')

By adding the continuative marker *-eoms* to the stem, the speaker requests the listener to act first.

*Gawl-**ams**-ila!* (굴앖이라!)   *Meog-**eoms**-ila!* (먹엾이라!)

talk-CONT-SE   eat-CONT-SE

'Start talking!'   'Start eating!'

Addition of the perfective marker to the stem signals a request to complete something before the speaker does or before starting something else.

*Meog-**eos**-ila!* (먹엇이라!)   *Chawj-**as**-ila!* (춪앗이라!)

eat-PFV-SE   search-PFV-SE

'Finish eating first!'   'Finish searching first!'

-*(eu)sim* ((으)심)

ALLOMORPHY:

- -*(i)sim* a stem that ends in *s*, *j*, or *ch*
- -*(u)sim* a stem that ends in a labial consonant
- -*sim* after a stem that ends in a vowel or *l*, which is then deleted

STEM TYPE: Type 1 (bare, or ending in -*eos* or -*eoms*).

USAGE: Used (mainly) by older women when speaking to a younger adult who is not old enough to merit a more honorific form and not young enough or close enough to the speaker to permit informal speech (S.-N. Lee 1957, 100; Y.-H. Park 1960, 346).

*Ssawl gwe-u-**sim**!* (쏠 궤우심!)   *Gawl-**eusim**!* (굴으심!)

rice   boil-CAUS-SE   speak-SE

'Boil the rice!'   'Speak!'

*Sim-**usim**!* (심우심!)   *Jilteu-**sim**!* (질트심!)

catch-SE   stretch-SE

'Catch it!'   'Stretch!'

In addition to its use with requests and proposals, -*(eu)sim* can also appear with statements and questions.

*Mikkang mawn tew-as-**sim**.* (미깡 몬 테왓심)

tangerine all   distribute-PFV-SE

'S/he distributed all the tangerines.'

Seonsuing-eun menal   eodeule dawd-sim? (선씽은 메날 어드레 돋심?)

teacher-TOP   everyday where run-SE

[or *dawl-eusim*]

'Where does the teacher go every day?'

Gasi-eomeong mulkkuleog meog-(eu)sim? (가시어멍 물꾸럭 먹(으)심?)

wife-mother octopus   eat-SE

'Does mother-in-law eat octopus?'

Other sentence enders that are used only by female speakers include *-sun, -son,* and *-sen* (S.-N. Lee 1957 100, 146; Y.-H. Park 1960 343, 346; S.-c. Jung 1985, 424).

4. Formal Sentence Enders

Jejueo does not traditionally have a subject honorific, but it does have an elaborate system of addressee honorification. The traditional sentence enders for use in formal situations and in the presence of people who are older or of higher social status all consist of three morphemes: the addressee honorific *-eub,* an evidentiality marker (*-de/di* versus *-ne/ni*), and a sentence ender (*-da* for statements and *-ga(ng)/kka(ng)* for questions).

Verb Stem–Addressee Honorific–Evidential Marker–Sentence Ender

Statement:	*-eub*	*-de/di* or *ne/ni*	*-da*
Question:	*-eub*	*-de/di*	*-ga(ng)*
		-ne/ni	*kka(ng)*

4.1 Formal Statements

-eub-de-da/-eub-di-da/-eob-de-da/-eob-di-da (읍데다, etc.)

ALLOMORPHY:

- *-ib*... after a stem that ends in *s, j,* or *ch*
- *-ub*... after a stem that ends in a labial consonant
- *-b*... after a stem that ends in a vowel or, possibly, *l* (which is then deleted)

STEM TYPE: Type 1 (bare, or ending in *-eos, -eoms,* or *-euk*).

USAGE: Used in formal situations for statements; has an evidential function, indicating that the statement is based on a direct past observation.

*Geu bas-dui   kawbdesani-n mag guj-**ib-di-da**.*

that field-place garlic-TOP   very bad-AH-EVI-SE

(그 밧듸 콥데사닌 막 굿입디다)

'(I noticed that) the garlic from that field is bad (in quality).'

*Gai mulkkuleog sim-**ub-de-da**.* (가이 물꾸럭 심웁데다)

3SG octopus   catch-AH-EVI-SE

'(I saw) him/her catching an octopus.'

*Mansu-ne asi   yeobcho   chawj-**ib-de-da**.*

Mansu-PL younger.sibling rolled.cigarette search-AH-EVI-SE

(만수네 아시 엽초 촛입데다)

'(I saw) Mansu's younger sibling looking for a cigarette.'

As is the case when *-de/di* stands alone (section 3.2), it is not a past-tense marker per se. Rather it simply signals that the speaker is basing his or her statement on a previously observed fact or report. A striking example of this comes from the following sentence, in which the speaker describes a possible *future* event whose likelihood of occurrence is based on a previous observation.

*Gasi-eomeong bue-na-n   dawgsegi dekki-k-**eub/eob-di-da**.*

wife-mother anger-come.out-CON egg   throw-PROSP-AH-EVI-SE

(가시어멍 부에난 둑세기 데끼큽/컵디다)

'(It seemed that) mother-in-law got angry, and she might throw
    away the eggs.'

The occurrence of *-eub-de/di-da* with a perfective marker, as in the next example, implies not just an observation of a past event, but that the event is in the more distant past.

*Abang dos-gwegi hayeong meog-eos-**ib-di-da**.*

father pig-meat a.lot   eat-PFV-AH-EVI-SE

(아방 돗궤기 하영 먹엇입디다)

'(I noticed that) father had eaten a lot of pork.'

-eub-ne-da/-eub-ni-da (읍네다/읍니다)

ALLOMORPHY:

- *-ib*. . . after a stem that ends in *s*, *j*, or *ch*
- *-ub*. . . after a stem that ends in a labial consonant
- *-b*. . . after a stem that ends in a vowel or, possibly, *l* (which is then deleted)

STEM TYPE: Type 1 (bare, or ending in *-eos* or *-eoms*).

USAGE: Used in formal situations for statements;[12] it has an evidential function, implying a prediction or inference based on prior knowledge.

The evidential function of *-ne/ni* can be discerned by considering contrasts with *-de/di* in patterns such as the following.

> *Geu sin   Mansu-sindi jog-eub-de-da.* (그 신 만수신디 족읍데다)
>
> that shoe Mansu-DAT   small-AH-EVI-SE
>
> '(I saw) those shoes were small for Mansu.'

> *Geu sin   Mansu-sindi jog-eub-ne-da.* (그 신 만수신디 족읍네다)
>
> that shoe Mansu-DAT   small-AH-EVI-SE
>
> '(I know) those shoes must be small for Mansu.'

Whereas the first sentence above implies that the speaker saw Mansu wearing shoes that are too small, the second one conveys a prediction or inference based on prior knowledge of Mansu's foot size.

The next pair of sentences exemplifies a parallel contrast.

> *Seong   nang geuchy-as-ib-de-da.* (성 낭 그챳입데다)
>
> older.brother tree   cut.down-PFV-AH-EVI-SE
>
> '(I noticed that) older brother cut down the tree.'

> *Seong   nang geuchy-as-ib-ne-da.* (성 낭 그챳입네다)
>
> older.brother tree   cut.down-PFV-AH-EVI-SE
>
> '(I know) older brother must have cut down the tree.'

---

12. The sentence ender can be used with a first-person subject, but only to express a fact about oneself and only if the verb is otherwise uninflected.

    Na gingi jal   meog-eub-ne-da. (나 깅이 잘 먹읍네다)
    1SG crab well eat-AH-EVI-SE
    'I eat crab a lot.'

In this case, the first sentence signals that the speaker directly observed his older brother cut down the tree, while the second sentence expresses an inference based on knowledge of the brother's intent.

Here are several more examples of *eub-ne-da* patterns.

*Halmang   menal   dawgsegi meog-**eub-ne-da**.*
grandmother everyday egg   eat-AH-EVI-SE
(할망 메날 둑세기 먹읍네다)
'(I know) grandmother eats eggs every day.'

*Bojegi   menal   gaekkaws-deole dawl-**eub-ne-da**.* [root = *dawd-*]
fisherman everyday seashore-DIR   run-AH-EVI-SE
(보제기 메날 개껏더레 둘읍네다)
'(I know) the fisherman goes to the seashore every day.'

*Geu bas-dui   nawmppi-n mag guj-**ib-ni-da**.* (그 밧듸 놈삔 막 궂입니다)
that field-place radish-TOP very bad-AH-EVI-SE
'(I know) the radish from that field is very bad (in quality).'

*Ga-ne-deol dolegi dunggeuly-eoms-**ib-ne-da**.* (가네덜 도레기 둥그렀입네다)
3-PL-PL   top   roll-CONT-AH-EVI-SE
'(I know) they must be rolling the top.'

*Seongje-ga   mikkang   mawn jus-eoms-**ib-ne-da**.*
siblings-NOM tangerine all   gather-CONT-AH-EVI-SE
(성제가 미깡 믄 줏없입네다)
'(I know) the siblings must be gathering all the tangerines.'

*Menal   geu-dui   ga-ng mulkkuleog sim-**ub-ne-da**.*
everyday that-place go-CON octopus   catch-AH-EVI-SE
(메날 그듸 강 물꾸럭 심웁네다)
'(I know) s/he catches octopus there every day.'

4.2 Formal Questions

-eub-de-ga(ng)/-eub-di-ga(ng) (읍데가, etc.)

ALLOMORPHY:

- *-ib*... after a stem that ends in *s, j,* or *ch*
- *-ub*... after a stem that ends in a labial consonant
- *-b*... after a stem that ends in a vowel or, possibly, *l* (which is then deleted)

STEM TYPE: Type 1 (bare, or ending in *-eos, -eoms,* or *-euk*).

USAGE: Employed in formal situations for *yes–no* and *wh* questions that can be answered based on information about a third party gathered from previous observation or experience.

> *Eomeong joban   meog-eub-di-ga?* (어멍 조반 먹읍디가?)
> mother   breakfast eat-AH-EVI-SE
> '(Did you see) mother eating breakfast?'

> *Eonchinag halmang   chib-ui   ga-b-de-ga/gang?*
> last.night   grandmother house-DIR go-AH-EVI-SE
> (언치낙 할망칩의 갑데가/강?)
> '(Did you see) someone go to grandmother's house last night?'

> *Haleubang geomjil mawn me-yeos-ib-di-ga/gang?*
> grandfather weed   all   pull-PFV-AH-EVI-SE
> (하르방 검질 믄 메엿입디가/강?)
> '(Did you notice whether) grandfather had pulled out all the weeds?'

> *Yecheong-deol   manong singg-eoms-ib-de-ga/gang?*
> married.woman-PL vegetable plant-CONT-AH-EVI-SE
> (예청덜 마농 싱겂입데가/강?)
> '(Did you see) the women planting vegetables?'

> *Abang eodeule   dawl-eub-di-ga?* (아방 어드레 돌읍디가?)
> father (some)where run-AH-EVI-SE
> [root = *dawd-*]
> '(Did you see) father going somewhere?'/'Where did father go?'

Mansu musigeo   *sichi-**b-de-ga**?* (만수 무시거 시칩데가?)

Mansu what/something wash-AH-EVI-SE

'(Did you see) Mansu washing something?'/'What did Mansu wash?'

As in the case of the statement marker *-eub-de/di-da*, *-de/-di* is concerned with evidentiality rather than tense or aspect. We therefore find examples such as the following, in which the speaker asks an addressee to make a prediction about a future event, based on previous observations.

Nal-i   *eol-k-**eub-di-ga**?* (날이 얼큽디가?)

day-NOM cold-PROSP-AH-EVI-SE

'(Based on your observation,) will the day be cold?'

-eub-ne-kka(ng)/-eub-ni-kka(ng) (읍네까, etc.)

ALLOMORPHY:

- *-ib...* after a stem that ends in *s, j,* or *ch*
- *-ub...* after a stem that ends in a labial consonant
- *-b...* after a stem that ends in a vowel or *l*

STEM TYPE: Type 1 (bare, or ending in *-eos* or *-eoms*).

USAGE: Used in formal situations for *yes–no* questions and *wh* questions that the addressee can be expected to answer based on information that need not involve direct observation.

Na-ga   *mawncheo aj-**ib-ne-kka**?* (나가 믄처 앚입네까?)

1SG-NOM first   sit-AH-EVI-SE

'Should I sit first?'

Na-ga   *halmang*   *dawl-ang ga-**b-ne-kka**?* (나가 할망 돌앙 갑네까?)

1SG-NOM grandmother bring-CON go-AH-EVI-SE

'Shall I bring grandmother?'

Jeoseul-e   *eotteong daws-**ib-ni-kka**?* (저슬에 어떵 돗입니까?)

winter-LOC how   warm-AH-EVI-SE

'How can it be warm in winter? (I doubt it.)'

*Ga-ng bo-min halmang-deol   mal   gawl-ams-**ib-ne-kka**?*

go-CON see-CON grandmother-PL speech speak-CONT-AH-EVI-SE

(강 보민 할망덜 말 굴았입네까?)

'When you go there, (do you usually see) grandmothers talking?'

*Ga-ng bo-min halmang   musigeo   meog-eos-**ib-ne-kka**?*

go-CON see-CON grandmother what/something eat-PFV-AH-EVI-SE

(강 보민 할망 무시거 먹엇입네까?)

'When you go there, (do you usually notice that) grandmother
    has eaten something?'/'When you go there, what has grand-
    mother (usually) eaten?'

4.3 Formal Imperatives

-eub-seo (읍서)

ALLOMORPHY:

- *-ibseo* after a stem that ends in *s, j,* or *ch*
- *-ubseo* after a stem that ends in a labial consonant
- *-bseo* after a stem that ends in a vowel or, possibly, *l* (which is
  then deleted)

STEM TYPE: Type 1 (bare, or ending in *-eos* or *-eoms*).
USAGE: Requests in formal situations.

*I-geo   meog-**eub-seo**.* (이거 먹읍서)

this-thing eat-AH-SE

'Please eat this.'

*Dawgsegi kkab chuli-**b-seo**.* (독세기 깝 추립서)

egg   price pay-AH-SE

'Please pay for the eggs.'

*Sawngki jus-eoms-**ib-seo**.* (숭키 줏었입서)

vegetable gather-CONT-AH-SE

'Please, get gathering vegetables (before me).'

*Paemanong jus-eos-**ib-seo**.* (패마농 줏엇입서)

green.onion gather-PFV-AH-SE

'Please, finish gathering green onions (before me).'

*Kong gwe-u-**b**-seo.* (콩 궤웁서)

bean boil-CAUS-AH-SE

'Please boil beans.'

Outside the family, in order to express deference to older people or when there is a greater social distance, the morpheme -*eusi* may be added.

-*eusi* (으시)

ALLOMORPHY:

- -*isi* after a stem ending in *s, j*, or *ch*
- -*usi* after a stem ending in a labial consonant
- -*si* after a stem ending in a vowel or in *l*, in which case the *l* is deleted

*Meog-**eusi**-b-seo.* (먹으십서)	*Aj-**isi**-b-seo.* (앚이십서)
eat-AH-AH-SE	sit.down-AH-AH-SE
'Please eat.'	'Please sit down.'
*Mom gawm-**usi**-b-seo.* (몸 곰우십서)	*Sim-**usi**-b-seo.* (심우십서)
body bath-AH-AH-SE	hold-AH-AH-SE
'Please take a bath.'	'Please hold it.'
*Singgeu-**si**-b-seo.* (싱그십서)	*Deu-**si**-b-seo.* (드십서)
plant-AH-AH-SE	eat-AH-AH-SE
'Please plant (it).'	[verb root = *deul-*]
	'Please eat.'

*Mal   gawl-**eusi**-b-seo.* (말 굴으십서) [root = *gawd-*]

speech speak-AH-AH-SE

'Please talk.'

*I   pen-deole do-**si**-b-seo.* (이펜더레 도십서) [root = *dol-*]

this side-DIR turn.around-AH-AH-SE

'Please, turn around to this side.'

The use of -*eusi* in Jejueo appears to be a quite recent phenomenon (J.-r. Hong 1975, 158; P.-h. Hyun 1977, 23). J.-W. Ko (pers. comm.) conjectures that the morpheme may have initially been brought from the mainland by exiled scholars and government officials at some point during the Joseon period; see also J.-h. Kim (2001, 17).[13]

4.4 A Mixed Honorific Pattern

In the preceding three sections, the addressee honorific *-eub* appears only with formal sentence enders. However, it is also able to appear with the less formal sentence ender *-ju*, first discussed in section 3.2.

-eub-ju (읍주)

ALLOMORPHY:

- *-ibju* after a stem that ends in *s, j, or ch*
- *-ubju* after a stem that ends in a labial consonant
- *-bju* after a stem that ends in a vowel or, optionally, *l* (which is then deleted)

STEM TYPE: Type 1 (bare, or ending in *-eos* or *-eoms*).

USAGE: Like *-(eu)ju*, *-eubju* expresses intention when there is a first-person subject and advice or judgments with subjects of other types.

*Na-ga gawl-**eub-ju**.* (나가 걀읍주)
1-NOM speak-AH-SE
'I will talk.'

*Samchun-i mulkkuleog sim-**ub-ju**?* (삼춘이 물꾸럭 심웁주?)
uncle-NOM octopus   catch-AH-SE
'Uncle, why don't you catch the octopus?'

*Geu-dui-n   mag neolleu-**b-ju**.* (그딘 막 널릅주)
that-place-TOP very spacious-AH-SE
'That place is very spacious.'

In addition, *-eubju* is commonly used to express proposals.

---

13. In the above examples, the subject is also the addressee. However, we have heard that some speakers use patterns such as the following, in which *-si* functions as a genuine Korean-like subject honorific, presumably as a result of contact.

*Sunsuing-nim o-**sy**-eon.* (선셍님 오션)
teacher-HON   come-HON-PST
'The teacher arrived.'

Ga-b-ju. (갑주)

go-AH-SE

'Let's go.'

Mulkkuleog sim-ub-ju. (물꾸럭 심웁주)

octopus   catch-AH-SE

'Let's catch the octopus.'

Jiseul   jus-ib-ju. (지슬 줏입주)

potato gather-AH-SE

'Let's gather the potatoes.'

Like *-(eu)ju* and parallel to imperative *-eubseo, -eubju* can be used with a perfective or continuative suffix in sentences expressing a proposal.

Ga-s-ib-ju. (갓입주)

go-PFV-AH-SE

'Let's be gone first.'

Ga-ms-ib-ju. (값입주)

go-CONT-AH-SE

'Let's get going (first).'

Moreover, as in the case of *-eubseo, -eusi* can be added if the addressee is older or of higher social status.

Gingi sim-usi-b-ju. (깅이 심우십주)

crab   catch-AH-AH-SE

'Let's catch crabs.'

5. The Addressee-Honorific Markers *-u* and *-euu*

Deference to an addressee can be expressed by using the honorific suffixes *-u* and *-euu*, in direct combination with a small number of sentence enders.

-u (우)

ALLOMORPHY: almost always -u,[14] but -su is used by some speakers after -eoms and -eos; see section 5.1.

STEM TYPE: Type 1 (bare, or ending in -eos, -eoms, or -euk).

USAGE: Attaches to the inflected stem of an action verb, a descriptive verb, or a copula, or to a bare copula. (As noted in chapter 6, section 2.4.3, we assume that -eulgeo is accompanied by an invisible copula.) The examples below all involve the sentence ender -(eu)da (see section 3.2), the most common option for this pattern. It is discussed in more detail in section 5.1.

> Sawdab haw-k-**u**-da. (ᄉ답ᇂ쿠다)
> laundry do-PROSP-AH-SE
> 'I will do the laundry.'

> Jog-euk-**u**-da. (족으쿠다)
> small-PROSP-AH-SE
> 'It will be small.'

> Jawdeul-as-**u**-da. (ᄌ들앗우다)
> worry-PFV-AH-SE
> 'S/he worried.'

> Daws-ams-**u**-da. (돗앖우다)
> warm-CONT-AH-SE
> 'It is becoming warm.'

> Gawl-eulgeo-**u**-da. (ᄀᆯ을거우다)
> talk-FUT-AH-SE
> 'S/he will talk.'

> Daws-ilgeo-**u**-da. (돗일거우다)
> warm-FUT-AH-SE
> 'It will be warm.'

> Mawl-i-yeos-**u**-da. (몰이엿우다)
> horse-be-PFV-AH-SE
> 'It was a horse.'

> Mawl-i-lgeo-**u**-da. (몰일거우다)
> horse-be-FUT-AH-SE
> 'It might be a horse.'

-euu (으우)

Used only with uninflected descriptive verbs, -euu has the intricate system of allomorphic options summarized in table 7.4 when the stem is bare.

---

14. J.-h. Kim (2001, 25) reports the use of -we as an alternative to -u; see also Y.-J. Hyun (2007), from whom the following examples are taken.

Eun-do   ma-**we**-da. (은도 마웨다)
silver-too don't.want-AH-SE
'(I) don't want silver too.' (Y.-J. Hyun 2007, 25)

Abanim-do   deog-i-**we**-da. (아바님도 덕이웨다)
father-too   grace-be-AH-SE
'Father is gracious too.' (Y.-J. Hyun 2007, 169)

Table 7.4   Allomorphy for -*euu* (uninflected descriptive verbs, regardless of sentence ender)

CONTEXT		EXAMPLES
-*euu*	default form	*Jog-euu-da.* (죽으우다) small-AH-SE 'It is small.'	*Bawlg-euu-da.* (붉으우다) bright-AH-SE 'It is bright.'
		Joh-euu-da. (좋으우다) good-AH-SE 'It is good.'	*Gawt-euu-da.* (곹으우다) same-AH-SE 'It is the same.'
-*iu*	after a stem ending in *s* or *j*	*Daws-iu-da.* (닷이우다) warm-AH-SE 'It is warm.'	*Guj-iu-da.* (궂이우다) deep-AH-SE 'It is bad (in quality).'
-*uu*	after a stem ending in a labial	*Jip-uu-da.* (짚우우다) deep-AH-SE 'It is deep.'	*Nop-uu-da.* (높우우다) high-AH-SE 'It is high.'
		Duteo-uu-da. (두터우우다) thick-AH-SE 'It is thick.' [root=*duteob-*]	*Yallu-uu-da.* (얄루우우다) thin-AH-SE 'It is thin.' [root=*yallub-*]
		Yawm-uu-da (욤우우다) ripen-AH-SE 'It is ripe.'	*Jeolm-uu-da* (젊우우다) yeong-AH-SE 'S/he is young.'
-*su*	alternative option after a stem ending in a conso- nant other than *l*	*Duteob-su-da.* (두텁수다) thick-AH-SE 'It is thick.'	*Yallub-su-da.* (얄룹수다) thin-AH-SE 'It is thin.'
		Daws-su-da. (닷수다) warm-AH-SE 'It is warm.	*Guj-su-da.* (궂수다) bad-AH-SE 'It is bad (in quality).'
		Jog-su-da. (죽수다) small-AH-SE 'It is small.'	*Bawlg-su-da.* (붉수다) bright-AH-SE 'It is bright.'
		Jip-su-da. (짚수다) deep-AH-SE 'It is deep'	*Joh-su-da.* (좋수다) good-AH-SE 'It is good.'
-*u*	after a stem ending in a vowel or *l* (with subse- quent deletion of *l*, as in *meol-da* 'far')	*Jjawlleu-u-da.* (쩔르우다) short -AH-SE 'It is short.' *Meo-u-da.* (머우다) far-AH-SE 'It is far.'	*Panchig-haw-u-da.* (판칙ᄒ우다) good.condition -do-AH-SE 'It is in good condition.'

A particularly striking example in table 7.4 is the verb meaning 'thin,' whose root is *yallub-* (얄릅). To derive the honorific form, the root *yallub-* requires the *-uu* allomorph of the addressee honorific, which in turn triggers deletion of the stem-final *b* (chapter 2, section 4.2.4), yielding the form *yallu-uuda*.

The addressee honorific is always immediately followed by a sentence ender whose properties are discussed in the next sections.

5.1 Statements Containing the Addressee Honorific *-u* or *-euu*

Several distinct statement patterns call for consideration.

Addressee honorific with *-(eu)da* (으다) (See Section 3.2)

When used with action verbs (which must always be inflected), the preferred form of the addressee honorific is *-u*.

> *Mul   jil-eos-u-da.* (물 질었우다)
> water draw-PFV-AH-SE
> 'S/he drew water.'

> *Chawlle   menggeul-ams-u-da.* (출레 멩글았우다)
> side.dish make-CONT-AH-SE
> 'S/he is making side dishes.'

> *Sigge-chib-ui*   *ga-k-u-da.* (식게칩의 가쿠다)
> ancestral.rites-house-DIR go-PROSP-AH-SE
> 'I will attend the ancestral rites.'

> *Gwegi kkab   chuli-lgeo-u-da.* (궤기깝 추릴거우다)
> meat   price pay-FUT-AH-SE
> 'S/he will pay for the meat.'

However, J.-h. Kim (2001) reports that some speakers use *-su* rather than *-u* after the suffixes *-eoms* and *-eos*.

> *Ije-sa   ol-ams-su-da.* (이제사 올았수다)
> now-just come-CONT-AH-SE
> 'S/he is coming just now.' (based on J.-h. Kim 2001, 19)

Descriptive and copula verbs, which may be either inflected or uninflected, take the honorific marker *-euu* and manifest the much more elaborate allomorphy described in table 7.4.

*Daws-**iu**-da*. (돗이우다)
warm-AH-SE
'It is warm.'

*Kobdag-haw-**u-da**.* (곱닥ㅎ우다)
beauty-do-AH-SE
'It is beautiful.'

*Ji-**u-da**.* (지우다) [root=*jil-*]¹⁵
long-AH-SE
'It is long.'

*Joh-**euu-da**.* (좋으우다)
good-AH-SE
'It is good.'

*Eodug-**euu-da**.* (어둑으우다)
dark-AH-SE
'It is dark.'

*Daws-as-**u-da**.* (돗앗우다)
warm-PFV-AH-SE
'It is warm.'

*Daws-ik-**u-da**.* (돗이쿠다)
warm-PROSP-AH-SE
'It will be warm.'

*Jog-**su**-da*. (족수다)
small-AH-SE
'It is small.'

*Jjawlleu-**u-da**.* (쫄르우다)
short-AH-SE
'It is short.'

*Deo-**uu-da**.* (더우우다)
hot-AH-SE
[root= *deob-*]
'It is hot.'

*guj-**iu-da**.* (궂이우다)
bad-AH-SE
'It is bad (in quality).'

*Duteob-**su**-da*. (두텁수다)
thick-AH-SE
'It is thick.'

*Daws-ams-**u-da**.* (돗앖우다)
warm-CONT-AH-SE
'It is getting warm.'

*Daws-ilgeo-**u-da**.* (돗일거우다)
warm-FUT-AH-SE
'It will be warm.'

Addressee honorific with *-ge/gwe* (게/궤)

ALLOMORPHY: None.

STEM TYPE: Type 1 (ending in *-eos, -eoms,* or *-euk*).

USAGE: To report new information to an older or socially superior listener; used *only* with verbs that are inflected with the perfective *-eos,* the continuative *-eoms,* or the prospective *-euk,* all of which trigger only the default *-u* form of the addressee honorific regardless of whether the verb denotes an action or a state.

---

15. A stem-final *l* is deleted in front of the addressee honorific *-u.*

Action verbs:

*Chawlle   menggeul-as-**u-ge/gwe**.* (출레 멩글앗우게/궤)
side.dish make-PFV-AH-SE
'(I) have made side dishes.'

*Pojang jjawl-ams-**u-ge/gwe**.* (포장 쭐랎우게/궤)
curtain cut-CONT-AH-SE
'(I) am cutting the curtain.'

*Gamjeo   kkab chuli-k-**u-ge/gwe**.* (감저깝 추리쿠게/궤)
sweet.potato price pay-PROSP-AH-SE
'You should have paid for the sweet potato.'

*Buleumssi haw-k-**u-ge/gwe**.* (부름씨 ㅎ쿠게/궤)
errand   do-PROSP-AH-SE
'You should have done the errand.'

Descriptive verbs:

*Eodug-eos-**u-ge/gwe**.* (어둑엇우게/궤)   *Eol-eoms-**u-ge/gwe**.* (얼없우게/궤)
dark-PFV-AH-SE   cold-CONT-AH-SE
'It is dark.'   'It is getting cold.'

*Jog-euk-**u-ge/gwe**.* (족으쿠게/궤)
small-PROSP-AH-SE
'It will be small'

Addressee honorific with -*kkwe* (꿰)

STEM TYPE: Type 1 (bare, or ending in -*eos* or -*eoms*).
USAGE: To report information or express an opinion to an older or socially superior listener. It seems to occur only with uninflected nonaction verbs, including the copula. As noted previously, the allomorphy found with uninflected descriptive verbs is unusually complex (see table 7.4).

*Jog-**euu-kkwe**.* (족으우꿰)   *Daws-**iu-kkwe**.* (돗이우꿰)
small-AH-SE   warm-AH-SE
'It is small.'   'It is warm.'

Guj-iu-kkwe. (궂이우꿰)
bad-AH-SE
'It is bad (in quality).'

Jip-uu-kkwe. (짚우우꿰)
deep-AH-SE
'It is deep.'

Panchig-haw-u-kkwe. (판칙ㅎ우꿰)
good.condition-do-AH-SE
'It is in good condition.'

Jjawlleu-u-kkwe. (쫄르우꿰)
short-AH-SE
'It is short.'

Ji-u-kkwe. (지우꿰) [root=*jil-*]
long-AH-SE
'It is long.'

Meo-u-kkwe. (머우꿰)
far-AH-SE
[root= *meol-*]
'It is far.'

Guj-su-kkwe. (궂수꿰)
bad-AH-SE
'It is bad (in quality).'

The following two patterns involve a copula with the default addressee honorific form *-u*. (Recall that *-eulgeo* is followed by an invisible copula; see chapter 6, section 2.4.3.)

Malchug-i-u-kkwe. (말축이우꿰)
grasshopper-be-AH-SE
'This is a grasshopper.'

Nel   na-ga   san-ui   ga-lgeo-u-kkwe. (넬 나가 산의 갈거우꿰)
tomorrow 1SG-NOM grave-DIR go-FUT-AH-SE
'I'm the one going to the grave tomorrow.'

The sentence ender *-kkwe* can express deference even without the presence of the honorific marker—but only when it is used with an uninflected descriptive verb or copula. When used in this way, its basic form is *-eukkwe*, with the following allomorphy.

- *-ikkwe* after a stem that ends in *s*, *j*, *or ch*
- *-ukkwe* after a stem that ends in a labial consonant
- *-kkwe* after a stem that ends in a vowel or *l* (which is then deleted)

*Jog-**eukkwe**.* (족으꿰)

small-SE

'It is small.'

*Daws-**ikkwe*** (둣이꿰)

warm-SE

'It is warm.'

*Guj-**ikkwe*** (궂이꿰)

bad-SE

'It is bad (in quality).'

*Jip-**ukkwe*** (짚우꿰)

deep-SE

'It is deep.'

*Panchig-haw-**kkwe**.* (판칙ᄒ꿰)

good.condition-do-SE

'It is in good condition.'

*Jjawlleu-**kkwe**.* (쫄르꿰)

short-SE

'It is short.'

*Ji-**kkwe**.* (지꿰) [root=*jil-*]

long-SE

'It is long.'

*Meo-**kkwe**.* (머꿰) [root=*meol-*]

far-SE

'It is far.'

*Malchug-i-**kkwe**.* (말축이꿰)

grasshopper-be-SE

'This is a grasshopper.'

*Nel   na-ga   san-ui   ga-lgeo-**kkwe**.* (넬 나가 산의 갈거꿰)

tomorrow 1SG-NOM grave-DIR go-FUT-SE

'I'm the one going to the grave tomorrow.'

5.2 Questions Containing the Addressee Honorific *-u* or *-euu*

Addressee honorific with *-gwa/gwang* or *-kkwa/kkwang* (과/광 or 꽈/꽝)

USAGE: *Yes–no* and *wh* questions; most widely used when addressing elders or social superiors, or in formal situations.

The form *-u-gwa(ng)* is generally used only with stems that are inflected for aspect or modality.

*Dawgsegi dekki-k-**u-gwa/gwang***? (둑세기 데끼쿠과/광?)

egg   throw-PROSP-AH-SE

'Will you throw away the eggs?'

*Dukke sichy-eos-**u-gwa/gwang***? (두께 시쳣우과/광?)

lid   wash-PFV-AH-SE

'Have you washed the lid?'

*Musingeo bongg-ams-**u-gwa/gwang**?* (무신거 봉값우과/광?)

what   gather-CONT-AH-SE

'What are you gathering?'

*Nal eodug-eoms-**u-gwa/gwang**?* (날 어둑없우과/광?)

day dark-CONT-AH-SE

'Is it getting dark?'

*Mawl-i-yeos-**u-gwa**?* (몰이엿우과?)

horse-be-PFV-AH-SE

'Was it a horse?'

In contrast, *-euu-kkwa(ng)* can be used with either inflected or uninflected descriptive verbs and copulas. (It cannot be used with uninflected action verbs.)

*Jog-eulgeo-**u-kkwa**?* (족을거우꽈?)

small-FUT-AH-SE

'Will it be small?'

*Si-**u-kkwa**?* (시우꽈?)   *Daw-**u-kkwa**?* (드우꽈?) [root=*dawl-*]

sour-AH-SE   sweet-AH-SE

'Is it sour?'   'Is it sweet?'

*Ji-**u-kkwa**?* (지우꽈?) [root=*jil-*] *Meo-**u-kkwa**?* (머우꽈?) [root=*meol-*]

long-AH-SE   far-AH-SE

'Is it long?'   'Is it far?'

*Daws-**iu-kkwa**?* (돗이우꽈?)   *Jip-**uu-kkwa**?* (짚우우꽈?)

warm-AH-SE   deep-AH-SE

'Is it warm?'   'Is it deep?'

*Jog-**euu-kkwa**?* (족으우꽈?)   or   *Deob-su-kkwa*? (덥수꽈?)

small-AH-SE   hot-AH-SE

'Is it small?'   'Is it hot?'

Guj-su-kkwa? (궂수꽈?)

bad-AH-SE

'Is it bad?'

Like its counterpart *-kkwe*, *-kkwa(ng)* can give an honorific interpretation to uninflected descriptive and copula verbs, even in the
absence of *-u*. When used in this way, its basic form is *-eukkwa*, with
the following allomorphy.

- *-ikkwa* after a stem that ends in *s, j,* or *ch*
- *-ukkwa* after a stem that ends in a labial consonant
- *-kkwa* after a stem that ends in a vowel or *l* (which is then
  deleted)

Si-kkwa? (시꽈?)

sour-SE

'Is it sour?'

Ji-kkwa? (지꽈?) [root=*jil-*]

long-SE

'Is it long?'

Daws-ikkwa? (둣이꽈?)

warm-SE

'Is it warm?'

Jog-eukkwa? (족으꽈?)

small-SE

'Is it small?'

Daw-kkwa? (드꽈?) [root=*dawl-*]

sweet-SE

'Is it sweet?'

Meo-kkwa? (머꽈?) [root=*meol-*]

far-SE

'Is it far?'

Jip-ukkwa? (짚우꽈?)

deep-SE

'Is it deep?'

I-geo   malchug-i-kkwa?

this-thing grasshopper-be-SE

(이거 말축이꽈?)

'Is this a grasshopper?'

Genan dul-i   seongje-kkwa? (게난 둘이 성제꽈?)

so   two-NOM sibling-SE

'So, are you two siblings?'

I-geo   eolme-kkwa? (이거 얼메꽈?)

this-thing how.much-SE

'How much is this?'

I-geo   musigeo-kkwa? (이거 무시거꽈?)

this-thing what-SE

'What is this?'

Jib-i   eodui-kkwa? (집이 어듸꽈?)

house-NOM where-SE

'Where is your house?'

6. An "All-Purpose" Formality Marker

Yet another strategy for signaling formality and deference has become popular, especially among younger speakers. It involves use of the "all-purpose" honorific marker *masseum* (마씀), also spelled and pronounced *massim* (마씸) and *massi* (마씨). (J.-h. Kim 2017, 237 suggests that this marker is derived from the Koreanic honorific form *malsseum* (말씀) 'speech.')

-masseum/massim/massi (마씀/마씸/마씨)

ALLOMORPHY: None.

USAGE: Can be added to phrases of various types to increase formality and deference.

In the following two examples, *-masseum* occurs with subsentential phrases.

Penji-masseum (펜지마씀)
letter-AH.SE
'A letter.' [In answer to 'What are you reading?']

I-chag-deule-masseum (이착드레마씀)
this-side-DIR-AH.SE
'Toward this side.' [In answer to 'Where should I put this?']

Jeo dam-u-ui dawlbengi-masseum. (저 담우의 돌벵이마씀)
that fence-top-LOC snail-AH.SE
'That is a snail on top of the fence.'

Adawl-deol san-ui ga-n-masseum? (아돌덜 산의 간마씀?)
son-PL grave-DIR go-PST-AH.SE
'Have (your) sons gone to the grave?'

Naws sichi-lgeo-masseum. (늣 시칠거마씀)
face wash-FUT-AH.SE
'I will wash my face.'

-masseum seems to be compatible only with the sentence enders listed in table 7.5.

Table 7.5   Sentence enders compatible with -*masseum*

STATEMENTS	QUESTIONS
-*di*	-*eo*
-*eo*	-*eumen*
-*(eu)ju*	-*ga*
-*eume*	-*go*
-*eumen*	
-*ge*	

*Na-ga   dawl-a-**masseum**?* (나가 돌아마씀?)

1SG-NOM run-SE-AH.SE

'Do you want me to run?'

*Gawchi   seodab-haw-ge-**masseum**!* (ᄀ치 서답ᄒ게마씀!)

together laundry-do-SE-AH.SE

'Let's do the laundry together.'

7. Emphatic Markers

Despite their name, sentence enders are not always the final item to occur in a sentence. Under appropriate circumstances, it is possible to add a "postsentential" particle for purposes of emphasis. There are three such particles.

-*i* (이), -*ge* (게), -*yang* (양)

ALLOMORPHY: None.

USAGE: All three particles assert and emphasize the speaker's belief or suggestion, with -*i* and -*yang* also calling for the listener's reaction. Only the suffix -*yang* can be used when the addressee has higher social status.

*Gai mag ganse-he-ms-jeo-**i/yang/ge**!* (가이 막 간세헸저이/양/게!)

3SG very lazy-do-CONT-SE-EMPH

'S/he is very lazy, right?/really!'

*Seodab-haw-le   ga-ge-**i/yang/ge**!* (서답ᄒ레 가게이/양/게!)

laundry-do-COM go-SE-EMPH

'Let's go do the laundry, okay?/really!'

Sentence enders vary in terms of their compatibility with particular emphatic markers. For example, only *-i* and *-ge* can appear with the informal imperative sentence ender *-eula*.

*Mikkang   jus-ila-**ge/i**!* (미깡 줏이라게/이!)

tangerine gather-SE-EMPH

'Pick up the tangerines, okay?/really.'

In contrast, only *-yang* or *-ge* can be used in more formal speech.

*Mikkang   jus-ib-seo-**yang/ge**!* (미깡 줏입서양/게!)

tangerine gather-AH-SE-EMPH

'Please pick up the tangerines, okay?/really.'

8

Connectives and Discourse Markers

1. Introduction

Various strategies are available for integrating clauses into larger sentences and for weaving sentences into discourse. Whereas discourse-related markers (discussed in section 5) tend to be sentence-initial adverbials, the markers used to combine clauses are all verbal suffixes.

Like sentence enders (see the previous chapter), most connectives can be placed into one of two groups, based on the type of stem with which they are compatible (table 8.1). Type 1 connectives can occur either with bare stems or with stems that end in *-eoms, -eos,* or (sometimes) *-euk.* In contrast, Type 2 connectives require a stem that ends in *-eun, -eon, -eul,* or *-eom.* In addition, a small number of connectives belong to a mixed type, with the ability to occur with an overlapping set of Type 1 and Type 2 stems.

Table 8.1   Two classes of connectives, depending on stem type

STEM TYPE 1	STEM TYPE 2
Can occur with a bare stem, or a stem ending in *-eos* or *-eoms* and sometimes *-euk.*	Requires a stem ending in *-eun, -eon, -eul,* or *-eom* (a variant of *-eoms;* see ch. 7, section 2.2).

There are just three Type 2 connectives: *-di, -disa,* and *-yen.*

2. Adnominal Clauses

Adnominal clauses combine directly with a following noun. Relative clauses are perhaps the most common type of adnominal clause, but we also include in this class less prototypical modifier patterns such as the following. (The noun *chim* 'value' in the second example is a bound morpheme; see chapter 3, section 4.4.)

dam   mawlaji-neu-n   soli (담 몰아지는 소리)
fence fall-INDC-NPST.CON sound
'the sound of the fence falling'

bo-l   chim (볼 침)
see-FUT.CON value
'the value of seeing'

As we will see next, adnominal clauses manifest a three-way tense-related contrast that is expressed by verbal suffixes that simultaneously serve as connectives: *-eun, -(eu)neun,* and *-eul.* Each of these suffixes is homophonous with a tense suffix that occurs in simple clauses, as discussed in chapter 6, section 2.4. In addition, adnominal clauses are able to express habituality via two strategies, one involving an auxiliary verb and the other involving a clause-final morpheme.

-eun (은)

ALLOMORPHY:

- *-in* after a stem that ends in *s, j,* or *ch* (for some speakers)
- *-un* after a stem that ends in a labial consonant (for some speakers)
- *-n* after a stem that ends in a vowel or *l.* When the stem ends in *l,* that segment is deleted (e.g., *jil-* 'long' + *-eun* > *ji-n*).

STEM TYPE: Type 1 (bare, or ending in *-eos* or *-eoms*).
USAGE: Connective for adnominal clauses denoting a past event in the case of action verbs and an achieved state in the case of descriptive verbs.

na-ga   ta-n   mikkang (나가 탄 미깡)
1SG-NOM pick-PST.CON tangerine
'the tangerine I picked'

uli   asi-ga   *sim-**un***   *malchug*

1PL younger.sibling-NOM catch-PST.CON grasshopper

(우리 아시가 심운 말축)

'the grasshopper that my younger sibling caught'

*geomeonghaw-**n** swe* (거멍흔 쉐)

black-PST.CON   cow

'a black cow'

*daws-**in***   *gudeul* (돗인 구들)

warm-PST.CON room

'the warm room'

-na-n (난) and *-dan* (단)

ALLOMORPHY: None

A habitual action in the past can be expressed in either of two ways: by the past tense adnominal form of the auxiliary *na-da* (chapter 5, section 2.3), or by the special adnominal connective *-dan*.

*denggy-eo-**na-n***   *usdeuleu* (뎅겨난 웃드르)

go-LV-HAB-PST.CON mountain.village

'the mountain villages (we) used to go to'

*denggi-**dan** usdeuleu* (뎅기단 웃드르)

go-HAB.CON mountain.village

'the mountain villages (we) used to go to'

The two forms can be used with descriptive verbs.

*daws-a-**na-n***   *gudeul* (돗아난 구들)

warm-LV-HAB-PST.CON room

'the room that used to be warm'

*daws-**dan***   *gudeul* (돗단 구들)

warm-HAB.CON room

'the room that used to be warm' (also: 'the room that was be-
    coming warm')

-*(eu)neu-n* ((으)는)

ALLOMORPHY:

- -*(i)neun* after a stem that ends in *s, j,* or *ch*
- -*(u)neun* after a stem that ends in a labial consonant
- -*neun* after a stem that ends in a vowel or *l*, which is then deleted

STEM TYPE: Type 1 (bare stem only).

USAGE: Connective for adnominal clauses denoting a nonpast (typically present) event or state, often with a habitual intepretation.

*a-**neu-n***   *yecheong* (아는 예청)

know-INDC-NPST.CON married.woman

'the woman who I know'

Mansu-ga   *ta-**neu-n***   *joyeongge* (만수가 타는 조영게)

Mansu-NOM ride-INDC-NPST.CON bicycle

'the bicycle that Mansu usually rides'/'the bicycle that Mansu is riding'

*gansehaw-**neu-n***   *sawnai* (간세ㅎ는 ㅅ나이)

dawdle-INDC-NPST.CON man

'a man who is dawdling'

*daw-**neu-n***   *mikkang* (ㄷ는 미깡) [root=*dawl-*]

sweet-INDC-NPST.CON tangerine

'sweet tangerines'

The association of -*(eu)neu-n* with habituality is also found with descriptive verbs, as the following contrast with -*eun* helps show.

With -*(eu)neu-n*:

*daws-**ineu-n***   *gudeul* (둣이는 구들)

warm-INDC-NPST.CON room

'the (usually) warm room'

With *-eun*:

daws-in   *gudeul* (돗인 구들)

warm-PST.CON room

'the (already) warm room'

-eul (을)

ALLOMORPHY:

- *-il* after a stem that ends in *s*, *j*, or *ch* (for some speakers)
- *-ul* after a stem that ends in a labial consonant (for some speakers)
- *-l* after a stem that ends in a vowel or *l*, which is then deleted

STEM TYPE: Type 1 (bare, or ending in *-eos* or *-eoms*).

USAGE: Connective for adnominal clauses denoting a future or conjectured situation.

tawd-eul   *sawngki* (톤을 숭키)

pick-FUT.CON vegetable

'vegetables that s/he will pick'

singgeu-l   *gojang* (싱글 고장)

plant-FUT.CON flower

'the flowers that s/he will plant'

sim-ul   *gawlgaebi* (심울 굴개비)

catch-FUT.CON frog

'a frog to catch'

Mansu-ga   *jus-il*   *gamjeo* (만수가 줏일 감저)

Mansu-NOM gather-FUT.CON sweet.potato

'the sweet potatoes that Mansu will gather'

geu-le   *dawl-as-il*   *sawnai* (그레 돌앗일 스나이)

that-DIR run-PFV-FUT.CON man

'a man who would have run there'

geu-le   *dawl-ams-il*   *sawnai* (그레 돌앖일 스나이)

that-DIR run-CONT-FUT.CON man

'a man who would be running there'

3. Reported Speech and Thought

A wide variety of connectives is available for speakers to report the speech and thoughts of others. As we will note as we proceed, many of these items can also be used as sentence enders, where they fulfill an explicitly evidential function by indicating that the information conveyed by the speaker comes from someone else.

-den/deng (덴/뎅)[1]

ALLOMORPHY: Allomorphic variation occurs only when the connective is added to the bare stem of a descriptive verb; see the discussion below.

STEM TYPE: Mixed (bare for a descriptive verb; ending in *-eun*, *-eos*, or *-eoms* for all verb types).

USAGE: Marks a reported statement or question; can also be used as a sentence ender.

When *-den/deng* is used with action verbs, the stem must be inflected.

Mansu unyeongpas-dui   *ga-s-**den**?* (만수 우녕팟듸 갓덴?)

Mansu vegetable.garden-place go-PFV-CON

'(Did s/he say that) Mansu went to the vegetable garden?'/
 '(Did Mansu say that) he went to the vegetable garden?'

Neu-ne ses-ttawl *geolssagjige geomjil me-n-**den** gawl-ala.*

2-PL second-daughter quickly weed pull-NPST-CON say-SE

(느네 셋뚤 걸쌕지게 검질 멘덴 굴아라)

'S/he said that your second-oldest daughter weeds quickly.'/
 'Your second-oldest daughter said that she weeds quickly.'

Mansu menal *geu-dui* *yewag-haw-le* *ga-n-**den** he-la.*

Mansu every.day that-place conversation-do-CON go-NPST-CON do-SE

(만수 메날 그듸 예왁ᄒ레 간덴 헤라)

'S/he said that Mansu goes there every day to talk.'/'Mansu
 said that he goes there every day to talk.'

---

1. Following King (1994, 26–30), we surmise that *-den* derives historically from the fusion of declarative marker *-da* and the reportive suffix *-en*, which also shows up in *-jen*, *-gen*, *-eulen*, and *-eolen* (see below).

*Gasi-abang-i   Cheolsu-n   yeosnal sun.gyeong-haw-yeo-na-s-**den***

wife-father-NOM Cheolsu-TOP past   policeman-do-LV-HAB-PFV-CON

gawl-ala. (가시아방이 철순 엿날 순경ㅎ여낫뎬 골아라)

say-SE

'Father-in-law said that Cheolsu used to work as a policeman in
  the past.'

*Mansu gengi neomui hayeong meog-eon gew-as-**den**   haw-yeola.*

Mansu crab overly a.lot   eat-PST   vomit-PFV-CON do-SE

(만수 겡이 너믜 하영 먹언 게왓뎬 ㅎ여라)

'S/he said that Mansu threw up because he ate too many crabs.'/
  'Mansu said that he threw up because he ate too many crabs.'

*Gai dos-gwegi kkab chuli-k-u-**den**   gawl-ala.*

3SG pig-meat price pay-PROSP-AH-CON say-SE

(가이 돗궤기깝 추리쿠뎬 골아라)

'S/he said that s/he would pay for the pork.'

In casual speech, *-den* is used as a de facto sentence ender, signaling
reported speech.

*Sunja mul   jil-eoms-**den**.* (순자 물 질없뎬)

Sunja water draw-CONT-CON

'(S/he said that) Sunja is drawing water.'/'(Sunja said that) she
  is drawing water.'

*Sunja sawdab haw-yeos-**den**.* (순자 ᄉ답 ㅎ엿뎬)

Sunja laundry do-PFV-CON

'(S/he said that) Sunja did the laundry.'/'(Sunja said that) she
  did the laundry.'

Descriptive verbs differ from action verbs in allowing *-den* even
when the stem is uninflected. When this happens, the following
pattern of allomorphic variation occurs.

- *-iden* after an uninflected stem that ends in *s, j,* or *ch*
- *-uden* after an uninflected stem that ends in a labial consonant
- *-den* after an uninflected stem that ends in a vowel or *l*

*Geu gudeul daws-**iden**?* (그 구들 돗이뎬?)
that room   warm-CON
'(Did s/he say that) the room is warm?'

*Geu-dui-n   mag hawkkeullag-haw-**den**.* (그뒨 막 ㅎ끌락ㅎ뎬)
that-place-TOP very small-do-CON
'(S/he said that) that place is very small.'

*I-geo   neomui   jjawlleu-**den**.* (이거 너믜 쫄르뎬)
this-thing too.much short-CON
'(S/he said that) it is too short.'

*Oneol-eun mag eol-**den**   gawl-ala.* (오녈은 막 얼뎬 ᄀᆯ아라)
today-TOP   very cold-CON   say-SE
'S/he said that today is very cold.'

*Yawm-**uden** haw-yeola.* (욤우뎬 ㅎ여라)
ripe-CON   do-SE
'S/he said that (it is) ripe.'

When the stem is inflected, *-den* has no allomorphic variation.

*Geu sin   jog-as-**den**   he-la.* (그 신 족앗뎬 헤라)
that shoe small-PFV-CON do-SE
'S/he said that those shoes were small.'

-disa (디사) 'whether'

ALLOMORPHY: None.
STEM TYPE: Type 2 (ending in *-eom, -eun, -eon,* or *-eul*).
USAGE: Signals a thought whose truth is unknown to the speaker; can also be used as a sentence ender.

*Neu-ne gasi-abang-eun mulkkuleog sim-eon-**disa**   molleu-k-yeo.*
2-PL   wife-father-TOP octopus   catch-PST-CON not.know-PROSP-SE
(느네 가시아방은 물꾸럭 심언디사 몰르켜)
'I don't know whether father-in-law has caught an octopus or not.'

*Yeongsu-n   jiseul   jus-eos-in-**disa**.* (영순 지슬 줏엇인디사)

Yeongsu-TOP potato gather-PFV-NPST-CON

'(I don't know) whether Yeongsu has picked potatoes or not.'

*Neu-ne abang-eun dos-gwegi meog-eul-**disa** molleu-k-yeo.*

2-PL   father-TOP pig-meat eat-FUT-CON   not.know-PROSP-SE

(느네 아방은 돗궤기 먹을디사 몰르켜)

'I don't know whether your father will eat pork or not.'

*Neu-ne eomeong-eun gingi gwe-w-ams-in-**disa**   molleu-k-yeo.*

2-PL   mother-TOP   crab boil-CAUS-CONT-NPST-CON not.know-PROSP-SE

(느네어멍은 깅이 궤왔인디사 몰르켜)

'I don't know whether your mother is boiling crabs or not.'

Because *-disa* requires a Type 2 stem, the continuative marker has
the form *-eom* and does not trigger tensing in examples such as the
following; see the discussion in chapter 7, section 2.2.

*Mansu buleumssi haw-**yeom-disa**   molleu-k-yeo.*

Mansu errand   do-CONT-CON   not.know-PROSP-SE

(만수 부름씨 ᄒ염디사 몰르켜)

'I don't know whether Mansu is doing an errand.'

-eolen (어렌)

ALLOMORPHY:

- *-alen* (vowel harmony; see chapter 2, section 4.2.4)
- *-len* after a stem ending in a vowel

STEM TYPE: Type 1 (bare, ending in *-eos*, *-eoms*, or *-euk*).

USAGE: To report a statement made in the past; can also be used
as a sentence ender.

Because it has an evidential function, *-eolen* is reserved for patterns in which the person being quoted (the father in the first
example below) has directly observed or experienced the reported
event.

*Abang-i   geu baechi-n   mag guj-**eolen** gawl-ala.*

father-NOM that cabbage-TOP very bad-CON say-SE

(아방이 그 배친 막 궂어렌 골아라)

'Father said that that cabbage was very bad (in quality).'

*Neu-ne abang-i   neu mag chawj-**alen** he-la.*

2-PL   father-NOM 2SG a.lot search-CON do-SE

(느네 아방이 느 막 촛아렌 헤라)

'S/he said that (s/he saw) your father looking hard for you.'

*Nongbani unyeongpas-deole   ga-**len** gawl-ala.*

farmer   vegetable.garden-DIR go-CON say-SE

(농바니 우녕팟더레 가렌 골아라)

'S/he said that (s/he saw) the farmer going to the vegetable garden.'

*Neu-ne eomeong-i   Cheolsu joban   chawlly-eoms-**eolen** he-la.*

2-PL   mother-NOM Cheolsu breakfast prepare-CONT-CON do-SE

(느네 어멍이 철수 조반 출렸어렌 헤라)

'Your mother said that (she saw) Cheolsu preparing breakfast.'

-*eub-sen* (읍센)

ALLOMORPHY:

- -*ibsen* after a stem that ends in *s, j, or ch*
- -*ubsen* after a stem that ends in a labial consonant
- -*bsen* after a stem that ends in a vowel or *l*

STEM TYPE: Type 1 (bare, or ending in -*eos* or -*eoms*).

USAGE: To indicate a message that is to be conveyed to an older or higher-ranked person.

The use of the addressee honorific in the examples below reflects the status of the person to whom the addressee is being asked to speak, not the status of the addressee himself/herself.

*Neu-ne gasi-abang-gawla mikkang ta-b-**sen**   haw-la.*

2-PL   wife-father-DAT   tangerine pick-AH-CON do-SE

(느네 가시아방ᄀ라 미깡 탑센 ᄒ라)

'Tell your father-in-law to pick some tangerines.'

*Halmang-sindi   gawse gob-ji-b-**sen**   gawl-eula.*

grandmother-DAT scissors hide-CAUS-AH-CON say-SE

(할망신디 ᄀ세 곱집센 굴으라)

'Tell grandmother to hide the scissors.'

*Gasi-abang-sindi bab   mawnyeo meog-eoms-ib-**sen** gawl-a-ju-b-seo.*

wife-father-DAT   meal first   eat-CONT-AH-CON say-LV-give-AH-SE

(가시아방신디 밥 몬여 먹없입센 골아줍서)

'Please tell father-in-law to get eating first.'

*Eomeong-sindi   mawnyeo ga-s-ib-**sen**   gawl-a-bul-la.*

grandmother-DAT first   go-PFV-AH-CON say-LV-COMPL-SE

(어멍신디 몬여 갓입센 골아불라)

'Tell mother to be gone first.'

-(eu)gen ((으)겐)[2]

ALLOMORPHY:

- *-(i)gen* after a stem ending in *s, j,* or *ch*
- *-(u)gen* after a stem that ends in a labial consonant
- *-gen* after a stem that ends in a vowel or *l*

STEM TYPE: Type 1 (bare, or ending in *-eos, -eoms,* or *-euk*).

USAGE: Used for action verbs that report a suggestion or a wish; can also be used as a sentence ender.

*Na-ga   mawncheo gingi sim-(**u**)**gen** gawl-as-jeo.*

1SG-NOM first   crab catch-CON   tell-PFV-SE

(나가 몬처 깅이 심(우)겐 골앗저)

'I suggested that we catch some crabs (together) first.'

*Mawncheo sawdab haw-yeoms-**igen** haw-yeos-jeo.*

first   laundry do-CONT-CON   do-PFV-SE

(몬처 ᄉ답 ᄒ없이겐 ᄒ엿저)

'I suggested that we get doing the laundry first (before others).'

*Na-ga   mawncheo gongbui-haw-yeos-**igen** gawl-as-jeo.*

1SG-NOM first   study-do-PFV-CON   tell-PFV-SE

(나가 몬처 공븨ᄒ엿이겐 골앗저)

'I suggested that we study first.'

---

2. Following the logic of note 1, we surmise that *-gen* derives historically from the
   fusion of the evidential marker *-ge* and the reportive suffix *-en,* which also shows
   up in *-jen, -den* and *-len.*

A future interpretation arises when *-gen* is replaced by *-ken,* which appears to incorporate the prospective marker *-(eu)k* (see chapter 6, section 2.3).

> *Unyeongpas-dui   gawjji   ga-**ken**   gawl-as-jeo.*
> vegetable.garden-place together go-PROSP.CON say-PFV-SE
> (우녕팟듸 ㄱ찌 가켄 굴앗저)
> 'I said that we will go to the vegetable garden together.'

-(eu)gwandi/(eu)gwande ((으)관디/(으)관데) [also spelled *-(eu)gwandui*]

ALLOMORPHY:

- *-(i)gwandi* after a stem that ends in *s, j, or ch*
- *-(u)gwandi* after a stem ending in a labial consonant
- *-gwandi* after a stem that ends in a vowel or *l*

STEM TYPE: Type 1 (bare, or ending in *-eos* or *-eoms*).
USAGE: Marks an embedded clause as a question; can also be used as a sentence ender.

> *Eolmena   deob-**gwandi** ttawm-eul heulli-neu-n-go?*
> how.much hot-CON   sweat-ACC drip-INDC-NPST-SE
> (얼메나 덥관디 뚬을 흘리는고?)
> 'You are dripping sweat, so (I wonder) how hot it is.' (Y.-H. Park 1960, 376)

> *Nuge-yeong mal   gawl-as-**(i)gwandi** yeong   bue-na-n?*
> who-with   speech speak-PFV-CON   like.this anger-come.out-PST
> (누게영 말 굴앗(이)관디 영 부에난?)
> 'You got this angry so (I wonder) who you were talking with.'

> *Musigeo meog-eos-**(i)gwandi** gyeong   be   ap-an   he-ms-in-go?*
> what   eat-PFV-CON   like.that stomach hurt-PST do-CONT-NPST-SE
> (무시거 먹엇(이)관디 경 베아판 헸인고?)
> 'Your stomach is hurting, so (I wonder) what you ate.'

> *Musigeo bongg-ams-**(i)gwande** gyeong   jikkeojy-eong he-ms-in-go?*
> what   gather-CONT-CON   like.that happy-CON   do-CONT-NPST-SE
> (무시거 봉갉(이)관데 경 지꺼정 헸인고?)
> 'S/he is happy like that, so (I wonder) what s/he is gathering.'

-(eu)jen/(eu)jeng ((으)젠/(으)젱)

ALLOMORPHY:

- -(i)jen after a stem ending in s, j, or ch
- -(u)jen after a stem that ends in a labial consonant
- -jen after a stem that ends in a vowel or l

STEM TYPE: Type 1 (bare, or ending in -eos or -eoms).

USAGE: Can be used as a connective or as a sentence ender, in either of the two senses described below.

When used with a bare verb stem, it has an anticipatory force, indicating that something is about to happen.

> *Songegi chawj-(i)jen haw-yeoms-jeo.* (송에기 촛(이)젠 ᄒ 엾저)
> calf   look.for-CON do-CONT-SE
> 'I am about to look for the calf.'

> *Neu nang singgeu-jen he-ms-in-ya?* (느 낭 싱그젠 헸인야?)
> 2SG tree plant-CON do-CONT-NPST-SE
> 'Are you about to plant a tree?'

> *Halmang   mom gawm-(u)jen haw-men.* (할망 몸 곰(우)젠 ᄒ 멘)
> grandmother body wash-CON   do-SE
> 'Grandmother is about to have a bath.'

On the other hand, when attached to a stem that carries the aspectual marker -eos or -eoms, -(eu)jen indicates a reported event and is often accompanied by *haw-da* 'do,' which is interpreted in this context as a verb of saying.

> *Neu-ne seong   jeongji-le   dawl-as-jen   (gawl-ala).*
> 2-PL   older.sibling kitchen-DIR run-PFV-CON (say-SE)
> (느네 성 정지레 돌앗젠 (굴아라))
> 'S/he said that your older sibling ran to the kitchen.'

> *Geu bibali sawngki   tawd-ams-jen   (he-n-ge).*
> that girl   vegetable pick-CONT-CON (do-PST-SE)
> (그 비바리 숭키 톤앖젠 (헨게))
> 'S/he said that the girl is picking vegetables.'

*Mansu-ga   abang-i   mulkkuleog sim-eoms-**jen**   gawl-ala.*
Mansu-NOM father-NOM octopus   catch-CONT-CON say-SE
(만수가 아방이 물꾸럭 심없젠 굴아라)
'Mansu said father is catching an octopus.' (based on S.-G. Jin
    1980, 25)

-eulen (으렌)

ALLOMORPHY:

• *-ilen* after a stem that ends in *s, j,* or *ch*
• *-ulen* after a stem that ends in a labial consonant
• *-len* after a stem that ends in a vowel or *l*

STEM TYPE: Type 1 (bare, or ending in *-eos, -eoms,* or *-euk*).
USAGE: Reports a command, intention, or possibility; can also be
used as a sentence ender.

*Mawncheo ga-s-**ilen**   gawl-ala.* (문처 갓이렌 굴아라)
first   go-PFV-CON say-SE
'S/he said to be gone first.'

*Joban   chawlli-**len**   haw-la.* (조반 출리렌 ᄒ라)
breakfast prepare-CON do-SE
'Tell him/her to prepare breakfast.'

*Gingi gwe-u-**len**   gawl-ala.* (깅이 궤우렌 굴아라).
crab   boil-CAUS-CON say-SE
'S/he said to boil the crabs.'

*Mawncheo nang singg-eoms-**ilen**   gawl-ala.* (문처 낭 싱겂이렌 굴아라)
first   tree   plant-CONT-CON say-SE
'S/he said to get planting the tree first.'

*Cheolsu nuilmoli   san-ui   ga-lgeo-**len** he-la.*
Cheolsu day.after.tomorrow grave-DIR go-FUT-CON do-SE
(철수 닐모리 산의 갈거렌 헤라)
'Cheolsu said that (he) will go to the grave the day after
    tomorrow.'

On occasion, *-eulen* can occur at the end of a sentence, implying the presence of an unstated verb of communication.

> *Halmang-i   neu yangji sichi-len.* (할망이 느 양지 시치렌)
> grandmother-NOM 2SG face   wash-CON
> 'Grandmother (said) to wash your face.'

> *Eomong-i   neu kong gawl-len.* (어멍이 느 콩 골렌)
> mother-NOM 2SG bean grind-CON
> 'Mother (said) to grind the beans.'

-(eu)nolen ((으)노렌)

ALLOMORPHY:

- *-(i)nolen* after a stem ending in *s*, *j*, or *ch*
- *-(u)nolen* after a stem that ends in a labial consonant
- *-nolen* after a stem that ends in a vowel or *l* (in which case the stem-final *l* is deleted)

STEM TYPE: Type 1 (bare, or ending in *-eos* or *-eoms*).
USAGE: Marks a clause in which the person describing the situation is also the referent of the subject.

> *Mansu-man swe jillu-nolen he-la.* (만수만 쉐 질루노렌 헤라)
> Mansu-only cow raise-CON do-SE
> 'Mansu said that only he raises cows.'

> *Mansu-man gongbui haw-nolen he-la.* (만수만 공븨 ᄒ 노렌 헤라)
> Mansu-only study   do-CON   do-SE
> 'Mansu said that only he (Mansu) is studying.'

> *Abang jang-ui   ga-nolen he-ms-jeo.* (아방 장의 가노렌 헸저)
> father market-DIR go-CON   do-CONT-SE
> 'Father is saying that he (father) is going to the market.'

> *Mansu bas ga-nolen he-ms-jeo.* (만수 밧 가노렌 헸저) [root=*gal-*]
> Mansu field plow-CON do-CONT-SE
> 'Mansu is saying that he is plowing the field.'

Halmang   kong sawlm-(u)nolen haw-yeoms-in-ge.

grandmother bean boil-CON   do-CONT-NPST-SE

(할망 콩 숢(우)노렌 ᄒᆞᆼ없인게)

'(I see that) grandmother is saying that she (grandmother) is
   boiling beans.'

Mansu songegi chawj-(i)nolen gawl-ams-in-ge.

Mansu calf   look.for-CON   say-CONT-NPST-SE

(만수 송에기 촟(이)노렌 ᄀᆞᆯ았인게)

'(I see that) Mansu is saying that he (Mansu) is looking for
   the calf.'

Sawmus   ji-ne-man   gob-nolen   he-ms-jeo. (ᄉᆞ뭇 지네만 곱노렌 헸져)

very.simply self-PL-only pretty-CON do-CONT-SE

'They are just very simply saying that only they are pretty.'

On occasion, *-(eu)nolen* can occur at the end of a sentence, implying
the presence of an unstated verb of communication.

Mansu ttawl   pawl-as-(i)nolen. (만수 ᄄᆞᆯ 폴앗(이)노렌)

Mansu daughter sell-PFV-CON

'Mansu (said) he married off his daughter.'

Haleubang-i   dam daw-ams-(i)nolen. (하르방이 담 다았(이)노렌)

grandfather-NOM fence build-CONT-CON

'Grandfather said that he (grandfather) is building the fence.'

-yen (옌)

ALLOMORPHY: None.

STEM TYPE: Mixed (ending in *-eun* or *-eon*; can take a bare stem
with a copula).

USAGE: Reports a statement or question; can also be used as a
sentence ender.

Geu-geo   setang-gawlu-yen   gawl-ala. (그거 세탕ᄀᆞ루옌 ᄀᆞᆯ아라)

that-thing candy-powder-CON say-SE

'S/he said that is sugar.'

*Geos-gawla jaeyeol-i-**yen***   *haw-neu-n-di.* (것?라 재열이옌 ᄒᆞᆫ디)
that-say   cicada-be-CON do-INDC-NPST-SE
'Talking about that, it's called a cicada.' (based on M.-S. Kwon 2011, 22)

Yeongi eomeong-i   *haleubang sabal-nawmawl jillu-neu-n-**yen***
Yeongi mother-NOM grandfather plate-vegetable   grow-INDC-NPST-CON
deul-eola. (영이 어멍이 하르방 사발ᄂᆞ물 질루는옌 들어라)
ask-SE
'Yeongi's mother asked (me) whether grandfather grows cabbage.'

Halmang-i   *oneol san-deole ga-k-eun-**yen***   *deul-eola.*
grandmother-NOM today grave-to   go-PROSP-NPST-CON ask-SE
(할망이 오널 산더레 가큰옌 들어라)
'Grandma asked (me) whether I want to go to the grave today.'

Yeongi-ga   *haleubang bal-mogegi gawmokk-as-in-**yen***   *deul-eola.*
Yeongi-NOM grandfather foot-neck   sprain-PFV-NPST-CON ask-SE
(영이가 하르방 발모게기 ?모깟인옌 들어라)
'Yeongi asked (me) whether grandfather sprained his ankle.'

Eonchinyag   *eoneuje chawlle   menggeul-as-in-**yen** deul-eola.*
yesterday.evening when   side.dish make-PFV-NPST-CON ask-SE
(언치냑 어느제 출레 멩글앗인옌 들어라)
'S/he asked (me) when you made the side dish(es) yesterday evening.'

Like *-den, -eulen, -eunolen,* and *-eolen, -yen* can occur at the end of a sentence, implying the presence of an unstated verb of speaking.

Yeongi eomeong-i   *Cheolsu hawgge jal   denggy-eoms-in-**yen**.*
Yeongi mother-NOM Cheolsu school   well attend-CONT-NPST-CON
(영이 어멍이 철수 흑게 잘 뎅겼인옌)
'Yeongi's mother asked whether Cheolsu is attending school well.'

I-geo-n   *chawmwe-n-yen?* (이건 춤웬옌?)[3]

this-thing-TOP melon-NPST-CON

'(Did she say) this thing is a melon?'

4. Other Connectives

Connectives fulfill a broad range of other functions in Jejueo, ranging from conjunction to the expression of temporal relations.

4.1 Conjunctions

-eong (엉) and *-eon* (언)

ALLOMORPHY:

- *-ang* and *-an* (vowel harmony; see chapter 2, section 4.2.4)
- *-ng* and *-n* after a stem ending in *a*: *ka-ng/ka-n* (캉/칸) 'burn'
- either *-ng/n* or *-yeong/yeon* after a stem ending in *e* or *ae*: *me-ng/ me-n* (멩/멘) or *me-yeong/me-yeon* (메영/메연) 'pull'
- *-yeong* and *-yeon* after a stem ending in *i* or *aw*: *haw-yeong/ haw-yeon* (ᄒᆼ영/ᄒᆼ연) 'do'

STEM TYPE: Bare.

USAGE: Expresses the relationship between overlapping or sequential actions. The contrast between *-eong* and *-eon* appears to be disappearing, and the distinctions that remain are subtle and variable. A number of different generalizations have been put forward in work by J.-h. Kang (1988), S.-N. Lee (1957), and S.-J. Song (2011), among others. The judgments reported here apparently reflect the views of liberal speakers.

When both actions lie in the future, only *-eong* is allowed.

Joyeongge ta-ng   *ga-la!* (조영게 탕 가라!)

bicycle   ride-CON go-SE

'Leave riding on a bike!' (based on S.-N. Lee 1957, 164)

Aj-ang *yeowagi-haw-k-yeo.* (앚앙 여와기 ᄒᆼ켜)

sit-CON conversation-do-PROSP-SE

'I will talk while sitting.'

---

3. The noun *chawmwe* 'melon' is followed by an unpronounced copula here, consistent with the usual generalization that *i-* 'be' is realized as zero after a noun ending a vowel.

*Mulkkuleog sim-**eong**   meog-**euk**-yeo.* (물꾸럭 심엉 먹으켜)

octopus   catch-CON eat-PROSP-SE

'I will catch an octopus and eat it.'

*Bawleum bul-**eong**   gasa   geokk-eo-ji-k-yeo.* (부름 불엉 가사 거꺼지켜)

wind   blow-CON umbrella break-LV-become-PROSP-SE

'The umbrella will/may get broken because of the wind
   blowing.'

*Bingegi hayeong sim-**eong**   ga-**ng**   jal   jillu-la.*

chick   a.lot   catch-CON go-CON well raise-SE

(빙에기 하영 심엉 강 잘 질루라)

'Catch a lot of chicks and go and raise them well.'

*San-ui   ga-**ng**   nangg-eul geuchy-**ang** o-la.*[4]

mountain-DIR go-CON tree-ACC   cut-CON   come-SE

(산의 강 낭글 그챵오라)

'Go to the mountain and cut down a tree and then bring
   it back.'

*Jegi   jegi   chawlly-**eong** ga-la.* (제기제기 출령 가라)

quickly quickly prepare-CON go-SE

'Get ready quickly and go.'

In contrast, when the two actions both happen in the past, either
-eong or *-eon* can be used.

*Joyeongge ta-**n/ng**   ga-s-jeo.* (조영게 탄/탕 갓저)

bicycle   ride-CON go-PFV-SE

'I got on the bicycle and left.'

*Ileosa-**n/ng**   jilt-eos-jeo.* (일어산/일어상 질 텃저)

stand.up-CON stretch-PFV-SE

'S/he stretched while standing up.'

---

4. The *g* that shows up in the second syllable of the word for 'tree' when the case
    marker is added is reminiscent of a similar phenomenon in Middle Korean in
    which a "hidden" stem-final *g* is heard only when the following syllable begins
    with a vowel (e.g., K.-M. Lee and Ramsey 2011, 184). An apparently similar
    example involves *bas.g-eulo* (밖으로) 'to the outside,' in which a hidden *g* at the
    end of *bas* 'field' is heard when followed by a vowel (J.-W. Ko 2014, p.48).

*Haleubang nawmppi awj-**eon/eong** w-as-jeo.*

grandfather radish take-CON come-PFV-SE

(하르방 놈삐 옷언/옷엉 왓저)

'Grandfather brought (us) radishes.'

Use of either connective is also possible when the second action is ongoing (J.-h. Kang 1988, 182).

*Sonang singg-**eon/eong** ga-ms-u-da.* (소낭 싱건/싱겅 갊우다)

pine.tree plant-CON go-CONT-AH-SE

'I planted the pine tree and am going.'

The same alternation also occurs when a sentence reports consecutive actions, whether in the past or the present, as long as the second action takes place in the speaker's sight.

*Gwegi jab-**an/ang** meog-eoms-eola.* (궤기 잡안/잡앙 먹없어라)

fish catch-CON eat-CONT-SE

'(I saw) him/her eating the fish after he caught (it).'

*Gwegi jab-**an/ang** meog-eoms-in-ge.* (궤기 잡안/잡앙 먹없인게)

fish catch-CON eat-CONT-NPST-SE

'(I see) you eating the fish after you caught it.'

-go/gog (고/곡) 'and'

ALLOMORPHY: None.

STEM TYPE: Type 1 (bare, or ending in *-eos* or *-eoms* for *-go*; bare only for *-gog*).

*Geomjil me-**gog** seodab-do haw-yeos-jeo.* (검질 메곡, 서답도 ᄒ엿저)

weed pull-CON laundry-too do-PFV-SE

'I weeded (the field), and also did the laundry.'

*Neu-ne ttawl nawmppi-do meog-**gog** manongji-do*

2-PL daughter radish-too eat-CON pickled.garlic-too

meog-eoms-jeo. (느네 똘 놈삐도 먹곡, 마농지도 먹없저)

eat-CONT-SE

'Your daughter is eating radish as well as pickled garlic.'

*Seong   gingi-do sim-eoms-**go**   mulkkuleog-do sim-eoms-jeo.*
older.sibling crab-too catch-CONT-CON octopus-too   catch-CONT-SE
(성 깅이도 심없고 물꾸럭도 심없저)
'My older sibling is catching crabs as well as octopus.'

*Gongbui haw-**gog** he-ng   ga-la!* (공븨 ᄒ곡 헹 가라!)
study   do-CON do-CON go-SE
'Study first and then go!'

*Nuil-lang   tal   ta-dang meog-eum-do haw-**gog** sul-do*
tomorrow-TOP wild.berry pick-CON eat-NMLZ-too do-CON   alcohol-too
dawnggeu-ge. (닐랑 탈 타당 먹음도 ᄒ곡 술도 둥그게.)
make-SE
'Tomorrow, after picking wild berries, let's eat (some) and
    make alcohol (with others).'

4.2 Conditionals and Concessives
-dagji (닥지) 'the more...the more'
ALLOMORPHY: None.
STEM TYPE: Bare.

*Cheong-eun meog-**dagji** mas-na-da.* (청은 먹닥지 맛나다)
honey-TOP   eat-CON   taste-come.out-SE
'The more you eat honey, the more delicious it is.' (based on
    Y.-H. Park 1960, 352)

*Sonang-eun   keu-**dagji** joh-a.* (소낭은 크닥지 좋아)
pine.tree-TOP big-CON   good-SE
'The bigger the pine tree is, the better it is.' (S.-J. Song 2007, 766)

*Geul-eun   haw-**dagji** neu-n-da.* (글은 ᄒ닥지 는다)
writing-TOP do-CON   improve-NPST-SE
'The more writing you do, the better it is.'

*Nol-**dagji**   geul-eun   mos   haw-n-da.* (놀닥지 글은 못ᄒ다)
idle.away-CON writing-TOP cannot do-NPST-SE
'The more (you) idle time away, the more (you) cannot study.'

-di-(do) (디(도)) 'even though'

ALLOMORPHY: None.
STEM TYPE: Type 2 (ending in *-eun*).

*Cheolsu-n menal gwegi meog-neu-n-**di-do*** *jile-ga an*
Cheolsu-TOP daily meat eat-INDC-NPST-CON-even height-NOM not
k-eoms-jeo. (철순 메날 궤기 먹는디도 지레가 안 컸저)
grow-CONT-SE
'Even though Cheolsu eats meat every day, he is not getting
   taller.'

*Jawm-eun hayeong ja-ms-in-**di-do**,* *musa yeong*
sleep-TOP a.lot sleep-CONT-NPST-CON-even why like.this
jolaw-ams-in-go? [root=*jolab-*] (줌은 하영 잢인디도, 무사 영 조라왎인고?)
sleepy-CONT-NPST-SE
'Even though I'm sleeping a lot, why am I so sleepy?'

*I-makke-n ji-n-**di**,* *jeo-geo-n* *jjawlleu-da.*
this-bat-TOP long-NPST-CON that-thing-TOP short-SE
(이 마껜 진디, 저건 쫄르다)
'This bat is long, but that one is short.'

*Jeo gudeul-eun daws-in-**di**,* *i-dui-n* *mag eol-da.*
that room-TOP warm-NPST-CON this-place-TOP very cold-SE
(저 구들은 돗인디, 이뒨 막 얼다)
'That room is warm, but here is very cold.'

-(eu)geollang ((으)걸랑) 'if'

ALLOMORPHY:

- *-(i)geollang* after a stem that ends in *s*, *j*, or *ch*
- *-(u)geollang* after a stem ending in a labial consonant
- *-geollang* after a stem that ends in a vowel or *l*

STEM TYPE: Type 1 (bare, or ending in *-eos*, *-eoms*, or *-euk*).

*Chogi ta-**geollang** hawssawl gawj-eong o-la.*
mushroom pick-CON a.little take-CON come-SE
(초기 타걸랑 ᄒ쓸 궂엉오라)
'If (you) pick some mushrooms, bring some.'

*Bojegi   badang-i ga-**geollang** jawch-ang ga-la.*

fisherman sea-LOC   go-CON   follow-CON go-SE

(보제기 바당이 가걸랑 조앙 가라)

'If the fisherman is on the way to the sea, follow him.'

*Abang jawnyag mawn meog-eos-(**i**)**geollang** sang seoll-eo-bul-la.*

father   dinner   all   eat-PFV-CON   table clean-LV-COMPL-SE

(아방 조냑 몬 먹엇(이)걸랑 상 설러불라)

'If father ate all his dinner, clean up the table.'

A future interpretation arises when *-geollang* is replaced by *-keollang*, which appears to incorporate the prospective marker *-(eu)k* (see chapter 6, section 2.3).

*Gingi meog-(**eu**)**keollang** gaekkaws-deole ga-ng   sim-eong   o-la.*

crab   eat-PROSP.CON   seashore-DIR   go-CON catch-CON come-SE

(깅이 먹(으)컬랑 개깟더레 강 심엉오라)

'If you want to eat crab, go to the seashore and catch some.'

*Gaekkaws-ui ga-**keollang**   iljjigengi chawlli-la.*

sea.shore-DIR go-PROSP.CON early   get.ready-SE

(개깟의 가컬랑 일찍엥이 출리라)

'If you want to go to the seashore, get ready early.'

-(eu)geon ((으)건) 'if, when'

ALLOMORPHY:

- *-(i)geon* after a stem that ends in *s, j, or ch*
- *-(u)geon* after a stem that ends in a labial consonant
- *-geon* after a stem that ends in a vowel or *l*

STEM TYPE: Type 1 (bare, or ending in *-eos, -eoms, or -euk*).

*Gingi-l   meog-**geon** mulkkuleog-eul meog-**geon** na-n*

crab-ACC eat-CON   octopus-ACC   eat-CON   1SG-TOP

molleu-n-da. (깅일 먹건 물꾸럭을 먹건 난 몰른다)

not.know-NPST-SE

'I don't care if/whether you eat crab or octopus.'

Sawdab mawn haw-yeos-(i)geon buleumssi haw-la.

laundry all do-PFV-CON errand do-SE

(ᄉ답 ᄆ ᄒ엿(이)건 부름씨 ᄒ라)

'If you have finished all the laundry, do the errand.'

Jiseul bonggeu-geon hawssawl te.u-la. (지슬 봉그건 ᄒ쏼 테우라)

potato gather-CON some distribute-SE

'When you gather the potatoes, distribute some of them.'

Dawlbengi da jus-eos-(i)geon ileosa-ng geol-la.

snail all gather-PFV-CON stand.up-CON walk-SE

(둘벵이 다 줏엇(이)건 일어상 걸라)

'If you have gathered all the snails, then get up and let's go.'

Eodug-geon bul ssa-b-seo. (어둑건 불 쌉서)

dark-CON light turn.on-AH-SE

'Turn the light on if it is dark.'

Sigge chawly-eoms-(i)geon na bulleu-la.

ancestral.rites prepare-CONT-CON 1SG call-SE

(식게 출렀(이)건 나 불르라)

'If (you) are preparing for the ancestral rites, call me.'

Nal daws-(i)geon joyeongge ta-ng badang-deole ga-sa-k-yeo.

day warm-CON bicycle ride-CON sea-DIR go-OBLG-PROSP-SE

(날 둣(이)건 조영게 탕 바당더레 가사켜)

'If the day is warm, (I) must go to the ocean by bicycle.'

Ga-ng bw-a-ng haleubang jingsim meog-eoms-(i)geon

go-CON see-LV-CON grandfather lunch eat-CONT-CON

chawlle-lado deo anne-la.

side.dish-even.just more give-SE

(강 봥 하르방 징심 먹없(이)건 출레라도 더 안네라)

'If grandfather is eating lunch when you get there, serve more
side dishes.'

A future interpretation arises when *-geon* is replaced by *-keon,* which
appears to incorporate the prospective marker *-(eu)k* (see chapter 6,
section 2.3).

*Gaekkaws-deole dawl-**eukeon**   jegi   chawlli-la.*

seashore-DIR   run-PROSP.CON quickly get.ready-SE

(개껏더레 돌으컨 제기 출리라)

'If you intend to go to the seashore, get ready quickly.'

-*(eu)godaena/(eu)godaego* ((으)고대나/(으)고대고) 'even if/whether or not'

ALLOMORPHY:

• -*(i)godaena* after a stem that ends in *s, j, or ch*
• -*(u)godaena* after a stem that ends in a labial consonant
• -*godaena* after a stem that ends in a vowel or *l*

STEM TYPE: Type 1 (bare, or ending in -*eos* or -*eoms*).

*Bi-ga   o-**godaena** naechang-ui   ga-ge.* (비가 오고대나 내창의 가게)

rain-NOM come-CON river(bed)-DIR go-SE

'Let's go to the river (bed) whether or not it rains.'

*Seong-i   an ga-**godaego** neu-man ga-la.*

elder.sibling-NOM not go-CON   2SG-only go-SE

(성이 안 가고대고 느만 가라)

'Even if your older sibling does not go, you should go alone.'

*Neu bab   meog-eos-**(i)godaego** i-geo-do   hawkkom deo*

2SG   meal eat-PFV-CON   this-thing-too a.little   more

meog-eula. (느 밥 먹엇(이)고대고 이거도 ㅎ끔 더 먹으라)

eat-SE

'Even though you have eaten a meal, eat a little more of
    this too.'

-*(eu)jeoman* ((으)저만)/*(eu)juman* ((으)주만) 'although, even though'

ALLOMORPHY:

• -*(i)jeoman* after a stem that ends in *s, j, or ch*
• -*(u)jeoman* after a stem that ends in a labial consonant
• -*jeoman* after a stem that ends in a vowel or *l*

STEM TYPE: Type 1 (bare, or ending in -*eos* or -*eoms*).

USAGE: Indicates a contrast between two clauses; often accompanied by the apparent topic marker -*eun*.

*Na-sa   babjuli   jal sim-**juman**-eun asi-n*

1SG-NOM dragonflies well catch-CON-TOP younger.brother-TOP

mos   sim-na. (나사 밥주리 잘 심주만은 아신 못 심나)

cannot catch-SE

'Although I can catch a lot of dragonflies, my younger brother
   can't.'

*Nunengi   hayeong meog-eos-**juman**-eun ije-do   be-ga*

scorched.rice a.lot   eat-PFV-CON-TOP   now-even stomach-NOM

gawlleu-den   he-la. (누넹이 하영 먹엇주만은 이제도 베가 골르덴 헤라)

hungry-CON do-SE

'Even though s/he ate a lot of scorched rice, s/he said that
   s/he is still hungry.'

*Geu   seongje-deol-eun unyeongpas-deole   jawju ga-ms-**juman***

those sibling-PL-TOP   vegetable.garden-DIR often go-CONT-CON

na-n   ani ga-n-da. (그 성제덜은 우녕팟더레 ᄌ주 갌주만 난 아니 간다)

1SG-TOP not go-NPST-SE

'Although those siblings go to the vegetable garden frequently,
   I don't.'

*Geu asi-n   Dakkeune-deole ga-lgeo-**juman**-eun na-n*

that younger.brother-TOP Dakkeune-DIR   go-FUT-CON-TOP   1SG-TOP

ai   ga-lgeo-yeo. (그 아신 다끄네더레 갈거주만 난 아이 갈 거여)

not go-FUT-SE

'Even though younger brother is going to Dakkeune village, I
   will not go.'

-eumin (으민) 'if/when'

ALLOMORPHY:

- *-imin* after a stem that ends in *s, j, or ch*
- *-umin* after a stem that ends in a labial consonant
- *-min* after a stem that ends in a vowel or *l*

STEM TYPE: Type 1 (bare, or ending in *-eos* or *-eoms*).

*Menal gyeong   il   haw-**min** buje   dwe-k-yeo.*
daily   like.that work do-CON   rich.person become-PROSP-SE
(메날 경 일 ᄒ민 부제 뒈켜)
'If (you) work like that every day, you will become rich.'

*Badang-deole ga-lgeo-**min** hawnjeo chawlli-la.*
sea-DIR   go-FUT-CON quickly   get.ready-SE
(바당더레 갈거민 ᄒ저 출리라)
'If (you) are going to the seashore, get ready quickly.'

*Nal daws-**imin** sedab   dam   u-tui   neol-la.*
day warm-CON laundry fence top-on hang-SE
(날 돗이민 세답 담우틔 널라)
'If the weather is warm, hang the laundry on top of the fence.'

*Tongsi-e   denggy-eo-w-as-**imin** son   kawlkawli sichi-la.*
toilet-LOC go-LV-come-PFV-CON hand cleanly   wash-SE
(통시에 뎅겨왓이민 손 콜콜이 시치라)
'If you have been to the toilet, wash your hands clean.'

*Ma-chi-**min**   gogseog mawn sseog-eum deu-n-da.*
rainy.season-hit-CON grain   all   rot-NMLZ enter-NPST-SE
(마치민 곡석 ᄆ 썩음 든다)
'When the rainy season begins, all the grains completely rot.'

*Hanui-bawleum bul-**min**   eol-eong san-ui   mos   ga-ju.*
north-wind   blow-CON cold-CON mountain-DIR cannot go-SE
(하늬ᄇ름 불민 얼엉 산의 못 가주)
'When/if the north wind blows, we cannot go to the mountain
    because it is cold.'

*Mileus w-as-**imin**   na-yeong hawndi yewag haw-yeos-ilgeo-n-di?*
early   come-PFV-CON   1SG-with together talk   do-PFV-FUT-NPST-SE
(미릇 왓이민 나영 ᄒ은디 예왁 ᄒ엿일건디)
'If you had come early, (you) could have talked with me
    together.'

-eun/neun/eul-chulug (추룩) 'appearance (as if)'

ALLOMORPHY: There is variation for *-eun* and *-eul*; see section 2.
STEM TYPE: Type 1 (bare, or ending in *-eos* or *-eoms*).

*Jai-n   ga-l   **chulug**   chawlly-eos-in-ge.*
3SG-TOP go-FUT.CON appearance prepare-PFV-NPST-SE
(자인 갈 추룩 출럇인게)
'(I see that) s/he has prepared as if s/he will go.'

*Seong-eun   gongbui haw-neu-n   **chulug**   gudeul-e*
older.sibling-TOP study   do-INDC-NPST.CON appearance room-LOC
si-n-ge. (성은 공븨ᄒᆞ는 추룩 구들에 신게)
be-NPST-SE

'(I see that) your older sibling is in his/her room as if s/he is
    studying.'

*Mansu nang singgeu-n   **chulug**   he-ms-jeo.*
Mansu tree   plant-PST.CON appearance do-CONT-SE
(만수 낭 싱근 추룩 헸져)
'Mansu is pretending as if he planted a tree.'

4.3 Reason and Purpose

-eobunan (어부난)/*-eononan* (어노난) 'because'

ALLOMORPHY:

- *-abunan/-anonan* (vowel harmony; see chapter 2, section 4.2.4)
- *-bunan/-nonan* after a stem that ends in a vowel

STEM TYPE: To be determined.

*Bawleum bul-**eobunan** sangbang-i   gudum-i sawmppag*
wind   blow-CON   living.room-LOC dust-NOM fully
deul-eo-w-as-jeo. (ᄇᆞ름 불어부난 상방이 구둠이 솜빡 들어왓져)
enter-LV-come-PFV-SE
'Because the wind blows, a lot of dust came into the living room.'

*Dawgmawleub ap-**anonan**,   bas-dui-l   ga-ji-l   mos*
knee   painful-CON field-place-ACC go-NMLZ-ACC cannot
he-ms-jeo. (독무릅 아파노난 밧딀 가질 못헸저)
do-CONT-SE
'(I) haven't been able to go to the field because my knee hurts.'

The form *-lanonan* (라노난) is used if the stem is the copula *i-*.

*Sunja-ga   keun-ttawl-i-**lanonan** il   hayeong haw-yeoms-u-ge.*
Sunja-NOM big-daughter-be-CON work a.lot   do-CONT-AH-SE
(순자가 큰 똘이라노난 일 하영 ᄒ엾우게)
'Because Sunja is the eldest daughter, she works a lot.'

-(eu)gwande/(eu)gwante/(eu)gwandi ((으)관데/(으)관테/(으)관디) 'since, because' (Y.-H. Park 1960, 376, 391; S.-J. Song 2007, 745)

ALLOMORPHY:

- *-(i)gwande* after a stem that ends in *s, j, or ch*
- *-(u)gwande* after a stem that ends in a labial consonant
- *-gwande* after a stem that ends in a vowel or *l*

STEM TYPE: Type 1 (bare, or ending in *-eos* or *-eoms*).

*Neu-ne manong jal   meog-**gwande** gawj-eo-w-as-jeo.*
2-PL   garlic   well eat-CON   take-LV-come-PFV-SE
(느네 마농 잘 먹관데 ᄀ어왓저)
'Since you guys eat a lot of garlic, I brought it here.'

*Mansu abang bab   meog-eoms-(i)**gwande** na-n*
Mansu father meal eat-CONT-CON   1SG-TOP
na-w-a-bi-s-jeo. (만수아방 밥 먹엾(이)관데 난 나와빗저)
out-come-LV-COMPL-PFV-SE
'Because Mansu's father was eating a meal, I came out.'

Sunja ju-jen   gamjeo   awj-eo-ga-n   bo-nan   bab

Sunja give-CON sweet.potato take-LV-go-CON see-CON meal

meog-eos-(i)gwande, awj-eong   w-a-bi-s-jeo.

eat-PFV-CON   take-CONT come-LV-COMPL-PFV-SE

(순자 주젠 감저 옺어간 보난, 밥 먹엇(이)관데, 옺엉 와빗저)

'When I brought sweet potatoes for Sunja, (I noticed that) she
   had eaten her meal so I brought them back.'

Bo-nan halmang(-i)-gwande   gob-a-bul-eos-u-da

see-CON grandmother(-be)-CON hide-LV-COMPL-PFV-AH-SE

(보난 할망(이)관데, 곱아불엇우다)

'Since I saw that it was grandmother, I hid.'

-eukabuden (으카부덴) 'I am worried about X, so Y.'

ALLOMORPHY:

- *-ikabuden* after a stem that ends in *s, j, or ch*
- *-ukabuden* after a stem that ends in a labial consonant
- *-kabuden* after a stem that ends in a vowel or *l* (and, idiosyncrati-
  cally, after the root *meog* 'eat')

STEM TYPE: Type 1 (bare, or ending in *-eos* or *-eoms*).

San-deole sonang-ppulli deul-eo-ga-kabuden sonang

grave-DIR pine.tree-root enter-LV-go-CON   pine.tree

geuchy-a-bul-eoms-u-ge. (산더레 소낭뿔리 들어가카부덴 소낭 그챠불없우게)

cut-LV-COMPL-CONT-AH-SE

'Because (I worry) the pine tree roots might get into the grave,
   (I) am cutting the pine tree.'

-(eu)kude ((으)쿠데) / (eu)kute ((으)쿠테) 'since, because'
(Y.-H. Park 1960, 349; P.-h. Hyun et al. 2009, 598)

ALLOMORPHY:

- *-(i)kude* after a stem that ends in *s, j, or ch*
- *-(u)kude* after a stem that ends in a labial consonant
- *-kude* after a stem that ends in a vowel or *l*

STEM TYPE: Type 1 (bare, or ending in *-eos* or *-eoms*).

Keun ttawl   Seoweol ga-ms-(i)kude, kawbdesani bonae-s-jeo.

big   daughter Seoul   go-CONT-CON   garlic   send-PFV-SE

(큰 뚤 서월 갆(이)쿠데 쿱데사니 보냇저)

'Because (my) oldest daughter was going to Seoul, I packed
  garlic and sent (it with her to Seoul).'

Abang Seoweol ga-s-(i)kude, bangdui sa-ng   o-len   he-s-jeo.

father Seoul   go-PFV-CON   toy   buy-CON come-CON do-PFV-SE

(아방 서월 갓(이)쿠데, 방듸 상 오렌 헷저)

'Since father went to Seoul, (I asked him to) buy a toy.'

Mansu-ga   gawse   chawj-(i)kude begjang u-ui   bo-len   he-s-jeo.

Mansu-NOM scissors look.for-CON   closet   top-LOC look-CON do-PFV-SE

(만수가 ᄀ세 촞(이)쿠데, 벡장 우의 보렌 햇저)

'Since Mansu was looking for the scissors, I told (him) to look
  at the top of the closet.'

-*eule* (으레) 'for the purpose of, in order to'

ALLOMORPHY:

- -*ile* after a stem that ends in *s, j, or ch*
- -*ule* after a stem ending in a labial consonant
- -*le* after a stem ending in a vowel or *l*

STEM TYPE: Type 1 (bare, or ending in -*eos* or -*eoms*).

Mikkang nang al-le   pachi   jus-ile   ga-ms-u-da.

tangerine tree   under-LOC fallen.tangerine gather-CON go-CONT-AH-SE

(미깡낭 알레 파치 춧이레 갆우다)

'I'm going to pick up fallen tangerines under the tangerine tree.'

Mom gawm-ule ga-ms-jeo. (몸 곰우레 갆저)

body wash-CON go-CONT-SE

'(I)'m going to take a bath.'

Bas gal-le   ga-ms-jeo. (밧 갈레 갆저)

field plow-CON go-CONT-SE

'(I) am on my way to plow the field.'

Jiseul   singgeu-le ga-ge. (지슬 싱그레 가게)

potato plant-CON go-SE

'Let's go to plant potatoes.'

-eum-e (음에) 'if, since, because, due to'[5]

ALLOMORPHY:

- *-ime* after a stem that ends in *s, j, or ch*
- *-ume* after a stem that ends in a labial consonant
- *-me* after a stem that ends in a vowel or *l*

STEM TYPE: Type 1 (bare, or ending in *-eos* or *-eoms*).

USAGE: Can also be used as a sentence ender (see chapter 7, section 3.2).

*Na-ga   chawj-ik-**eum-e**   jawdeul-ji mal-la.*

1SG-NOM find-PROSP-NMLZ-due.to worry-NMLZ not.do-SE

(나가 촞이큼에 ㅈ들지 말라)

'Since I will find (it), don't worry.'

*Neu-n   mawn meog-eos-**im-e**   ileosa-la!* (는 믄 먹엇임에 일어사라)

2SG-TOP all   eat-PFV-NMLZ-due.to stand.up-SE

'Since you've finished eating, you should stand up (and go)!'

*Na-do ije ga-ms-**im-e**   jegi   chawlli-la.*

1SG-too now go-CONT-NMLZ-due.to quickly get.ready-SE

(나도 이제 값임에 제기 출리라)

'Since I'm going now, (you should) get ready quickly.'

*Abang-eun uldam daw-ams-**im-e**   gwendang chib-ilang*

father-TOP fence stack-CONT-NMLZ-due.to relative   house-TOP

na-ga   ga-k-u-da. (아방은 울담 다왏임에 궨당칩이랑 나가 가쿠다)

1SG-NOM go-PROSP-AH-SE

'Because father is building a wall, as for my relative's house, I'll go.'

---

5. We follow N.-S. Sung (1982, 5) and J.-h. Kang (1987, 525) in taking *-eume* to consist of the nominalizer *-eum* and the postposition *-e*, as indicated in our spelling. In contrast, we spell the more fully grammaticalized evidential sentence ender *-eume* as 으메 (chapter 7, section 3.2).

Geu saleum jo-n   *saleum-i-**m**-e*   *mid-eo-bo-b-seo.*

that person good-NPST.CON person-be-NMLZ-because trust-LV-see-AH-SE

(그 사름 존 사름임에 믿어봅서)

'Because that person is a good person, you should try to trust
   him.' (based on J.-h. Kang 1987: 525)

-eunan (으난) 'because'

ALLOMORPHY:

- *-inan* after a stem that ends in *s, j,* or *ch*
- *-unan* after a stem that ends in a labial consonant
- *-nan* after a stem that ends in a vowel or *l* (in which case the
  stem-final *l* is deleted)

STEM TYPE: Type 1 (bare, or ending in *-eos* or *-eoms*).

*Yog   meog-**eunan** ul-eoms-u-ge.* (욕 먹으난 울없우게)

criticism eat-CON   cry-CONT-AH-SE

'Because s/he has been scolded, s/he is crying.'

*Eomeong ga-**nan** il-haw-yeoms-eo.* (어멍 가난 일ᄒ엾어)

mother   go-CON   work-do-CONT-SE

'Because Mom has left, (s/he) is doing the work.'

*Nal daws-as-**inan** sedab   dol   u-teule neol-ge.*

day warm-PFV-CON laundry stone top-DIR spread-SE

(날 ᄃᆞᆺ앗이난 세답 돌 우트레 널게)

'Because the weather is warm, let's spread the laundry on top
   of the stone.'

*Gasi-eomeong gingi gwe-w-ams-**inan**   i-le   o-b-seo.*

wife-mother   crab boil-CAUS-CONT-CON here-DIR come-AH-SE

(가시어멍 깅이 궤왒이난 이레 옵서)

'Because mother-in-law is boiling crabs, (please) come here.'

*Oneol san-ui   ga-lgeo-**nan** hawnjeo chawlli-la.*

today grave-DIR go-FUT-CON quickly get.ready-SE

(오널 산의 갈거난 ᄒᆞ저 출리라)

'(We) are going to the grave, so get ready quickly.'

-gola/gawla (고라/ㄱ라) 'because (maybe)'

ALLOMORPHY: None.
STEM TYPE: Mixed (bare, or ending in *-eos*, *-eoms*, or *-eun*).
USAGE: Used to express reasons.

Ga-ne mal   da gawl-as-in-gola   sogsom-he-ms-jeo.
3-PL   speech all talk-PFV-NPST-CON quiet-do-CONT-SE
(가네 말 다 굴앗인고라 속솜헸저)
'Because they may have finished talking, they are quiet.'

Ije-do   mal   gawl-ams-in-gola   mag sikkeuleo-un-ge.
now-too speech talk-CONT-NPST-CON very noisy-NPST-SE
(이제도 말 굴앖인고라 막 시끄러운게)
'(I notice that) because they may be still talking, it is very noisy.'

Ga-ne ije-sa   yewag haw-yeoms-in-gawla jeongji-seo   musin soli
3-PL   now-just talk   do-CONT-NPST-CON   kitchen-LOC some   sound
na-ms-jeo.[6] (가네 이제사 예왁ㅎ없인ㄱ라 정지서 무신 소리 낲저)
come.out-CONT-SE
'Because they may be talking now, there is some noise from the
   kitchen.'

Ga-ne bab   meog-eulgeo-n-gola sang chawly-eoms-eola.
3-PL   meal eat-FUT-NPST-CON   table prepare-CONT-SE
(가네 밥 먹을건고라 상 출렸어라)
'(I saw that) they were preparing a table because they are about
   to eat.'

4.4 Temporal

-dan (단) and *-dang* (당) 'after, while, if'

STEM TYPE: Type 1 (bare, or ending in *-eos* or *-eoms*).
USAGE: Combines with a bare stem to express the relationship
between overlapping or sequential actions. As in the case of *-eon* and
-eong (section 4.1), the contrast between *-dan* and *-dang* appears to

---

6. When *-gola* immediately follows the continuative marker, as in *yewag haw-yeom-gola*, there is no tensing.

be disappearing, and the distinctions that remain are subtle and variable. A variety of different generalizations has been put forward in work by J.-h. Kang (1988), S.-N. Lee (1957), and S.-J. Song (2011), among others. The judgments reported here may reflect the views of liberal speakers.

When the actions lie in the future, only -*dang* is allowed.

*Hawssawl gongbui haw-**dang** buleumssi haw-la.*
a.little   study   do-CON   errand   do-SE
(ᄒ쌀 공븨ᄒ당 부름씨ᄒ라)
'Do the errand after studying for a little.'

*Ganse-haw-**dang** nom-sindi guche-bo-n-da.* (간세ᄒ당 놈신디 구체본다)
idle-do-CON   other-DAT   embarrassment-see-NPST-SE
'If you get lazy, you could be embarrassed.'

*Neomui   deulagki-**dang** bal-mogegi gawmokkeu-ju.*
too.much jump-CON   foot-neck   sprain-SE
(너믜 들락키당 발모게기 ᄀ모끄주)
'If you jump too much, (you could) sprain your ankle.'

*I-geo   neomui ole   sawlm-**dang** ka-bu-n-da-i.*
this-thing too   long boil-CON   burn-COMPL-NPST-SE-EMPH
(이거 너믜 오레 숢당 카분다이)
'If you boil it too long, it could get completely burned.'

*Gyeong   jegi dawd-**dang** pudeoji-n-da.* (경 제기 돋당 푸더진다)
like.that fast run-CON   fall.down-NPST-SE
'If (you) run that fast, (you) could fall down.'

*U-nyeog-chib-uiseo   nol-**dang**   ga-k-yeo.* (우녁칩의서 놀당 가켜)
above-side-house-LOC hang.out-CON   go-PROSP-SE
'I will go after hanging out at the (neighbor's) mountainside
    house.'

In contrast, when the two actions both happen in the past, either -*dang* or -*dan* can be used, according to many speakers. (However, it also seems to be the case that some speakers permit only -*dan*.)

Mansu heoteu-n   *dui beli-**dang/dan** pudeojy-eos-jeo.*
Mansu pointless-NPST.CON place see-CON   fall.down-PFV-SE
(만수 허튼 듸 베리당/단 푸더졋저)
'Mansu fell down while his eyes were wandering.'

Yecheong   *kong gawl-**dan/dang** u-nyeog-chib-ui*   *ga-s-jeo.*
married.woman bean grind-CON   above-side-house-DIR go-PFV-SE
(예청 콩 굴단/당 우녁칩의 갓저)
'The woman was grinding beans, and then she went to the
    (neighbor's) mountainside house.'

*Ogoseng-i aj-as-**dan/dang** w-as-u-da.* (오고셍이 앚앗단/당 왓우다)
still-ADV   sit-PFV-CON   come-PFV-AH-SE
'(I) sat still and then came back.'

Nal-do eo-n-di   *yallu-n*   *os*   *ib-eos-**dan/dang** goppul*
day-too cold-NPST-CON thin-NPST.CON clothes wear-PFV-CON   cold
deul-ly-eos-jeo. (날도 언디 얄룬 옷 입엇단/당 고뿔 들렷저)
enter-CAUS-PFV-SE
'Because I wore thin clothes even though the weather was cold,
    I got a cold.'

Similarly, when the first action is completed, and the second action
is ongoing, *-dan* and *-dang* can be used interchangeably.

I-dui-seo   *yewag-haw-**dang/dan** ga-ms-u-da.*
this-place-LOC conversation-do-CON go-CONT-AH-SE
(이듸서 예왁ᄒ당/단 감우다)
'I am leaving after talking here.'

-dangeune (당은에) / *dageune* (다근에)

ALLOMORPHY: None.
STEM TYPE: Type 1 (bare, or ending in *-eos* or *-eoms*).
USAGE: Expresses an action that occurs after the completion of
another action, with the possible implication that the second action
is caused by the first action. (Some speakers allow only *-dageune* in
these patterns.)

*Cheolsu deulleogki-**dangeune/dageune** pudeojy-eo-bul-eon.*

Cheolsu jump-CON   fall.down-LV-COMPL-PST

(철수 들럭키당은에/다근에 푸더져불언)

'While jumping, Cheolsu fell down.'

*Mansu abang-eun mengtengi jeol-**dangeune/dageune***

Mansu father-TOP basket   weave-CON

eos-eo-jy-eos-in-ge. (만수 아방은 멩텡이 절당은에/다근에 엇어겻인게)

not.be-LV-become-PFV-NPST-SE

'(I notice that) Mansu's father disappeared while he was
     weaving the basket.'

*Neu sswette gyeong   gawj-eong denggi-**dangeune/dageune***

2SG key   like.that have-CON walk.around-CON

ij-eo-bu-n-da-i. (느 쒜떼 경 곶엉 뎅기당은에/다근에 잊어분다이)

lose-LV-COMPL-NPST-SE-EMPH

'While carrying around your key like that, you could lose it.'

*Gingi sim-eos-**dangeune** son   jawb-ji-n-da.* (깅이 심엇당은에 손 줍진다)

crab catch-PFV-CON   hand pinch-PASS-NPST-SE

'If you caught a crab, you could get pinched.'

-eon-ge (언게) 'noticed/experienced..., and then'

ALLOMORPHY:

- *-an-ge* (vowel harmony; see chapter 2, section 4.2.4)
- *-n-ge* after a stem ending in *a: ka-n-ge* (칸게) 'was burning'
- either *-n-ge* or *-yeon-ge* after a stem ending in *e* or *ae: we-n-ge*
  (웬게) or *we-yeon-ge* (웨연게) 'was shouting'
- *-yeon-ge* after a stem ending in *i* or *aw: haw-yeon-ge* (ㅎ연게) 'was
  doing'

STEM TYPE: Type 1 (bare, or ending in *-eos, -eoms,* or *-euk*).

USAGE: This combination of the past tense suffix *-eon* and the
evidential marker *-ge* is used as a connective to indicate evidentiality,
with the semantic effects previously discussed in chapter 6, section 3,
and in chapter 7, section 3.2.

*Acheog-eun   hawssol eol-**eon-ge**   he-tteu-nan   mag daws-da.*
morning-TOP little   cold-PST-CON sun-rise-CON very warm-SE
(아척은 흣쏠 얼언게 헤뜨난 막 둣다)

'(I noticed/felt) it was a little cold in the morning, but then
   after the sun rose (it) is very warm.'

*Gai inchigi penji ig-**eon-ge**-man   ul-eo-bu-b-di-da.*
3SG earlier letter read-PST-CON-only cry-LV-COMPL-AH-EVI-SE
(가이 인칙이 펜지 익언게만 울어붑디다)

'Earlier, (I saw that) s/he just read the letter, then (s/he) cried.'

*Mansu abang-eun dosegi geos ju-eoms-**eon-ge**   Mansu-n*
Mansu father-TOP pig   food give-CONT-PST-CON Mansu-TOP
eodui ga-b-di-ga? (만수 아방은 도세기 것 주없언게 만순 어듸 갑디가?)
where go-AH-EVI-SE

'(I saw that) Mansu's father was feeding the pig, but then
   where did Mansu go (did you see)?'

Mansu-n   duli-n   ttae jile-ga   mag
Mansu-TOP young-NPST.CON time height-NOM very
*keu-k-eul-**an-ge**   hawneosi an k-eos-eola.*
tall-PROSP-FUT-PST-CON so.much not grow-PFV-SE
(만순 두린 때 지레가 막 크클안게 흔엇이 안 컷어라)

'(I noticed that) when Mansu was a child, it seemed that he
   would grow tall, but then (I saw that) he did not grow tall
   at all.'

-eongeune (엉은에) / *eogeune* (어근에) **'and then'** (S.-J. Song 2007, 878)

ALLOMORPHY:

- *-angeune* (vowel harmony; see chapter 2, section 4.2.4)
- *-ngeune* after a vowel

STEM TYPE: Type 1 (bare, or ending in *-eos* or *-eoms*).
USAGE: Indicates that one event in a sequence of events ends and
is followed by another.

*Joban   meog-**eongeune/eogeune*** *naechang-ui   ga-ge.*
breakfast eat-CON   river(bed)-DIR go-SE
(조반 먹엉은에/먹어근에 내창의 가게)
'Let's go to the river(bed) after eating breakfast.'

*Sawdab haw-**yeongeune/yeogeune*** *w-as-u-da.*
laundry do-CON   come-PFV-AH-SE
(ᄉ답ᄒ영은에/ᄒ여근에 왓우다)
'(I) came after doing the laundry.'

-*eumeong* (으멍) 'while, although'

ALLOMORPHY:

- -*imeong* after a stem ends in *s, j,* or *ch*
- -*umeong* after a stem that ends in a labial consonant
- -*meong* after a stem that ends in a vowel or sometimes *l*

STEM TYPE: Type 1 (bare, or ending in -*eos* or -*eoms*).

*Yeongi-yeong mal   gawl-(**eu**)**meong** jib-i   ga-s-jeo.*
Yeongi-with speech say-CON   home-DIR go-PFV-SE
(영이영 말 굴(으)멍 집이 갓저)
'I went home while talking with Yeongi.'

*Baleu   chab-eule ga-**meong** jolag   as-ang   ga-s-u-da.*[7]
seafood catch-CON go-CON   small.basket have-CON go-PFV-AH-SE
(바르 찹으레 가멍 조락 앗앙 갓우다)
'While going to catch seafood, I brought a small basket.'

*Si-e   ga-lgeo-**meong** musa gyeong   mongke-ms-in-i?*
city-to go-FUT-CON   why like.that take.so.long-CONT-NPST-SE
(시에 갈거멍 무사 경 몽퀘인이?)
'Why are you taking so long even though you are going to the city?'

---

7. The intial consonant of the verb is aspirated because of a "hidden *h*" at the end of *baleu;* see chapter 2, section 4.2.1.

*Menal unyeongpas-dui ga-ms-**imeong** geomjil-do an*

everyday vegetable.garden-place go-CONT-CON weed-even not

me-s-eo? (메날 우녕팟듸 값이멍 검질도 안멧어?)

pull-PFV-SE

'Although you are going to the vegetable garden every day, haven't you weeded it?'

Noun + *huje*; V root + *-eun huje* (N 후제/V은 후제) 'after'

ALLOMORPHY:

- *-in huje* after a stem that ends in *s, j,* or *ch*
- *-un huje* after a stem that ends in a labial consonant
- *-n huje* after a stem that ends in a vowel or *l*

*Naj **huje**-lang gingi sim-ule ga-ge.* (낮 후제랑 깅이 심우레 가게)

noon after-TOP crab catch-CON go-SE

'Let's go catch crabs in the afternoon.'

*Buleumssi haw-n **huje** daejugppulegi singgeu-la.*

errand do-PST.CON after corn plant-SE

(부름씨 혼 후제 대죽뿌레기 싱그라)

'Plant the corn after doing the errand.'

Noun + *jeon*; Verb root + *-gi jeon* (N 전/V기 전) 'before'

ALLOMORPHY: None.

*Seol **jeon-i** sedab da he-sa-k-yeo.*

New.Year's.Day before-LOC laundry all do-OBLG-PROSP-SE

(설 전이 세답 다 헤사켜)

'(I) should do all the laundry before New Year's Day.'

In the next example, the suffix *-gi* converts a verb into a noun, to which *jeon* is then added.

*Awmong-haw-**gi jeon-i** chaebi jal haw-la.*

move-do-NMLZ before-LOC preparation well do-SE

(오몽ᄒ기 전이 채비 잘 ᄒ라)

'Before you leave, prepare well.'

5. Discourse Markers

Discourse markers, which are typically expressed as sentence-initial adverbials in Jejueo, serve to organize and clarify the flow of speech by indicating the relationship between sentences, as well as the speaker's attitude and intent.

5.1 Conjunctive

Gegog/gego (게곡/게고) **'and, also'**

>*Na bas-dui   ga-ms-ime   hawnjeo joban   meog-eula.* **Gegog**
>1SG field-place go-CONT-CON quickly   breakfast eat-SE   also
>
>*sedab   he-ms-ila-i.* (나 밧듸 갉이메 혼저 조반 먹으라. 게곡 세답 헸이라이)
>laundry do-CONT-SE-EMPH
>
>'I am going to the field, so eat breakfast quickly. Also, start doing the laundry.'

Gyeonghawgo (g) (경ᄒ고/경ᄒ곡) **'and, in addition'**

>*Hwag ileosa-ng   buleumssi haw-la.* ***Gyeong-haw-gog****, gwegi*
>at.once stand.up-CON errand   do-SE   like.that-do-and   meat
>
>*hawssawl gawj-eong o-la.*
>a.little   have-CON   come-SE
>
>(확 일어상 부름씨 ᄒ라. 경ᄒ곡 궤기 ᄒ쏠 궂엉 오라)
>
>'Stand up at once and do an errand. And bring a little meat here.'

>*Na-n   jang-e   ga-n   kobdesani-yeong nawmppi*
>1SG-TOP market-DIR go-CON garlic-and   radish
>
>*sa-w-as-jeo.   **Gyeong-haw-gog**, gasi-abang-eun dos-gwegi*
>buy-come-PFV-SE like.that-do-and   wife-father-TOP pig-meat
>
>*hayeong sa-w-as-jeo.*
>a.lot   buy-come-PFV-SE
>
>(난 장에간 콥데사니영 눔삐 사왓저. 경ᄒ곡 가시아방은 돗궤기 하영 사왓저.)
>
>'I went to a market and bought some garlic and radish. In addition, father-in-law bought a lot of pork.'

5.2 Contrastive

Daelyeog(eulo) (대력(으로)) 'instead'

> ***Daelyeog*** *neu-ga   haw-la.* (대력, 느가 ᄒ라)
> instead   2SG-NOM do-SE
> 'Instead, you'd better do it.'

Doliyeo (도리여) 'to the contrary, instead'

> *Gyeong-haw-dang* ***doliyeo*** *neu-ga   danghaw-neu-n*
> like.that-do-CON   instead 2SG-NOM suffer-INDC-NPST.CON
> *su-ga   is-jeo.* (경ᄒ당 도리여 느가 당ᄒ는 수가 잇저)
> possibility-NOM be-SE
> 'If you keep doing that, you could be hurt instead.'

Gemulo(sa) (게무로(사)) 'no way, nonetheless'

> *Jile-ga   jjawlleu-juman,* ***gemulo-sa,***   *i   nang-do mos*
> height-NOM short-CON   however-really this tree-even cannot
> *ssa-k-eun-ya?* (지레가 쫄르주만, 게무로사 이 낭도 못 싸큰야?)
> cut-PROSP-NPST-SE
> 'Although s/he is short, can't s/he cut down even this tree?'

> ***Gemulo*** *eos-den   haw-k-yeo.* (게무로 엇덴 ᄒ켜)
> no.way   not.be-CON do-PROSP-SE
> 'There is no way (s/he) will say no.'

Genajeona (게나저나) 'anyway, by the way, anyhow'

> ***Genajeona,*** *swindali-na hawn sabal deuleussa-la.*
> anyway   swindali-just one   bowl drink-SE
> (게나저나, 쉰다리나 ᄒ 사발 드르싸라)
> 'Anyhow, just drink a bowl of *swindali*.' (*Swindali* is a fermented
>   rice beverage.)

> ***Genajeona*** *gopang-ui   jegi   ga-ng bo-la.*
> by.the.way storeroom-DIR quickly go-CON see-SE
> (게나저나 고팡의 제기 강 보라)
> 'By the way, go to the storeroom quickly and check.'

Gyeonghawndi (경훈디) 'but, however'

Gyeong-haw-n-di   *neu-ne seong*   *mes*   *sawl-go?*
like.that-do-NPST-CON 2-PL   older.sibling how.many year-SE
(경훈디 느네 성 멧 술고?)
'However, how old is your older sibling?'

Gyeonghedo/gyeonghawyeodo (경혜도/경후여도) 'but, despite, however, nonetheless'

Gyeong-he-do   *jal*   *sal-a-ji-n-da.* (경혜도 잘 살아진다)
like.that-do-even well live-LV-become-NPST-SE
'Despite that, you can live well.'

Gyeonghawjuman (경후주만) 'but, however, although'

Mansu gongbui hayeong haw-yeos-ju. ***Gyeong-haw-juman*** *jeomsu-ga*
Mansu study   a.lot   do-PFV-SE   like.that-do-CON   score-NOM
an   na-w-an-ge. (만수 공븨 하영 후엿주. 경후주만 점수가 안 나완게)
not out-come-PST-EMPH
'Mansu has studied hard. But his grades did not come out (well).'

Tawnage gawlabomin/tawlo gawleumin/tawnage gawdnenhawmin (투나게 골아보민/투로 골으민/투나게 골넨후민) 'to put it differently, that is, in other words'

Taw-na-ge   ***gawl-a-bo-min*** *neu-ga*   *jillung*
difference-come.out-ADV say-LV-try-CON 2SG-NOM best
yawmang-ji-da. (투나게 골아보민 느가 질룽 우망지다)
smart-be-SE
'To put it differently, you are the smartest.'

Yakan (야칸) 'anyway, by the way, anyhow'

Yakan, *uli-ga*   *mawncheo* *ga-ge-masseum.* (야칸, 우리가 문처 가게마씀)
anyway 1PL-NOM first   go-SE-AH.SE
'Anyway, let's go first.'

5.3 Reason and Purpose

Genan (게난) 'therefore, so'

Genan *gasi-eomeong-i   mawn gawl-a-bul-eos-ju-ge.*

so   wife-mother-NOM all   say-LV-COMPL-PFV-SE-EMPH

(게난 가시어멍이 믄 골아불엇주게)

'So, mother-in-law has told everything.'

Gyeonghawnan (경ᄒᆞ난) 'therefore, so, that's why, because of'

Gyeong-haw-nan   *jal   seoll-eo-bul-la.* (경ᄒᆞ난 잘 설러불라)

like.that-do-because well clean.up-LV-COMPL-SE

'Therefore, clean up well.'

Seong-eun   neujigi amawng-haw-yeos-ju. **Gyeong-haw-nan**

older.sibling-TOP late   move-do-PFV-SE   like.that-do-because

neuj-eos-ju-ge. (성은 느직이 ᄋᆞ뭉ᄒᆞ엿주. 경ᄒᆞ난 늦엇주게)

late-PFV-SE-EMPH

'My older sibling had left late. That's why he was late.'

Gyeonghebunan (경헤부난) 'because of that'

Gai ttawsi teol-eo-jy-eos-den-yang.   **Gyeong-he-bu-nan**

3SG again fall-LV-become-PFV-CON-EMPH like.that-do-COMPL-because

bue-man   nae-ms-ju. (가이 뜨시 털어졋덴양. 경헤부난 부에만 냇주)

anger-only come.out-CONT-SE

'He failed again, you know. That's why he is just getting angry.'

5.4 Conditional

Gemin (게민) 'if, then'

Gemin, *eotteong haw-neu-n-i?* (게민 어떵 ᄒᆞ는이?)

then   how   do-INDC-NPST-SE

'Then, what shall (we) do?'

Gyeonghawmin (경ᄒᆞ민) 'if so, so then'

Gawppul deul-eos-in-ge.   **Gyeong-haw-min**   *o-ji*   *mal-la.*

cold   enter-PFV-NPST-SE. like.that-do-because come-NMLZ not.do-SE

(ᄀᆞ뿔 들엇인게. 경ᄒᆞ민 오지 말라)

'You have a cold. So then, do not come.'

Gyeong-haw-min,   *jegi*   *o-la-i.* (경ㅎ민, 제기 오라이)
like.that-do-because quickly come-SE-EMPH
'If so, you'd better come quickly.'

5.5 Temporal

Mawncheom/mawnyeo (ᄆ첨/ᄆ여) 'first of all'

Mawncheom, *nang ssa-le*   *ga-sa-k-u-da.* (ᄆ첨 낭 싸레 가사쿠다)
first.of.all   tree   cut.down-CON go-OBLIG-PROSP-AH-SE
'First of all, I must go to cut down a tree.'

Tal   ***mawncheom*** *ta-sa-ju.* (탈 ᄆ첨 타사주)
wild.berry first   pick-OBLG-SE
'You have to pick wild berries first.'

Menkkeusgaengi/maljai (멘끗갱이/말자이) 'finally'

Menkkeusgaengi, *ttaw-na-n*   *iwag-eul haw-ju.*
finally   difference-come.out-NPST.CON talk-ACC do-SE
(멘끗갱이, 뜨난 이왁을 ㅎ주)
'Finally, let's have another talk.'

5.6 Attitude and Manner

Chawm (춤) **'truly, really':** generally appears at the end of a sentence
and reflects the speaker's overall attitude (good or bad) toward
what he or she is reporting.

Mansu-n   *musa gyeong*   *ganse-he-ms-in-jisa,*   ***chawm.***
Mansu-TOP why   like.that lazy-do-CONT-NPST-SE really
(만순 무사 경 간세헸인지사, 춤)
'I wonder why Mansu is so lazy, really.'

Chawmmallo (춤말로) 'in fact/really'

Chawm-mal-lo *Mansu malchug*   *sim-ule*   *ga-s-in-ga-massi?*
truth-speech-by Mansu grasshopper catch-CON go-PFV-NPST-SE-AH.SE
(춤말로 만수 말축 심우레 갓인가마씨?)
'(Do you think) Mansu really went to catch grasshoppers?'

Geuja (그자) 'just, only, always, all the time'

Uli sonji-n **geuja** *eomeong-man jideulli-n-da.*

1PL grandchild-TOP always mother-only wait-NPST-SE

(우리 손진 그자 어멍만 지들린다)

'My grandchild always waits for only his mother.'

Nawsi (느시) 'at any cost, at all'

Mansu-ne gasi-abang-eun **nawsi** *an w-ams-jeo.*

Mansu-PL wife-father-TOP at.all not come-CONT-SE

(만수네 가시아방은 느시 안 왔저)

'Mansu's father-in-law is not coming at all.'

Ttog (똑) 'surely, certainly'

Mansu-n **ttog** *gyeong haw-n-da.* (만순 똑 경 흔다)

Mansu-TOP certainly like.that do-NPST-SE

'Mansu certainly does like that.'

5.7 Degree

Ameng (아멩) 'no matter (how/what)'

Ameng *gawl-a-do na-n molleu-k-yeo.* (아멩 골아도 난 몰르켜)

whatever talk-LV-even 1SG-TOP not.know-PROSP-SE

'However much you talk (to me), I don't understand.'

Amenghedo (아멩헤도) 'somehow, no matter what'

Ameng-he-do *molleu-k-yeo.* (아멩헤도 몰르켜)

whatever-do-even not.know-PROSP-SE

'No matter what I do, I do not understand.'

Giyeongjeoyeong (기영저영) 'somehow, one way or another'

Yeosnal-e-n **gi-yeong-jeo-yeong** *sal-as-jeo.*

the.old.days-LOC-TOP that-CON-that-CON live-PFV-SE

(옛날엔 기영저영 살앗저)

'In the old days, (we) lived somehow.'

***Kkawttag* (ᄁᆞ딱) 'move a little/slightly'**

Mansu-n ***kkawttag*** *an haw-yeola.* (만순 ᄁᆞ딱 안 ᄒᆞ여라)

Mansu-TOP slightly not do-SE

'(I saw that) Mansu didn't even move slightly.'

***Weon.gan/weonchae* (원간/원채) 'so, very'**

Mansu-ne gasi-abang ***weon.gan*** *buje-la.* (만수네 가시아방 원간 부제라)

Mansu-PL wife-father very rich-SE

'Mansu's father-in-law is very rich.'

9

The Future of Jejueo

Jejueo is an important part of the cultural and linguistic heritage not only of Jeju Island, but of all Korea. With a history dating back to at least the Goryeo dynasty (918–1392), Jejueo is older than many of Korea's official national treasures, including major landmarks of culture and history such as *Namdaemun* (South Gate), first constructed in 1398; the *Hunminjeongeum*, the document promulgating Hangeul that was published in 1446; and *Pansoli*, a type of musical storytelling whose origins date to the seventeenth century.

No one thinks of the *Hunminjeongeum* as part of the cultural heritage just of Andong, even though that is where the only surviving full copy was discovered. And no one considers *Namdaemun* to have historic value only to Seoul, even though that is where it is located. For the same reason, Jejueo should not be thought of as a mere regional language, let alone a dialect. It is in fact a *national* treasure, a precious contribution to the rich fabric of Korea's culture and history.

Unlike many languages, including English, Spanish, Mandarin, and Swahili, Korean does not have a large number of close linguistic relatives. Indeed, the Koreanic family of languages currently has only two known members—Korean and Jejueo. It may someday be possible to confirm that Hamgyeong, which is still reportedly used by elderly speakers in parts of North Korea and China, also deserves to be recognized as a separate language. For the moment, there is no practical way to confirm this, but the status of Jejueo at least should be acknowledged immediately.

Communities that lose their language almost always end up regretting the loss at some point, and many groups are now attempting to recover their linguistic heritage (Grenoble & Whaley 1998; Hinton & Hale 2001; Harrison 2010; Hinton 2013). This is the case on Jeju Island too. The *Jejueo Bojeonhoe* (제주어보전회) 'The Jeju Language Preservation Society' was founded in 2008 and has been active in defending and revitalizing the island's language. Jejueo has also been receiving increasing attention in the media, and the local KBS station has aired several documentaries on the language's plight and the options for revitalizing it.

The results of a major public opinion survey conducted by Yang and Yang (2013) are also revealing. The survey, which questioned 688 residents of Jeju Island (ranging from teenagers to senior citizens), sought to assess the respondents' attitudes about Jejueo and its future. A strong positive feeling about the language was evident among respondents of all ages (table 9.1). There was an equally strong feeling among all groups that it was important to ensure that Jejueo will be passed on to the next generation in light of its importance to the culture of Jeju Island (table 9.2).

In response to popular sentiment, the provincial government of Jeju Island promulgated the Language Act for the Preservation and Promotion of Jejueo in 2007; a revised version of the act was approved four years later. Since 2011, the Jeju Office of Education has released a General Plan for Jejueo Conservation and Education at regular intervals, and various pedagogical materials are now available, with still more in preparation; see https://sites.google.com/a/hawaii.edu/jejueo/jejueo-revitalization for updates.

Language loss is a major problem in the twenty-first century. Hundreds of languages have already disappeared, and approximately 40 percent of the world's surviving seven thousand languages are in jeopardy (Crystal 2000; Nettle & Romaine 2000; Harrison 2007, 2010; Campbell et al. 2013). Many will be lost within a matter of decades.

Progressive governments have already initiated efforts to preserve the linguistic heritage of their communities. For example, in 1992, the Council of Europe adopted the European Charter for Regional or Minority Languages, recognizing that languages are "expressions of cultural wealth" that should be preserved (https://www.coe.int/en/web/european-charter-regional-or-minority-languages). Many European countries encourage the use of minority languages alongside the national language and provide funding for a wide range of educational and cultural programs. Korea has much to learn from these efforts.

Table 9.1   Feelings toward Jejueo by its speakers

"Jejueo sounds familiar and friendly in everyday conversations."

Age	Strongly agree	Agree	Neutral	Disagree	Strongly disagree	Total
Teens	76 (27.1%)	131 (46.8%)	43 (15.4%)	23 (8.2%)	7 (2.5%)	280
20s	45 (30%)	69 (46%)	29 (19.3%)	7 (4.7%)	0	150
30s	23 (35.9)	28 (43.8%)	12 (18.8%)	0	1 (1.6%)	64
40s	28 (37.3%)	33 (44%)	12 (16%)	2 (2.7%)	0	75
50s	33 (54.1%)	18 (29.5%)	9 (14.8%)	0	1 (1.6%)	61
60+	19 (33.3%)	26 (45.6%)	11 (19.3%)	1 (1.8%)	0	57
Total	224 (32.6%)	305 (44.4%)	116 (16.9%)	33 (4.8%)	9 (1.3%)	687

Table 9.2   Attitudes about the preservation of Jejueo

"Jejueo has to be passed down as part of Jeju culture."

Age	Strongly agree	Agree	Neutral	Disagree	Strongly disagree	Total
Teens	118 (42%)	93 (33.1%)	55 (19.6%)	10 (3.6%)	5 (1.8%)	281
20s	51 (34.2%)	60 (40.3%)	28 (18.8%)	6 (4%)	4 (2.7%)	149
30s	23 (35.9%)	25 (39.1%)	14 (21.9%)	2 (3.1%)	0	64
40s	26 (34.7%)	37 (49.3%)	12 (16%)	0	0	75
50s	26 (43.3%)	26 (43.3%)	5 (8.3%)	3 (5%)	0	60
60+	33 (60%)	15 (27.3%)	6 (10.9%)	0	1 (1.8%)	55
Total	277 (40.5%)	256 (37.4%)	120 (17.5%)	21 (3.1%)	10 (1.5%)	684

The 2003 United Nations Convention for the Safeguarding of Intangible Cultural Heritage identifies the importance of language, calling for its preservation, promotion, and transmission (http:// www.unesco.org/new/en/santiago/culture/intangible-heritage /convention-intangible-cultural-heritage/). The Republic of Korea signed the convention in 2006, and quickly assembled a list of more than one hundred examples of the nation's intangible cultural heritage that it considered worthy of preservation. Of these, just four came from Jeju Island: a shamanic exorcism ritual (*Jeju chilmeolidang-gus*), the making of *Mangeon* headbands (*manggeonjang*), the making of *Tangeon* hats (*tanggeonjang*), and several folk songs (*Jeju minyo*). However, in the spring of 2015, the National Assembly extended the definition of intangible cultural heritage to include the country's linguistic diversity (without acknowledging that Jejueo is a language in its own right). This decision opens the door to possible action to address the plight of Jejueo.

A considerable investment is required to save a language. Indeed, many countries devote millions of dollars annually to the preservation of their linguistic heritage. For example, the government of Scotland budgeted £21.2 million ($33 million) to support efforts to teach and promote the Gaelic language for the 2014–2015 fiscal year alone. This investment can be put into perspective by noting that the cost of restoring *Namdaemun* was approximately $25 million, and that the budget of Korea's Cultural Heritage Administration (the *Munhwajaecheong*), the agency charged with promoting and preserving the nation's cultural heritage, is $500 million (https://martinroll .com/resources/articles/asia/korean-wave-hallyu-the-rise-of-koreas -cultural-economy-pop-culture/).

Many attempts at language revitalization in communities around the world fail, often because of a shortage of resources, an absence of commitment, or a lack of expertise. Fortunately, for several reasons, the situation in Jeju Island is significantly different; indeed, the conditions are virtually ideal for a successful program of language revitalization.

1. There is strong and growing support on Jeju Island for the revitalization and preservation of the community's language.
2. Sufficient documentation of the vocabulary and grammar of Jejueo exists to support the creation of high-quality teaching materials.
3. Jeju Island has a well-funded system of public education

that could accommodate a curriculum designed to teach Jejueo to children and adolescents.

4. The island has a publicly funded national university (Jeju National University) that could offer postsecondary courses in Jejueo, as well as training for teachers of the language.
5. Because Jejueo is closely related to Korean, it is realistic to think that students could achieve basic fluency in the language in a relatively short period of time.
6. The prosperity of contemporary South Korea, including Jeju Island, creates the potential for funding from government agencies, foundations, and private individuals.
7. The national government has proclaimed a policy of cultural diversity that allows for minority-language education and, as noted above, has recently recognized language as part of the nation's intangible cultural heritage.

The conditions are therefore in place for an exemplary revitalization effort that would not only save Jejueo, but also serve as an example to communities around the world who wish to preserve their own endangered languages.

We therefore end on an optimistic note. It is not impossible to imagine a day when Jejueo will once again be spoken by young people, who will go on to be its teachers and protectors. Revived and revitalized, the language will become a source of pride in the community, and the fluency of its new speakers will create a cascade of opportunities for its wider use at home, in schools, in the media, in the arts, and in a full range of social situations. This will not be the end, of course, but it will be a very good beginning.

References

Campbell, Lyle, Raina Heaton, Nala Lee, Eve Okura, Sean Simpson, Kaori Ueki, and John Van Way. 2013. "New Knowledge: Findings from the *Catalogue of Endangered Languages* ('ELCat')." Presentation, the 3rd International Conference on Language Documentation and Conservation, Honolulu, HI, February 28. PowerPoint slides available at: http://scholarspace.manoa.hawaii.edu/bitstream/handle/10125/26145/26145.pdf.

Casad, Eugene. 1974. *Mutual Intelligibility Testing.* Dallas, TX: Summer Institute of Linguistics.

Chafe, Wallace. 1980. *The Pear Stories: Cognitive, Cultural, and Linguistic Aspects of Narrative Production.* Norwood, NJ: Ablex.

Cho, Taehong, Sun-Ah Jun, Seung-chul Jung, and Peter Ladefoged. 2001. "The vowels of Cheju." *Korean Journal of Linguistics* 26(4): 801–819.

Cho, Taehong, Sun-Ah Jun, and Peter Ladefoged. 2000. "An Acoustic and Aerodynamic Study of Consonants in Cheju." *Speech Sciences* 7:109–141.

Choe, Sang-Hun. 2014. "Hardy Divers in Korea Strait, 'Sea Women' Are Dwindling." *New York Times*, March 29. http://www.nytimes.com/2014/03/30/world/asia/hardy-divers-in-korea-strait-sea-women-are-dwindling.html.

Choi, Hak-Kyoo. 1989. "Jeju bangeon-ui seobeob chegye yeongu- eomal eomi whalyong-eul jungsim-eulo" 제주방언의 서법체계 연구-어말어미 활용을 중심으로 [A study of mood patterns in the Jeju dialect]. Master's thesis, Jeju National University.

Choo, Miho, and Hye-Young Kwak. 2008. *Using Korean: A Guide to Contemporary Usage.* Cambridge: Cambridge University Press.

Choo, Miho, and William O'Grady. 2003. *The Sounds of Korean: A Pronunciation Guide.* Honolulu: University of Hawai'i Press.

Chung, Sung-Yeo. 2017. "Korean Interrogative Sentences: Nominalization and Cross-Dialectal Perspectives." Presentation, Workshop on Nominalizations and Related Phenomena UCLA, March 17.

Comrie, Bernard. 1976. *Aspect: An Introduction to the Study of Verbal Aspect and Related Problems.*Vol. 2. Cambridge: Cambridge University Press.

Crystal, David. 2000. *Language Death*. Cambridge: Cambridge University Press.

Dahl, Östen. 1985. *Tense and Aspect Systems*. Oxford: Basil Blackwell.

———— (ed.). 2000. *Tense and Aspect in the Languages of Europe*. Hawthorne, NY: Walter de Gruyter.

————. 2014. "The Perfect Map: Investigating the Cross-Linguistic Distribution of TAME Categories in a Parallel Corpus." In *Aggregating Dialectology, Typology, and Register Analysis: Linguistic Variation in Text and Speech, within and across Languages*, edited by Benedikt Szmrecsanyi and Bernhard Wälchli, pp. 268–289. Hawthorne, NY: Walter de Gruyter.

Feffer, John. 2012. "South Korea's Jeju Island, Paradise with a Dark Side." *Washington Post,* April 20. http://www.washingtonpost.com/lifestyle /travel/south-koreas-jeju-island-paradisewith-a-dark-side/2012/04/19 /gIQAVlFaVT_story.html.

Gooskens, Charlotte. 2013. "Experimental Methods for Measuring Intelligibility of Closely Related Language Varieties." In *The Oxford Handbook of Sociolinguistics,* edited by R. Bayley, R. Cameron, and C. Lucas, pp. 195–213. Oxford: Oxford University Press.

Grenoble, Lenore A., and Lindsay J. Whaley, eds. 1998. *Endangered Languages: Language Loss and Community Response*. Cambridge: Cambridge University Press.

Han, Yeong-Gyun. 1984. "Jeju bangeon dongmyeongsa eomi-ui tongsa gineung" 제주방언 동명사 어미의 통사 기능 [The syntactic function of verbal noun suffixes in the Jeju dialect]. *Gugeohag* 국어학 13:229–252.

Harrison, K. David. 2007. *When Languages Die: The Extinction of the World's Languages and the Erosion of Human Knowledge*. Oxford: Oxford University Press.

————. 2010. *The Last Speakers: The Quest to Save the World's Most Endangered Languages*. Washington, DC: National Geographic Society.

Hinton, Leanne, ed. 2013. *Bringing Our Languages Home*. Berkeley, CA: Heyday.

Hinton, Leanne, and Ken Hale, eds. 2001. *The Green Book of Language Revitalization in Practice*. San Diego: Academic Press.

Hockett, Charles. 1958. *A Course in Modern Linguistics*. New York: Macmillan.

Hong, Jong-rim. 1975. "Jejudo bangeon-ui uimunbeob-e daehan gochal: Seolon" 제주도방언의 의문법에 대한 고찰: 서론 [A study on the interrogative mood in the Jeju dialect: Introduction]. *Hangugeo gyoyug haghoe* 한국어교육학회 8:151–226.

————. 1987. "Jeju bangeon-ui aspect hyeongtae-e daehayeo" 제주방언의 아스펙트 형태에 대하여 [A study on aspectual morphology in the Jeju dialect]. *Gugeo gugmun haghoe* 국어국문학회 98 (12): 185–209.

————. 1993. *Jeju bangeon-ui yangtae-wa sang* 제주방언의 양태와 상 [A study on modality and aspect in the Jeju dialect]. Korea: Hansin munhwasa 한신문화사.

————. 1998. *"Jeju bangeon-ui 'h' maleum myeongsa-e daehan gochal"* 제주방언

의 'ㅎ' 말음 명사에 대한 고찰 [A study on nouns ending in 'h' in the Jeju dialect]. *Tamna Munhwa* 탐라문화 19:1–25.

Hsiao, Suying. 2013. "The Grammatical Temporal System from Middle Mongolian to Modern Mongolian." *Language and Linguistics* 14:1075–1103.

Hyun, Pyung-hyo. 1962. *Jejudo bangeon yeongu* 제주도 방언연구 [A study of the Jeju dialect]. Korea: Jeongyeonsa 정연사.

———. 1974. "Jejueo bangeon-ui jeongdongsa eomi yeongu" 제주도 방언의 정동사어미 연구 [A study on verbal suffixes in the Jeju dialect]. PhD diss., Dongkuk University.

———. 1976. *Jejudo bangeon-ui jeongdongsa eomi yeongu* 제주도방언의 정동사어미연구 [A study of finite verbal endings in the Cheju Island dialect]. Seoul: Asia Culture Press.

———. 1977a. "Jejudo bangeon-ui jondaebeob" 제주도 방언의 존대법 [Honorifics in the Jeju dialect], *Gugeo gugmunhag* 국어국문학 74:1–36.

———. 1977b. "Jejudo bangeong-ui '-jeo, -ju' eomi-e daehayeo" 제주도 방언의 '-저, -주' 어미에 대하여 [A study on *-jeo* and *-ju* in the Jeju dialect]. *Eomun nonjib* 어문논집:239–250.

———. 1979. "Jejudo bangeon yeongu-e daehan geomto" 제주도 방언연구에 대한 검토 [Evaluation of studies of the Jeju dialect]. *Dialects* 방언 1:35–55.

———. 1982. "Jejudo bangeon gaegwan: Jejudoji Ha" 제주도방언개관.제주도지 하 [Overview of Jejudo dialect: A record of Jejudo Vol. 2]. Jeju City, Jeju Province.

———. 1985. *Jejudo bangeon yeongu: Nongopyeon* 제주도 방언 연구: 논고편 [Research on the Jeju Island dialect: Essays]. Seoul: Iuchulpansa 이우출판사.

Hyun Pyung-hyo, Jong-Cheol Kim, Yeong-Don Kim, Yeong-bong Kang, Kwang-Min Ko, and Chang-myeong Oh. 1995. *Jejueo sajeon* 제주어 사전 [Jejueo Dictionary]. 제주대학교 박물관. Jeju National University Museum.

Hyun, Pyung-hyo, Jong-Cheol Kim, Yeong-Don Kim, Yeong-bong Kang, Gwang-min Ko, Chang-myeong Oh, Seunghun Oh, and Sun-Ja Kim. 2009. *Gaejeong jeungbo Jejueo sajeon* 개정증보 제주어 사전 [Revised Jejueo dictionary]. Jeju City: Jeju Special Self-Governing Province.

Hyun, Woo-Jong. 1988. "Jejuedo bangeon ⌈·⌋eumga-ui eumseonghagjeog yeongu" 제주도 방언⌈·⌋음가의 음성학적 연구 [A phonetical study of the *alae a* sound in the Jeju dialect]. *Tamna munhwa* 탐라문화 7:25–57.

Hyun, Yong-Jun. 2007. *Jejueo musog jaryo sajeon* 제주도무속자료사전 [Dictionary of Jeju shamanic materials]. Jeju City: Gag 각.

Jensen, John. 1989. "On the Mutual Intelligibility of Spanish and Portuguese." *Hispania* 72:848–52.

Jung, Seung-chul. 1985. "Jejudo bangeon-ui uimunbeob eomi-e daehan ilgochal" 제주도 방언의 의문법 어미에 대한 일고찰 [A study on interrogative mood in the Jeju dialect]. *Gwanag eomun yeongu* 관악어문연구 10:415–427.

———. 1999. "Jeju bangeon-ui eumjo-wa eumjo-gun" 제주방언의 음조와 음조군 [Pitch and pitch group in the Jeju dialect]. *Jindanhagbo* 진단학보 88:543–554.

————. 2000. "Jeju bangeon-ui eumunlon" 제주방언의 음운론 [Phonology of the Jeju dialect]. *Tamna munhwa* 탐라문화 21:179–189.

————. 2001. "Jeju bangeon" 제주방언 [Jeju dialect]. *Bangeonhag sajeon* 방언학 사전 [The dictionary of dialectology], edited by B.-K. Lee, C.-K. Kwak, B.-K. Kim, O.-W. Kim, J.-T. Kim, J.-P. Kim, C.-S. Kim, et al., pp. 305–314. Seoul: Taehagsa 태학사.

Jung, Un-Taek. 1983. "Jejudo bangeon-ui gyeog eomi yeongu" 제주도 방언의 격어미 연구 [A study on the case endings of the Jeju dialect]. Master's thesis, Jeju National University.

Jung, Yeong-Jin. 1983. "Jeju bangeon-ui jonggyeol eomi yeongu-dongsa-ui jonggyeol eomi jungsim-eulo" 제주방언의 종결어미 연구-동사의 종결어미 중심으로 [A study on final endings in the Jeju dialect with a focus of final endings of verbs]. *Hangugeo munhag yeongu haghoe* 한국어문학연구 학회 18:307–342.

Kang, Chung-Hee. 1983. "Jeju bangeon-ui myeongsaryu jeobmisa-e gwan-han yeongu" 제주방언의 명사류 접미사에 관한 연구 [A study of the noun class suffix in the Jeju dialect]. PhD diss., Ewha Womans University, Seoul.

Kang, Jeong-hui. 1982. "Jeju bangeon-ui munbeobwha gwajeong-e daeha-yeo" 제주 방언의 문법화 과정에 대하여—중세국어와의 대응을 중심으로 [A study on Jeju dialect and grammaticalization with a focus on the corre-spondence with Middle Korean]. *Gugeohag* 국어학 11:71–87.

————. 1987. "Jeju bangeon-ui jeobsog eomi-wa dongjag-sang eomi-wa-ui sanggwnseong-e daehaye" 제주방언의 접속어미와 동작상어미와의 상관성 에 대하여 [A study on the relationship between conjunctional suffixes and aspectual suffixes in the Jeju dialect]. *Gugeohag* 국어학16:521–541.

————. 1988. *Jeju bangeon yeongu* 제주방언연구 [A study on the Jeju dialect]. Daejeon: Hannam daehaggyo chulpanbu 한남대학교 출판부.

Kang, Nam-Gook. 2000. "Jeju bangeon-ui myeongryeong whahaeng yeongu" 제주 방언의 명령 화행 연구 [A study on imperative speech acts in the Jeju dialect]. Master's thesis, Jeju National University.

Kang, Yeong-bong. 1983. "Jejudo bangeon-ui hueum" 제주도방언의 후음 [Glottal sounds in the Jeju dialect]. *Tamna munhwa* 탐라문화 2:29–43.

————. 2007. *Jejueo* 제주어 [Jeju language]. Seoul: National Folk Museum of Korea.

————. 2013. *Jeju iiyeogeo jeonsa bogoseo* 제주 지역어 전사 보고서 [A report on the transcription of the Jeju local language]. Seoul: National Institute of the Korean Language.

Kim, Jee-hong. 2001. "Jeju bangeon daeubeob yeongu-ui myeoj gaji munje" 제주 방언 대우법 연구의 몇가지 문제 [A few issues in studies of deference in the Jeju dialect]. *Baeglog Eomun* 백록어문 17:7–35.

————. 2014a. "Eogan-gwa eomi" 어간과 어미 [Stems and suffixes]. In *Jejueo pyogibeob haeseol* 제주어 표기법 해설 [Explanation of the writing system ofthe Jejueo language]. edited by J.-W. Ko, S.-J. Song, J.-H. Kim, D.-H.

Ko, C.-M. Oh, S.-D. Moon, and S.- H Oh, pp. 115–190. Jeju City: Jeju Development Institute.

———. 2014b. *Jeju bangeon-ui tongsa gisul-gwa seolmyeong* 제주방언의 통사기술과 설명 [Explanation and description of syntax of the Jeju dialect]. Seoul: Gyeongjin chulpan 경진출판.

———. 2014c. "Jeju bangeon tongsa yeongu-eseo-ui hyeonwhang-gwa gwaje" 제주방언 통사 연구에서의 현황과 과제 [The status quo and issues in syntactic studies on the Jeju dialect]. In *Jeju bangeon yeongu-ui eoje-wa naeil* 제주방언 연구의 어제와 내일 [Yesterday and tomorrow of studies of the Jeju dialect]. edited by D.-H. Ko, S.-C. Jung, S.-J. Song, Y.-J. Ko, J.-H. Kim, C. M. Oh, and S.-D. Moon, pp. 178–314. Jeju: Jeju Development Institute.

———. 2016. "Jeju bangeon-ui seoneomal eomi-wa jonggyeol eomi chegye" 제주 방언의 선어말 어미와 종결어미 체계 [On prefinal and final ending systems in Jeju Korean]. *Han-geul* 한글 313:109–171.

———. 2017. "Non-canonical ending systems in Jeju Korean." *Bangeonhag* 방언학 26:29–260.

Kim, Kwang-Woong. 2001. *Jeju jiyeogeo-ui eumunlon* 제주 지역어의 음운론 [A phonological study of the Jeju regional dialect]. Jeju National University.

Kim, S.-T. 1972. "Jejudo bangeon-ui eomi whalyong-e daehayeo" 제주도 방언의 어미활용에 대해서 [About conjugation in the Jejudo dialect]. *Gug-munhagbo* 국문학보 4:67–82.

Kim, Soon-Ja. 2014. "Jejudo bangeon-ui danwi uijon myeongsa" 제주도 방언의 단위 의존명사 [Counting units in the Jeju dialect]. *Hangugeohag* 한국어학 63:133–169.

———. 2016. *Jejuin-ui salm-gwa dogu* 제주인의 삶과 도구 [Jeju Islanders' life and tools]. Jeju: Jeju Folklore and Natural History Museum.

Kim, Sung-ryong. 2004. *"Jeju bangeon sulyangsa eohwi yeongu"* 제주방언 수량사 어휘 연구 [A study of the quantifiers in the Jeju dialect]. Master's thesis, Jeju National University.

———. 2008. "Jeju bangeon-ui sulyang myeongsa-wa sudanwi uijon myeong-sa eohwi yeongu" 제주방언의 수량명사와 수단위 의존명사 어휘 연구 [A study on the numeral-qualitative nouns and numeral-unit-dependent nouns of the Jeju dialect]. *Youngju eomun* 영주어문 16:5–41.

Kim, Won-Bo. 2005. "Jeju bangeon moeum-ui eumhyang bunseog" 제주 방언 모음의 음향분석 [The acoustic analysis of diphthongs in the Jeju dialect]. *Eoneohag yeongu* 언어학연구 10(2): 161–174.

———. 2006. "Jeju bangeon hwaja-ui sedae-byeol (20dae, 50dae, 70dae) danmoeum-ui eumhyang bunseog-gwa moeum chegye" 제주방언화자의 세대별 (20대, 50대, 70대) 단모음의 음향분석과 모음체계 [The acoustic analysis of monophthongs in Jeju dialect speakers in their 20s, 50s, and 70s and their vowel inventories]. *Eoneo gwahag yeongu* 언어과학연구 39:125–136.

Kim, Yeong-Don. 1957. "Jeju bangeon-ui eomi hwalyong (2)" 제주방언의 어미활용(2) [Conjugation in the Jeju dialect]. *Hangeul* 한글 121:366–377.

King, Ross. 1994. "History of Reported Speech in Korean." *Korean Linguistics* 8:1–38.

———. 2006. Dialectal variation in Korean. In *Language in Korean Culture and Society*, edited by Ho-min Sohn, pp. 264-280. Honolulu: University of Hawaii Press.

———. 2007. North and South Korea. *Language and National Identity in Asia*, edited by A. Simpson, pp. 200–234. Oxford: Oxford University Press.

Ko, Dong-Ho. 2008. "Jeju bangeon ' ` ' ui sedae-byeol byeonwha yangsang" 제주 방언 ' ` '의 세대별 변화 양상 [The study of *arae-a* in Jejueo in different generations]. *Hangug eoneo munhag* 한국언어문학 65:55–74.

Ko, Dong-Ho, Seung-cheol Jung, Sang-Jo Song, Yeong-Jin Ko, Jee-hong Kim, Chang-myeong Oh, and Soon-Deok Moon. 2014. *Jeju bangeon yeongu-ui eoje-wa naeil* 제주방언 연구의 어제와 내일 [Yesterday and tomorrow in studies on the Jeju dialect]. Jeju City: Jeju Development Institute.

Ko, Jae-Whan. 2011a. *Jejueo gaelon* 제주어 개론 [Introduction to Jejueo]. Vol. 1. Seoul: Bogosa 보고사.

———. 2011b. *Jejueo gaelon* 제주어 개론 [Introduction to Jejueo]. Vol. 2 Seoul: Bogosa 보고사.

Ko, Jae-Whan, Sang-Jo Song, Jee-hong Kim, Dong-Ho Ko, Chang-myeong Oh, Soon-Deok Moon, and Seunghun Oh. 2014. *Jejueo pyogibeob haeseol* 제주어 표기법 해설 [Explanation of the writing system of the Jeju language]. Jeju City: Jeju Development Institute.

Ko, Young-jin. 2007. "Jejudo bangeon-ui hyeongyongsa-e natana-neun du gaji hyeonjae sije-e daehayeo." 제주도 방언의 형용사에 나타나는 두 가지 현재 시제에 대하여 [Two present tenses of adjectives in Cheju dialect]. *Hangeul* 한글 3:77–106.

Ko, Young-lim. 2009. "Jeju bangeon-ui daehwache damhwa-e natana-n eogyang yeongu—chilsib-dae isang golyeong hwaja-leul jungsim-eulo" 제주 방언의 대화체 담화에 나타난 억양 연구 – 70대 이상 고령 화자를 중심으로. [Intonation characteristics in conversational discourse of Cheju Dialect—Case study on speakers older than 70]. *Hangug eoneo munhwa* 한국언어문화 40:5–28.

Koo, Bon-Kwan. 1999. "Chugso jeobmisa-e daehan yeongu" 축소 접미사에 대한 연구 [A study on diminutives]. *Gugeohag* 국어학 34:109–141.

Kwon, Mi-So. 2011. "Jejudo bangeon-ui siljae sigan gyeonggwa-e ttaleun eoneo byeoni yangsang yeongu" 제주도방언의 실재시간 경과에 따른 언어 변이 양상 연구 [The study of linguistic variation according to the passing of real time in the Jeju dialect]. Master's thesis, Jeju National University.

Lee, Iksop, and S. Robert Ramsey. 2000. *The Korean Language*. Albany: State University of New York.

Lee, Ki-Moon. 1985. "Nogdae-wa gadal-e daehayeo" 녹대와 가달에 대하여
   [About *nogdae* and *gadal*]. *Gugeohag* 국어학14:9–18.
———. 1993. *"Jejubangeon-gwa gugeosa yeongu"* 제주방언과 국어사 연구 [A
   study on the Jeju dialect and Korean language history]. *Tamna munhwa*
   탐라문화 13:145–154.
Lee, Ki-Moon, and S. Robert Ramsey. 2011. *A History of the Korean Language.*
   Cambridge: Cambridge University Press.
Lee, Nam-Duk. 1982. "Jeju bangeon-ui dongsa jonggyeol eomi byeonwha-e
   natana-n sisang chegye-e daehayeo" 제주방언의 동사 종결어미 변화에 나타
   난 시상체계에 대하여 [A study on the tense-aspect system found in finite
   verb inflection in the Jeju dialect]. *Hangug munhwa yeonguwon nonchong*
   한국문화연구원논총 40:7–54.
Lee, Siwon. 2013. "Multicultural Education and Language Ideology in
   South Korea." *Working Papers in Educational Linguistics* 28:43–60.
Lee, Sook-hyang. 2014. "Jejueo gangsegu-ui eogyang" 제주어 강세구의 억
   양 [The intonation patterns of accentual phrases in the Jeju dialect].
   Malsoli-wa eumseong gwahag 말소리와 음성과학 6(4): 117–123.
Lee, Sung-Nyeong. 1957. "Jejudo bangeon-ui hyeongtaelon-jeog yeongu"
   제주도 방언의 형태론적 연구 [Morphological research on the Jeju Island
   dialect]. *Dongbang hagji* 동방학지 3:39–193.
Martin, Samuel E. 1992. *A Reference Grammar of Korean: A Complete Guide to
   the Grammar and History of the Korean Language.* North Clarendon, VT:
   Tuttle.
Moon, Do-Yong. 2004. "Jeju bangeon-ui hyeonjaesije hyeongtaeso-e daehayeo" 제주 방언의 현재시제 형태소에 대하여 [On the present tense morpheme in the Jeju dialect of Korean]. *Hyeongtaelon* 형태론 6(2): 293–316.
Moon, Kab-Soon. 2006. "Jeju bangeon busa yeongu" 제주방언 부사연구 [A
   study of adverbs in Jejueo]. Master's thesis, Jeju National University.
Moon, Soon-Deok. 1987. "Jejudo bangeon-ui hyeongtaeso '-se'-e gwanhan
   yeongu" 제주도 방언의 형태소 '-서'에 관한 연구 [Studies on the mor-
   pheme *-se* in the dialect of Jeju Island]. Master's thesis, Jeju National
   University.
———. 1999a. "Jeju bangeon-ui bujeong pyohyeon yeongu" 제주 방언의 부
   정 표현 연구 [A study of negative expressions in the Jeju dialect]. PhD
   diss., Jeju National University.
———. 1999b. "Jeju bangeon-ui janghyeong bujeongmun sogo" 제주 방언
   의 장형 부정문 소고 [A study on long-form negation in the Jeju dialect].
   Yeongju eomun 영주어문 1:19–44.
———. 2002. "Jeju bangeon bojojosa-ui damhwa gineung" 제주방언 보조
   조사의 담화기능 [Discourse functions of particles in the Jeju dialect].
   Yeongju eomun 영주어문 4:71-84.
———. 2005. "Jeju bangeon nopimmal cheomsa-ui damwha gineung" 제
   주방언 높임말 첨사의 담화 기능: '마씀, 양, 예'를 중심으로 [The discourse

function of honorific particles in the Jeju dialect with special reference to *masseum, yang,* and *ye*]. *Eoneo yeongu* 언어연구 20 (3): 71–87.

Moon, Soon-Deok, Chang-myeong Oh, Won-Bo Kim, and Woo-Bong Shin. 2015. "Jejueo pyogibeob jamo-ui silje baleum-gwa eumseong bunseog yeongu" '제주어표기법' 자모의 실제 발음과 음성 분석 연구 [The actual pronunciation of vowels and consonants acknowledged in the transcription regulation for the Jeju language and their phonetic analysis]. Jeju City: Jeju Development Institute.

Moon, Suk-Young. 1998. *Jejudo bangeon-ui sisang hyeongtae-e daehan yeongu.* 제주도 방언의 시상 형태에 대한 연구. [A study on tense-aspect morphemes in the Jeju dialect] Unpublished master's thesis, Seoul National University.

Nettle, Daniel, and Suzanne Romaine. 2000. *Vanishing Voices. The Extinction of the World's Languages.* Oxford: Oxford University Press.

O'Grady, William, Yang, Changyong, and Yang, Sejung. 2018. "Integrating Analysis and Pedagogy in the Revitalization of Jejueo." Presented at the 25th Japanese/Korean Linguistics Conference, Honolulu, October.

Ogura, Shinpei. 1944. *Chōsengo hōgen no kenkyū: Study of Korean dialects.* Vol. 2. Iwanami Shoten.

Oh, Seunghun, Dong-Ho Ko, Sang-Jo Song, Chang-myeong Oh, and Soon-Deok Moon. 2015. *Jejusmal-ui ihae* 제줏말의 이해 [Understanding Jeju speech]. Jeju City: Jeju Development Institute.

Oh, Seunghun, and Soon-Deok Moon. 2013. *Jejueo gicho eowhi seonjeong mich hwalyong bangan* 제주어 기초어휘 선정 및 활용방안 [Selection of basic vocabulary of the Jeju dialect and plans for practical use]. Jeju City: Jeju Development Institute.

Oh, Seunghun, Chang-myeong Oh, and Soon-Deok Moon. 2016. *Jeju sanan Jejussaleum* 제주 사난 제줏사름 [Jeju persons living in Jeju]. Jeju City: Jeju Development Institute.

Okura, Eva. 2015. "Language Versus Dialect in Language Cataloguing: The Vexed Case of Otomanguean Dialect Continua." *University of Hawaiʻi at Mānoa Working Papers in Linguistics* 46:1–19.

Park, Yong-Hu. 1960. *Jeju bangeon yeongu* 제주방언 연구 [A study of the Jeju dialect] Seoul: Dongwonsa 동원사.

———. 1988. *Jeju bangeon yeongu: Jalyopyeon* 제주방언 연구: 자료편 [A study of the Jeju dialect: a collection of data]. Seoul: Godae minjog munhwa yeonguso chulpansa 고대민족문화연구소 출판사.

Saltzman, Moira. 2014. "Language Contact and Morphological Change in Jejueo." Master's thesis, Wayne State University.

Seok, Ju-Myeong. 1947. *Jejudo bangeonjib* 제주도 방언집 [A collection of Jejudo dialect]. Seoul: Seoul sinmunsa chulpanbu 서울신문사 출판부.

Shin, Woo-bong. 2015. "Jejubangeon pyeongseomun-e natana-neun eogyang yeonsgu: eomaleomi –an/eon, eumen-eul jungsim-eulo" 제주방언 평서문과 의문문에 나타나는 억양연구 [(An) Intonation study of pred-

icate ending and interrogative ending in Jeju dialect: ʌn/ɑn, ɯmɛn].
  Yeongju eomun 영주어문 31:87–109.

Sohn, Ho-Min. 1999. *The Korean Language*. Cambridge: Cambridge University Press.

Song, Sang-Jo. 1991. "Jejudo baneon-ui jeobmi pasaengeo yeongu" 제주도 방언의 접미 파생어 연구 [A study on Jejueo suffixal derivatives]. PhD diss., Dong-A University, Busan.

———. 1993. "Hyeongtaeso '-ng, -n'-gwa anmaejeumssikkeut-ui hoeung" 형태소 '-ㅇ, -ㄴ'과 안맺음씨끝의 호응' [Agreement between the morphemes '-*ng* and–*n*' and prefinal endings]. *Tamna munhwa* 탐라문화 13:1–30.

———. 1994. "Hyungtaeso '-eong'-e daehan gochal" 형태소 '엉'에 대한 고찰 [A study on the morpheme '-*eong*']. *Tamna munhwa* 탐라문화 14:21–41.

———. 2007. *Jejumal keun sajeon* 제주말 큰사전 [Jeju speech dictionary]. Seoul: Hangug Munhwasa 한국문화사.

———. 2011. *Jejumal-eseo ttaegalimso, '-ng, -n'-gwa ssikkeut-deul-ui hoeung* 제주말에서 때가림소 '-ㅇ, -ㄴ'과 씨끝들의 호응. [Interaction between –*ng*, –*n* and enders in Jeju Speech]. Seoul: Hangug munhwasa 한국문화사.

Sung, Nag-Soo. 1982. Jejueo bangeon-ui jeobsongsa yeongu 제주도 방언의 접속사 연구 [A study on conjunctions in the Jeju dialect]. *Hangeul* 한글 176:3–39.

Van Valin, Robert D., and Randy J. LaPolla. 1997. *Syntax: Structure, Meaning, and Function*. Cambridge: Cambridge University Press.

Weinreich, Max. 1945. "The YIVO Faces the Post-War World." *YIVO Bleter: Journal of the Yiddish Scientific Institute* 25:3–18.

Woo, Chang-Hyeon. 1995. "Jeju bangeon-ui sisang seoneomal eomi-e dahayeo-2inching uimunmun-e natana-neun sisang chegye-leul jungsim-eulo" 제주방언의 시상선어말 어미에 대하여- 2인칭 의문문에 나타나는 시상 체계를 중심으로 [A study on tense and aspectual suffixes with a focus on the tense and aspect system in interrogatives with a 2nd person subject]. *Seogang eomun* 서강어문 11:37–60.

Woo, Chang-Hyun. 2005. "Jeju bangeon-ui '-neu'-e daehayeo: '-neu'-wa '-n'-ui sanggwanseong-eul jungsim-eulo" 제주방언의 '-느-'에 대하여: '-느-' 와 '-ㄴ-'의 상관성을 중심으로 [A study of -*neu* in Jeju dialect: Focusing on the relationship between '-*neu*' and '-*n*']. *Hyeongtaelon* 형태론 7(2): 387–402.

———. 2016. "Jeju bangeon gyeogjosa gyoyugeul wihan gicho yeongu" 제주 방언 격조사 교육을 위한 기초 연구 [Fundamental research on Jeju dialect case particles education] *Gugje eomun* 국제어문 70:29–50.

Woo, Kyung-Sik, Young-Kwan Sohn, Seok-Hoon Yoon, Ung-San Ahn, and Andy Spate. 2013. *Jeju Island Geopark: A Volcanic Wonder of Korea*. New York: Springer.

Yang, Changyong. 2014. "Jejueo: Its History and Attitudes". Presented at the 7th World Congress of Korean studies, Honolulu, November.

Yang, Changyong, William O'Grady, and Sejung Yang. 2017. "Toward a

Linguistically Realistic Assessment of Language Vitality: The Case of Jejueo. *Language Documentation and Conservation* 11:103–113.

Yang, Changyong, William O'Grady, Sejung Yang, Nanna Hilton, Sang-Gu Kang, and So-Young Kim. 2019. "Revising the Language Map of Korea." *Handbook of the Changing World Language Map,* edited by Stanley D. Brunn and Roland Kehrein. Berlin: Springer.

Yang, Changyong, and Sejung Yang. 2013. "A Study on Jejueo Use and Attitudes Toward Jejueo." Unpublished paper, College of Education, Jeju National University.

Yang, Sejung. 2018. "Assessing Language Knowledge in Jeju: Vocabulary and Verbal Patterns in Jejueo and English." PhD diss., University of Hawai'i. Available at http://ling.hawaii.edu/wp-content/uploads/SejungYangFinal.pdf.

Yeon, Jaehoon. 2012. "Korean Dialects: A General Survey." In *The Languages of Japan and Korea,* edited by N. Tranter, pp. 168–185. Abingdon and New York: Routledge.

Morpheme Index

Topic Index

About the Authors

Changyong Yang (PhD, University of Florida) is professor of education at Jeju National University. A native of Jeju Island, he was a founding member of the Jeju Language Preservation Society and has long been a leader in ongoing efforts to revitalize Jejueo.

Sejung Yang (PhD, University of Hawai'i at Mānoa) is a native of Jeju Island, whose interests range from the grammar of Jejueo to techniques for teaching it as a second language.

William O'Grady (PhD, University of Chicago) is professor of linguistics at the University of Hawai'i at Mānoa. He has written extensively on Korean and has authored numerous articles and books on the language. He began to work on Jejueo in 2014.